THE NEW FACE OF POLITICAL CINEMA

THE NEW FACE OF POLITICAL CINEMA
Commitment in French Film since 1995

Martin O'Shaughnessy

Berghahn Books
NEW YORK · OXFORD

First published in 2007 by

Berghahn Books

www.berghahnbooks.com

© 2007 Martin O'Shaughnessy

Library of Congress Cataloging-in-Publication Data
O'Shaughnessy, Martin (Martin P.)
The new face of political cinema : commitment in French film since
1995 / Martin O'Shaughnessy.
    p. cm.
Includes bibliographical references and index.
ISBN-13: 978-1-84545-322-0 (hardback : alk. paper)
1. Motion pictures--France--History. 2. Motion pictures--Political
aspects--France--History. I. Title.
PN1993.5.F7O84 2007
791.43'6580944--dc22
                                        2007035170

British Library Cataloguing in Publication Data
A catalogue record for this book is available from the British Library

Printed in the United States on acid-free paper

ISBN 978-1-84545-322-0 (hardback)

To Gloria, Ana Sofia, John, Michael and Kay

CONTENTS

ACKNOWLEDGEMENTS

Warm thanks are due to the Arts and Humanities Research Council and to Nottingham Trent University for providing me with research time that was so vital for this book. My thanks also go to the anonymous reader whose comments were such a judicial mix of support and advice. Thanks too to Graeme Hayes, Carrie Tarr, Florian Grandena, Patricia Caillé, Sylvie Agard, Gill Allwood, Winifred Woodhull and Martine Beugnet for productive dialogue and kind assistance at various stages of my research. My warm appreciation goes to all at Berghahn books, especially Anna Wright, for their help and support, and to Philip Thomas for his careful copyediting. I am grateful too to Dominique Cabrera and to Agat films for their permission to use the image from *Nadia et les hippopotames*. Thanks finally to Gloria, my wife, without whose constant support the book might never have made it.

INTRODUCTION

At the beginning of Haitian film-maker Raoul Peck's French-funded and tellingly entitled documentary *Le Profit et rien d'autre (Profit and Nothing But)* (2000), a whispering voice tells us that capital has won.[1] Capital seems to have won a definitive victory leaving no room either for radical political opposition or for a political cinema as earlier generations would have understood it. Were this the case, there would be nothing for an oppositional cinema to do but fall silent or engage in a critique that, condemned never to open onto a politics, would ultimately be sterile. Yet has capital simply won? The last ten years or so have seen the revival of political opposition in France. It began with the mass public sector revolt of late 1995 against the weakening of the social security regime, a revolt that, although it failed to spread to a cowed private sector, attracted enormous public support and forced a government retreat. It came resoundingly to the surface again with the triumph in 2005 of the 'No' vote in the referendum on the European constitution, a result which, while it dismayed mainstream parties rallied to the neo-liberal consensus, voiced a determined collective refusal of the European Union's apparently unstoppable neo-liberal drift. It continued in 2006 with the mass student mobilization against the CPE (*Contrat Première Embauche*), a piece of legislation that sought to 'help' young people into work by removing employment rights from them. It has also made itself felt through the considerable strength of the counter-globalization movement, something underlined by the foundation of ATTAC (Association pour la Taxation des Transactions pour l'Aide aux Citoyens) in 1998. Further evidence of revolt can be seen in the nationwide explosion of rioting in 2005 that was the latest and most spectacular but far from the only outpouring of anger that France has seen in its *banlieues* or outer-city estates. If, since the co-optation of the leading anti-racist organization, SOS-Racisme, by the Socialist government in the 1980s,

French people with immigrant roots have struggled to have any meaningful political voice, there has been ample evidence of their collective refusal of racialized marginalization and discriminatory policing.

Has this revival of wide-scale opposition found an adequate response in French cinematic production? The response, although not unqualified, is yes. One of the most striking features of both fictional and documentary production in the last decade has been the rebirth of a committed cinema. In documentary, this rebirth is most eloquently expressed in the surge of anti- and counter-globalization films. In the fiction films that are the concern of this volume, it most obviously makes itself felt in a return to the 'real' as expressed in a focus on workplace oppressions, unemployment, social 'exclusion', racism, migration, ethnicity and social class. Despite opinions to the contrary, film-makers' leading role in 1997 in defence of the *sans-papiers*, the people deemed by the then French government not to have the required documentation to be allowed to stay in the country, was not some mere flash in the pan nor a cynical search for publicity.[2] It was part of a broader return to socio-political engagement that inevitably generated comparisons with the previous, post-1968 flowering of political cinema. But just as, operating in the shadow of a massive defeat, a contemporary leftist politics must take new forms, so too must a radical cinema. Post-1968 film was able to feed off and prolong a vibrant radical politics. Contemporary political film is condemned to work in a very different context. It must seek to exist productively somewhere in the difficult space between the politics that was and an emergent new politics. While some have seen in it above all the shadow of a defeat and condemned it for its alleged political inadequacy, it is more interesting and more productive to assess it in terms of the effectiveness of the resistances that it mounts and its capacity to prepare the grounds for an emergent new politics. This is the task that this book sets itself.

The book's structure is as follows. Chapter 1 provides the necessary contextualization for what is to come by underlining the radical newness of both the larger socio-political terrain and the narrower cinematic one. Chapter 2 discusses important responses to the films in journals such as *Cahiers du Cinéma* and *Positif* as a way of establishing some of the key debates in relation to which this book will situate itself. Chapter 3 develops the core observation that, given the radically new situation, a committed cinema can no longer take the same forms or be judged by the same criteria as its cinematic predecessors. By exploring contrasts between two legendary pieces of post-1968 cinema, Jean-Luc Godard's and Jean-Pierre Gorin's *Tout va bien* (1972) and Marin Karmitz's *Coup pour coup* (1971) on the one hand and Hervé Le Roux's seminal documentary *Reprise* (1995) and the Dardenne brothers' little known early works on the other, it traces the consequences of the disappearance of the old, universalizing leftist dramaturgy of struggle while developing a genealogy for the raw, mute and corporeal social suffering and struggle that is such a characteristic feature of contemporary production.

Building on this contrastive and genealogical work, the next three chapters explore the two main strands of contemporary engaged cinema. Mapping the considerable body of films that seek to restore currency to a polemical, class-driven framing of the social, chapters 4 and 5 show how, even if an epic dramaturgy of class has been shattered, its dispersed pieces can be put to good use, re-establishing grounds for critique and configuring the socio-political terrain in the kind of antagonistic terms without which an oppositional politics makes no sense. Complementing this discussion, chapter 6 moves on to examine what happens when all access to a totalizing dramaturgy of the social has been lost. It examines a body of films that seek productive ways to occupy the wasteland between the politics that was and the politics yet to come by figuring the fragmentary stories of small groups and marginalized individuals evicted from broader solidarities, stripped of a public voice and subject to the brutal, uncushioned impact of the economy. Merely to occupy this space would of course be politically sterile. The chapter shows that the films' political use-value lies in their capacity to resist the disintegration that they record by restoring a sense of value and ethical agency where none seem to exist while reconnecting the violences of the margins to the systemic. In many ways this chapter is the heart of the book. It develops the notion of an *aesthetic of the fragment*, a term meant to suggest not simply social fragmentation (although that is undeniably important), but rather a sea change in the cinematic face of socio-political struggle represented by the passage from a universalizing, discursively mediated vision to one marked by a newly raw and near mute corporeality. Chapter 7 then shows how the films discussed have a general recourse to melodramatic strategies in order to restore eloquence and significance to struggles seemingly condemned to silence and meaninglessness. Melodrama has often been despised by proponents of a radical political cinema both because of the emotional involvement it generates and because of its tendency to focus on individuals, the interpersonal and the familial instead of the systemic. The chapter argues, however, that it is a key part of the films' effectiveness and notes how, despite the ideological risks involved, a focus on individuals and families allows both for an acerbic critique of individualism and for a dramatization of the monstrosity of the current order. Chapter 8 engages with the films' spatial economy. Consistent with a more general analysis that seeks to understand the films' newness, the chapter underlines the radical novelty of their spatiality, a novelty that cannot be accounted for by any suggestion that they simply reorientate our attention within a familiar national frame. The chapter suggests instead that, given the collapse of a totalizing leftist narrative and the weakening of the nation's symbolic protection, the films are threatened by an inability to locate causes or connect them to consequences. Unless they can find novel ways to combat this radical spatial dislocation, they are condemned to political impotence. If the macro-spatial level is thus a key dimension of their symbolic geography, the chapter also analyses the work they do at the micro-spatial level both to highlight profoundly unequal mobilities and to show how the capacity of the dominated to refuse immobilization becomes a sign of recalcitrant political agency. Taken together, the different chapters aim to provide an analysis of contemporary committed fiction cinema in France, explaining its context, originality and potential limitations as well as the different strategies it mobilizes to restore a political voice, meaning and visibility to social suffering and struggle.

The book seeks to marry close analysis, contextualization and relevant theoretical understandings. It draws, where relevant, on critical writings that suggest productive ways to approach the films. It draws too on recent sociological writings by leading figures such as Robert Castel, Stéphane Beaud and Michel Pialoux. However, its major debt is perhaps to political philosophers and analysts such as Luc Boltanski, Eve Chiapello, Etienne Balibar, Alain Badiou and Jacques Rancière, figures who, despite their clear differences, share a refusal to accept the foreclosing of the space of the political and a determination to challenge the apparently consensual triumph of the neo-liberal order. The work of Rancière plays a particularly central role. It reminds us that a true politics is one rooted in radical disagreement over the distribution of social roles and places and the right to public speech.   A radical cinema cannot simply seek to represent contemporary reality, to be 'realist', no matter how dark the tones that it employs. It must bring disagreement over the order of things to the surface, defining the dominated not by their subordination but by their capacity to challenge it while pushing its audience back towards a politics. The centrality Rancière accords to the regulation of access to the *logos*, the language of legitimate public deliberation, is particularly productive at a time when those at the bottom are routinely objectified and have lost access to any overarching oppositional language with which to express their situation. In the face of this silencing, the capacity of films to make the voice of the voiceless heard and to constitute them as political agents and not as social objects for our voyeuristic or 'humanitarian' contemplation would seem a central concern of critical analysis. Finally, Rancière's insistence on the necessary *theatricality* of an authentic politics – its capacity to offer an alternative dramaturgy characterized by a reordering of social roles, places and scripts – is useful both for thinking through the consequences of the loss of an established leftist dramaturgy of the social (chapter 3) and for developing an appreciation of films' capacity to improvise an oppositional drama even where no stage seems to exist (chapter 7).

The book is particularly concerned with filmic responses to the contemporary triumph of aggressive, neo-liberal capitalism. It does not seek to provide a rounded picture of French cinema's interventions in the full range of current struggles. Thus, although the emergence, since the later 1980s, of a *Beur* cinema giving expression to the voices of those of North African origin (Tarr 2005) is something of undoubted interest, there is no attempt to give it a rounded treatment here. Similarly, while the sharp increase in recent years in the number of women directors and their production, at times, of strikingly original work (Tarr and Rollet 2002) underlines the necessity of attention to the gendered dynamics of cinema, this book does not make gender a core concern. Rather, it engages with questions of gender and ethnicity as and where they intersect with its own chosen subject matter. This procedure is not, of course, without potential pitfalls. Hopefully the book retains sufficient awareness of them.

In the choice of films to discuss, a balance is sought between works familiar to viewers and students of French film outside France and those that may be relatively unknown. To simply concentrate on films that have achieved international distribution would be to produce a very partial picture, yet it is important at the same time to connect to that which people know. Thus, a good deal of space is devoted to discussion of Mathieu Kassovitz, Laurent Cantet, the Dardenne brothers, Bruno Dumont, Robert Guédiguian, Bertrand Tavernier and Erick Zonca, all film-makers with a solid international profile. But space is also given to less prominent figures such as Jean-François Richet, Laetitia Masson, Dominique Cabrera, Bénédicte Liénard, Rabah Ameur-Zaïmeche, Jean-Marc Moutout, Mehdi Charef, Claire Devers and Manuel Poirier, directors whose work has played a central role in the re-emergence of commitment. Because the book does not seek to be a survey of contemporary directors but is structured by a developing argument about the nature of contemporary committed film, directors and films are not treated as discrete units but are referred to as and when relevant for the needs of the evolving discussion. Although the book does refer to documentary, notably in chapters 3 and 8, its core concern is fiction cinema. The relative neglect of documentary is not meant to imply a dismissal of its impact but reflects a desire to do justice to the importance and the originality of the fiction. Positions developed are hopefully based on rigorous argument and analysis, but there is no pretence at a 'neutral' approach to the films. The aim throughout is to explore and develop their radical potential while maintaining the degree of critical distance necessary to draw out what limitations they may have and to establish robust criteria by which to evaluate their general effectiveness as political cinema.

Notes

1. The dates given for films when they are first mentioned reflect the year when they acquired an official existence as projects and not the date of their release.

2. While Judith Cahen (1997) suggested that the film-makers' general failure to engage with contemporary issues in their works undermined their commitment to the *sans-papiers*, a sceptical Judith Lazar (2000) attributed their mobilization to self-promotion.

1

CONTEXTS

⟨decorative ornament⟩

This chapter provides a concise account of the current state of the French socio-political and cinematic terrains. If it is driven, above all, by a sense of the urgent need to map and understand the present situation, it is also convinced that the present can only be understood, questioned and challenged if one has a clear sense of its historical roots. The chapter's turn to the past is both explanatory and contrastive; that is, history is used both to point to the origins of the current situation and to underline its newness. If the 1968 period is privileged in this chapter, and indeed in the next, it is because it represents a high point of socio-political and cinematic radicalism. The contrast between 1968 and the present risks working in a purely negative way, underlining the profundity of the left's political defeat and the apparent relative timidity of contemporary committed cinema. Hopefully more positive, the intention here is to take sobre stock of the present in the knowledge that strategies deployed by committed cinemas can only be gauged productively in terms of the effectiveness and timeliness of their responses to specific contexts.

Shifting Socio-political Contexts

In their highly influential *Le Nouvel Esprit du capitalisme*, Boltanski and Chiapello (1999) provide us with two 'snapshots' that are a useful starting point in an assessment of the present socio-political context. The first snapshot is of the period 1968–1975, a time when the authors note the activity of a social movement on the offensive, active trade unions and a consistent reference to social class in political debate. The second snapshot is of 1985–1995 when the authors find a quiescent social movement, disoriented unions and, significantly, a near disappearance of public reference to class. What happens in between, and what their work explains, is a seismic shift in the relationship between capital, labour and society more broadly. Boltanski and Chiapello suggest that capital underwent a crisis both of legitimacy and profitability in the period around 1968 when it was increasingly pressurized in Western societies by organized labour and subjected to a combination of what the authors call *la critique artiste* and *la critique sociale*. Generated by cultural producers and radical leftists, the former associates capital with unfreedom and alienating inauthenticity. Originating above all from the institutional left and trade unions, the latter targets the exploitation and poverty associated with the capitalist mode of production. The authors suggest that capitalism triumphed over both critiques, essentially by absorbing the values associated with the former and by disarming the latter. Thus, the old, massive, rigid and bureaucratic capitalist organization broke itself up and declared itself open to networking, creativity, intuition and difference in a way that made the critique of alienation and unfreedom harder to enforce. At the same time, the social critique was disabled as job security and collective drives to equality were undermined by individualization of rewards, fear of unemployment, and the loss of what had seemed a right to a full-time, permanent job. Subcontracting and outsourcing of work allowed collective agreements and labour protection laws to be bypassed and customer pressure to be applied to an atomized workforce at each stage of the production process. This dual process of co-option and disabling allowed capital to successfully reinvent itself and outflank opposition. Its success was marked – and this returns us to the snapshots – by the steady erasure of the discourse of class that had allowed the social to be described in terms of exploitation and its replacement by the politically disabling language of exclusion and inclusion. The latter locates those with full-time work among the privileged while presenting exclusion as a general social pathology and not as exploitation (Boltanski and Chiapello 1999). It was this sense that work was somehow a privilege that allowed for the disqualification by important sectors of political and intellectual opinion of the 1995 public sector strikes in defence of social security rights. Deemed to be 'included', striking workers were accused of a selfish disregard for those truly in need, the excluded.

If one side of the current picture is the successful self-reinvention of capital, the other is the dismantling of the organized working class. Although the story of labour is present in Boltanski and Chiapello's analysis, it is more central to Beaud and Pialoux's *Retour sur la condition ouvrière* (1999). This already classic study is specifically based on the Peugeot factory at Sochaux, but many of the transformations its authors describe have been played out across the world of work in general. They describe how the period since the 1970s has seen the dismantling of a working class that had been painfully built through the struggles of the mid-

1930s Popular Front and the post-war periods. This process had been accompanied by mass unemployment, the erosion of working-class bastions, the collapse of the Communist Party and the sharp decline of trade union membership. Whereas the workers had previously been able to defend themselves by drawing on the substantial political, cultural and symbolic capital embodied in their associations, group pride and union and party representation, they were now becoming objects of compassion. Taylorist production lines had once built solidarity off which union delegates could feed. Now, although the lines are often still there, the shift to flexible working patterns, to electronic monitoring and to financial incentives for teams and individuals has helped undo the old collectivist culture and replaced it with competition and mutual surveillance. The language and practices of struggle and solidarity have come to seem outdated, something associated with an older generation of workers and union militants to which the young cannot relate. Usually employed on short-term contracts by subcontractors, the latter lack the security to buy a home or procure loans and more broadly to project themselves into the future. Although they face naked social domination they have (and this will be a key point for my own argument) no symbolic tools, no collective words to think themselves as a class or to express their disarray (Beaud and Pialoux 1999: 358). Whereas older workers can still struggle to defend group honour, the young can only fight to escape at an individual level from a succession of menial jobs (Beaud and Pialoux 1999: 360). Taken in conjunction, the works cited show the profundity of the changes to the socio-political domain since the 1970s. Not only has capital successfully revolutionized itself and substantially dismantled the organized working class, there is now no shared language to name what has happened, to label current oppressions and to federate individual grievances. This is a deeply hostile symbolic terrain for an oppositional cinema.

The work of Badiou and Balibar can help both to elucidate the consequences of this loss of an overarching oppositional political language and to bring in the vital international dimension. Writing in the mid-1980s, and thus even before the fall of the Berlin Wall in 1989, Badiou suggested that a radical leftist, predominantly Marxist, worldview had imploded. This worldview had rested on three pillars: existing socialist states, Third World national liberation struggles, and the workers' movement with its party and union components. Each of the pillars had collapsed, as emblematic examples showed. China and the USSR had become counter-examples not models. Vietnam, once the epitome of a popular struggle for liberation, had become statist. The Solidarity movement in Poland had brought home the divorce between a militant workers' movement and a Marxism that could no longer claim to be in the vanguard of history (Badiou 1985). While the examples are, of course, from a particular historical moment, the underlying and still valid point is that a Marxist or related viewpoint is no longer available to provide an overarching, totalising vision that can connect local and specific struggles to a broader narrative of emancipation.

Balibar complements Badiou's analysis by pointing to the rise of 'useless' violence in the contemporary world. Class and colonial oppressions and resistances to them were violences that could be incorporated within a positive historical narrative of emancipation. Not only is a leftist narrative no longer available to give meaning to contemporary struggles, the world now sees the elimination of large sectors of population from the productive economy. These newly 'disposable' masses can no longer imagine themselves positively as political subjects capable of emancipating humanity as colonized peoples or the working class might once have done. Thus, the violence done to them through their economic marginalization no longer seems open to productive narration. The often violent, identitarian responses to capitalist globalization are similarly resistant to incorporation within a narrative of progressive politics (Balibar 1997: 23–26). Castel brings some of Balibar's conclusions closer to home. He points to the contemporary return of mass socio-economic vulnerability to Western societies who thought they had moved beyond it during the years of full employment and strong welfare states. As those previously in possession of stable employment are destabilized and others are locked into social precariousness, there is an increasing rationing of socially productive statuses and a concomitant growth in the number of 'useless people' or *inutiles au monde* (Castel 1995: 662), isolated individuals who are called upon to bear personal responsibility for their socially generated marginalization. Whereas the position of the old working class could be productively named as exploitation or as domination in ways that opened onto a challenge to the social structure, the diverse *inutiles au monde* are currently packaged together under the pathologizing term of social 'exclusion'. Rather than being used to question those (central) social processes that generate it, their marginality is seen as something that must be treated so that they can become part of a society that is not itself placed in question. Castel's *inutiles au monde* and Balibar's 'disposable' masses point to a sea change in the representation of the social, both within a national frame and at an international level, a shift that has its clear roots in the processes of globalizing capital and in the implosion and forcible undoing of the erstwhile leftist grand narrative of opposition. This profoundly disabling configuration of the social is something that a committed cinema must challenge.

The collapse of grand narratives has been a commonplace of intellectual discussion since the 1980s and notably since the publication of Lyotard's seminal *The Postmodern Condition* (1984). To the extent that grand narratives are oppressive and constraining (leaving no room for diversity and foreclosing alternative possibilities), their collapse can be seen as opening space for the emergence of a multiplicity of smaller, more diverse, less deterministic stories that, permitting choice and debate, are implicitly more democratic. While not entirely rejecting such a position, the argument developed in this book will follow very different lines. Firstly, its core concern is not the undoing of grand narratives as a generic category but the consequences of the collapse of an overarching leftist worldview. Secondly, while it is acutely conscious of the tyrannical potential of grand narratives in general and a leftist grand narrative in particular, it is profoundly unconvinced that, under current conditions of neo-liberal triumph, the collapse of the leftist imaginary has opened a space in which liberatory smaller stories can develop. Rather, in ways that will be developed in chapter 3, the suggestion will be that it has become difficult to tell any progressive story at all. The leftist imaginary that once gave a language, meaning and direction to struggles and brought oppressions to visibility is no longer available. It leaves in its wake not a space of freedom but one characterized by meaninglessness, isolation, silencing and invisibility. Operating on this scarred terrain, a committed cinema can no longer be the same. It must be a cinema that registers defeat but that also resists it by refusing the invisibility of class, by reconnecting marginalization to the central processes that drive it and by finding ways to restore meaning to 'useless' suffering and struggle.

Le Mouvement Social and the Revival of Opposition

The picture of political defeat and social retreat, disarray and fragmentation that emerges above needs to be balanced by the revival of a diverse socio-political opposition that has made its presence increasingly felt since the mid-1990s and notably since the public sector strikes of December 1995 signalled a collective refusal of neo-liberal policies. This opposition is sometimes gathered under the umbrella term, *le mouvement social*. Such an appellation bears the risk of implying an organizational unity and ideological discipline that a relatively fragmented oppositionality clearly neither has nor necessarily wants (Crettiez and Sommier 2002: 20–24). However, it does usefully indicate the divide, if not the divorce, between oppositional groups and those party and union actors who might traditionally have structured them. The social movement is not simply social because it as yet lacks an overarching political project, it is also social because the conventional political arena of state and parties seems unable or unwilling to challenge the neo-liberal consensus.

The social movement needs to be apprehended both in its diversity and in certain convergences. First the diversity: 1995 suggested a renewal of combativeness amongst public sector workers, an attitude maintained, although with less dramatic impact, by subsequent mobilizations by teachers, researchers, railway workers and others to defend jobs and pension rights and to resist creeping privatization of the state sector. However, the private sector failed to mobilize in 1995 and is largely the site of local and sometimes desperate defensive actions that take place against a background of a broader passivity and demoralization. In contrast, other groups traditionally thought incapable of mobilizing – the unemployed and the homeless – have undertaken highly visible actions, sometimes strictly local, sometimes national in their dimensions and sometimes (the European unemployment marches of 1997 and 1999) international. At the same time, the counter-globalization movement has grown in strength and visibility. ATTAC is its most prominent organization and the internationally circulated *Le Monde Diplomatique* one of its chief intellectual forums. French counter-globalization has been strongly represented in successive World and European Social forums. Repeated actions have also taken place in opposition to government policies perceived as racist as well as against the extreme rightist Front National that consistently registers electoral scores in the high teens. There has been, for example, a long-established campaign against the *double peine*, a discriminatory statute whereby non-French nationals can be doubly punished for crimes, first by imprisonment and then by expulsion from France. There has also been, as we noted at the beginning of this chapter, a sometimes little reported and sometimes high profile campaign in support of the *sans-papiers*. Anti-racism and anti-fascism, the constant motivation of campaigning by groups such as the Ligue des Droits de l'Homme, attract short-lived mass mobilization at times of perceived urgency, such as when, against expectations, the Front's leader, Jean-Marie Le Pen made it into the second round of the French presidential elections in 2002. France has also seen repeated mobilization around issues such as gay rights and environmentalism. If feminism can no longer claim the impact it enjoyed in the heady days of the 1970s, it has certainly not been quiescent in recent years. The campaign for political parity may in the end have had a somewhat disappointing outcome, with legislation being insufficiently radical to challenge the more important bastions of male political power. It nonetheless served to bring at least some of the questions raised by feminism back to the fore. At the same time, there have been other lower profile but nonetheless important feminist campaigns, triggered notably by threats to welfare regimes and reproductive rights and by enhanced awareness of the level of violence against women.

Despite the range of the above mobilizations – and the list is far from complete – certain commonalities can be identified (Crettiez and Sommier 2002: 20–22). As we have noted, these diverse movements all tend to operate with considerable independence from traditional union and party actors. Their distance from conventional political mobilization is accentuated by a refusal of centralized and hierarchical organizations and a marked preference for decentralized networks and direct democracy. The 1995 strikes were faithful to this pattern. They were led from the base and not from the top, and were driven by the cross-union and cross-trade 'co-ordinations' which first emerged in the 1980s and whose preferred mode of deliberation and decision making was the daily general assembly in which all had a voice. The 1995 strikes were also typical of other components of the social movement in that, although they began to evolve a set of principles in clear opposition to neo-liberalism, they had no longer-term social project. Other elements of the social movement also typically mobilize around specific goals rather than broader social projects. These shared features suggest some of the limitations and ambiguities of contemporary social mobilization. Seen in one way, the social movement might seem to present the politics of the future, one that has learned from the errors of the past and can see the undemocratic or even totalitarian potential of hierarchical organizations, pro-grammatic politics and grand narratives of emancipation. Yet seen in another way, the movement might seem to highlight the current lack of serious opposition to globalizing capital. Short-term, local struggles without broader ambitions and defensive and broadly consensual anti-fascism hardly suggest a truly radical social programme while the unstructured multiplicity of groups makes joint mobilization problematic. The radical credentials of the social movement are thus, as a number of commentators have noted (e.g., Hewlett 2004: 9–10), profoundly ambiguous. A strengthening of the politics of counter-globalization in both its anti-capitalist and internationalist dimensions would seem to be the obvious way for this ambiguity to resolve positively by allowing for the federation of core contemporary struggles against fascism, racism and social exclusions and in defence of migrants, state sector workers and egalitarian public service provision.

Taking in conjunction, the different changes evoked point to the radical newness of the socio-political terrain, a newness whose key points might be summarized as follows:

1. The traumatic undoing of the organized working class and the massive loss of influence of those institutions (the unions, the Communist Party or PCF) which both represented it and framed its struggles.
2. The collapse of a leftist, predominantly Marxist, grand narrative of opposition that connected local, national and international dimensions and past and present instances of resistance within an overarching frame.
3. The displacement of a polemical, class-based vision of the social by a politically disabling narrative of exclusion.
4. The fragmented, often individualized face of contemporary social suffering and its substantial loss of an adequate voice.
5. The rise of 'useless' suffering and violence no longer open to productive incorporation within a progressive narrative.
6. The emergence of an as yet fragmented and ambiguous but also vibrant and assertive social movement substantially disconnected from institutional politics.

Collectively, these changes constitute a radical transformation of the broader socio-political context in which a committed cinema must work and to which it must respond. But as we shall now see, they are paralleled by a similarly radical transformation of the cinematic terrain since the heyday of committed cinema in the years following 1968.

A Transformed Cinematic Terrain

The radical cinema that so flourished in the years after 1968 was one that saw itself as part of a broader project of socio-political transformation. Its double ambition was to make itself a vehicle for this broader project and to revolutionize its own means of production, expression, exhibition and reception. It was a cinema that found itself in frontal opposition to a state that was essentially considered to be a guarantor of the power of capital, still exercised direct political censorship and maintained a stranglehold on television, the public's principle source of information. It was a cinema too that was able, to some extent, to by-pass commercial channels of production, distribution and exhibition due to the existence of a vibrant associative sector, political and union actors (essentially the PCF and CGT or Confédération Générale du Travail) with a tradition of strong support for film production and exhibition, and a national network of non-commercial viewing sites associated with the same actors but also workplace councils. This was a context in which a counter-cinema could flourish and reach a cinematically literate audience disposed towards actively political reception.

Almost everything is now different. The large, parallel circuit of distribution and exhibition finally died out around the beginning of the 1980s, around the period when the left, after so many years in opposition, finally came to power, only to be driven to political 'realism' by the pressure of the markets. The collectivist production that grew out of 1968 in the shape of groups such as Dziga-Vertov, Medvedkine and Cinélutte came apart as the 1970s wore on and it became clear that the radical change that 1968 had seemed to announce was not a present possibility. Production returned to more conventional modes with film-makers again making films in their own name and not in that of a group. Those collectives that did survive mutated into small production companies run along more conventional lines.[1] At the same time, the PCF and the CGT, once mainstays of militant film production, recognized that film was no longer the best vehicle for reaching their in any case diminished publics.[2] Other militants also realized that television and the media more broadly were now the sites where public visibility was produced and thus where efforts had to be concentrated despite the accompanying risks of distortion related to the media's taste for the instantaneous and the graphic (Denis 2005: 118–122).

A lifeline was thrown to independent production in the mid-1980s as the state broke up the monopolies of big television companies and opportunities arose for external suppliers to provide programmes. New satellite and cable technologies brought an explosion in the number of television channels that went from two in the late 60s to over one hundred now. This proliferation meant vastly increased demand for new programmes. Although television largely buys entirely conventional programming, there is a fragile space at the system's margins for the making of committed documentary. At the same time, support mechanisms and exhibition quotas meant that France has been able to continue to make and show a large number of fiction films each year in a way that makes it by far the strongest industry in Europe. Television companies – notably Canal Plus – have been legally obliged to divert a percentage of their income into film production thus providing substantial funds but also exercising obvious commercial pressures on what kind of film can get made. Not only is there clearly the finance for a diverse range of films to be made, but, given that France retains a sizeable arts circuit open to independent productions, there is also a (threatened) space for them to be shown. These factors do not of themselves explain the return of a socio-politically engaged cinema, but they show that there is room within the French industry for such a thing to exist, given the right audience. They also remind us that it is not currently possible to imagine a radical cinema entirely free from state interference and commercial ties. Oppositional cinema, especially its fictional variant, now exists largely within the commercial sector, albeit often at its edges, and depends substantially on state quotas and subsidy mechanisms. Some prominent directors like Guédiguian, Tavernier and the Dardenne brothers have guaranteed themselves a degree of independence by working to set up production companies (Agat Films, Little Bear and Les Films du Fleuve respectively) and other younger directors have made films on a shoestring (Richet, Chibane and Ameur-Zaïmeche being three notable cases), but these are ways of evading systemic pressures and not direct challenges to the system.

Given the disappearance of the old parallel circuits of distribution and exhibition, it is also clear that a committed cinema can no longer find its core audience in the old ways. The return of combativeness signalled by the 1995 strikes, the dynamism of the social movement, the powerful rise of French counter-globalization and the more recent resounding 'no' in the referendum over the European constitution suggests that there clearly is public demand, but it is now met in new ways. At a routine level, it works through the arts circuit and thus clearly struggles to meet the popular public that the old militant cinema could reach through political party involvement and workplace penetration. In a less routine way, it increasingly functions through what one might call 'special events' such as cinema festivals and debates or study sessions structured around film viewings. The most emblematic, but far from the only example of the former, is the tellingly named *Résistances* festival sponsored by veteran oppositional film-makers Ken Loach and Bertrand Tavernier. The latter – the film-debate – is almost impossible to track, but is an important phenomenon of the last decade whereby film projections, whether in cinemas or in alternative venues, are used to open up debates, sometimes with the presence of members of the production team, sometimes with academic experts or social movement and political actors. The film-debate points to an important convergence of interests between independent exhibition and the directors of small and medium budget films. While the latter can use the debate to raise the profile of films with restricted promotional budgets, the former can draw upon them to underline how the cinematic experience they offer is qualitatively different to the standard multiplex fare. More broadly, the film-debate formula underlines how cinema can still play a public and political role.

Film has been a key tool in certain socio-political struggles. It has, for example, become a major pedagogic tool in struggles around globalization (Marie 2005). More specifically, ATTAC, the counter-globalization movement now routinely uses it – usually but not exclusively in the form of documentary – to structure and inform public discussion (Heller 2004). ATTAC now runs three quite sizeable annual film festivals, in Paris, Strasbourg and the Isère *département*. The film-makers 1997 intervention in the *sans-papiers'* struggle and their subsequent production of a widely seen short is another important example, but one could also cite Tavernier's *Histoires de vies brisées* (2001), Jean-Pierre Thorn's *On est pas des marques de vélo* (2002) and Ameur-Zaïmeche's *Wesh wesh, qu'est-ce qui se passe?* (2001), all films in protest against the *double peine*, the first of which played a key role in bringing the campaign to public attention.[3] One could cite too the multiple debates organized around Agnès Varda's *Les Glaneurs et la glaneuse* (1999) with its apparently gentle but ultimately devastating exploration of the violences of mass consumption or the way in which Le Roux's enormously successful *Reprise* became a focus for debates around France about both workplace struggle and the need to move beyond a society centred on waged labour (see chapter 3). Put briefly, because of its capacity to gather publics and inform debate, film has been an important vector of opposition over the last decade.

If cinema has been involved with a range of extra-cinematic socio-political struggles, it has also been involved in its own battles. The most prominent of these has been that concerning the *exception culturelle*, the fight to prevent cultural production and notably cinema from being classified as just one more product that should be opened up to 'free' competition, with the inevitable conclusion that the French system of support and quotas would have been dismantled with disastrous consequences not only for French film-making but also for all those many international directors who now call upon French funding. While it has vigorously defended its own cultural interests, France has also played a leading role, seconded by countries like Canada, in the broader, international campaign to achieve recognition for cultural exceptionalism. This has recently borne fruit with the ratification by the United Nation's cultural wing, UNESCO, of a charter enshrining culture's exceptional nature. Cultural exceptionalism is, of course, a problematic notion. It is clearly open to accusations of identitarian nationalism and of corporatist protectionism, and can be a high-minded alibi for the defence of narrow self-interest. It is perhaps for these reasons that it has more recently mutated into a defense of 'cultural diversity', a notion that is more fashionably open to difference and thus less national in its connotations. But, whatever name one gives it, and although it is clearly not the avowed intention behind it, exceptionalism has undoubtedly helped to preserve the space (the support mechanisms, the policies) in which a critical cinema can survive if not flourish.

If the main thrust of cultural exceptionalism has been at the level of production, a convergent battle has been against increased concentration of distribution and exhibition and more specifically over the predatory spread of multiplexes and the accompanying threat to the very existence of an independent cinema circuit. The struggle finds its institutional expression in organizations such as the ACID (L'Agence du Cinéma Indépendant pour sa Diffusion), an organization seeking to help promote the distribution of independent films with prominent leftist film-makers Guédiguian and Thorn amongst its founders, and, more locally, in battles to prevent the building of new multiplexes that bring together independent cinemas and spectators' associations (Hayes 2005). Like cultural exceptionalism, this struggle has its own ambiguities. The defence, for example, of high-brow, city-centre, art-circuit film theatres against multiplexes that may help bring cinema back to less central locations is clearly vulnerable to accusations of elitism and of the corporate self-interest of the owners of threatened cinemas. Yet, both cultural diversity and resistance to monopoly pressures and narrow commercialism in exhibition can be articulated in more radical ways when connected to an anti-globalization with a strongly anti-capitalist dimension. One can suggest with some confidence that the clear threats to French cinema's independence and diversity have helped sensitize film professionals to broader failings of the globalizing capitalist economy and provided a clear radicalizing pressure.[4]

In the case of fiction film, the threat to diversity is particularly sharply felt at the distribution and exhibition stage. A plentiful supply of French and foreign films, notably Hollywood ones, means that those films without large promotional budgets may struggle to remain on cinema screens for more than a few days. Thus, while 'blockbuster' releases aiming for maximum short-term returns increasingly tie down the lion's share of the nation's screens, other less commercial and less promoted films may not ever reach a wider national audience if their initial box office takings in Paris are poor. The rather absurd 1999 polemic that set many film-makers against those cinema critics who were felt to 'kill' films before they could find their audience was in good part a symptom of how desperate the struggle for screen space had become (O'Shaughnessy 2001). A more productive response was the publication in leading newspaper *Le Monde* (4 March 2004) of a public appeal written by the ACID and signed by nearly 200 film-makers. Entitled *Libérons les écrans* (Liberate the screens), it protested that the very existence of French cinema in its current diverse form was threatened by the monopolization of screens by big budget releases. In the first week of January 2004, it noted, four films (*Finding Nemo, Lord of the Rings, Scary Movie 3* and *Les Ripoux*) were occupying 3,022 of the nation's 5,280 screens. It therefore called upon the regulatory system to ensure that no film was shown on more than 10 per cent of screens.

A more recent, bitter and, at time of writing, still continuing struggle has been over the social security regime of the *intermittents du spectacle*, that is, of all those working in the cultural industries who typically undergo periods of unemployment between projects. In recent times the regime has come under enormous pressure, partly due to strong growth in the cultural sector and partly due to the increasing tendency for major media players to avoid giving permanent contracts, thus perversely passing on their costs to a social security regime designed to support freelance workers. Under pressure from the employer's organization, the MEDEF (Le Mouvement des Entreprises de France), the rightist government has installed a less generous system, thus provoking fierce resistance amongst cultural workers. Although there is widespread support for the *intermittents*, it has been less enthusiastic where action has threatened to disrupt shooting or interrupt festivals. Cultural workers have played a key role in the development of cultural wings of organizations like ATTAC with their own precarious status clearly providing an impetus to their involvement (Agard 2004). The precarious status of many of these same workers also opens up clear possibilities for alliances with other groups mobilizing around unemployment, unstable employment or welfare rights.

Cultural exceptionalism, battles over exhibition and the rights of cultural workers are all ambiguous struggles. If framed narrowly and disconnected from other causes, they may appear essentially corporatist and driven by self-interest. However, they are also clearly available for articulation within a broader politics that places defence of a diverse, democratic public sphere and egalitarian public welfare provision near its heart. They can thus clearly be connected to other struggles we have identified, notably over globalization and resistance to a neo-liberal hollowing out of the public sector. At the current time, one can probably say that this connection is emergent rather than a given, something that is being developed as cultural producers and workers become more closely involved in other struggles, as organizations such as ATTAC develop their cultural wings, or as cinemas, such as the independent Utopia network, open their doors to the anti-globalization movement even as they defend themselves against the predation of multiplexes (Hayes 2005).

It is in the emergent and often very local nature of this connectivity that lies one of the key differences between current cinematic commitment and earlier variants, particularly around 1968. In the period following 1968 a fully developed politics, albeit one riven by division and by debates, preceded mobilizations in the cinematic sphere. Although it might be recognized that a political cinema had to work in a way that recognized the specificity of film as cultural practice, the underlying logic of the cinematic struggle came from the broader political arena, even when cinema was not simply instrumentalized by political actors, as with the *film militant* (see chapter 2). The situation is now very different. As I have noted, the broader struggle itself is characterized by greater diversity and fragmentation with no fully elaborated politics at its disposal and with each struggle being suspended between the more systemic challenge to which it could become attached and more local, tactical goals. Cinema's 'internal' struggles follow a similar pattern, certainly being available for connection to a broader radicalism but not finding their origin within such a thing. Where cinema becomes involved in the struggles of others, its interventions are of necessity local and ambiguous given the current fragmented state of the social movement and the generally limited nature of its interventions. Cinema, taken in the round, is thus involved in a diverse series of struggles that have not yet been articulated within an overarching frame, although the potential for that is clearly there. Committed film is thus part of a broader, as yet inchoate and necessarily ambiguous socio-political striving.

Conclusion

We are now able to situate the current wave of socio-politically committed cinema with more precision. While it is unwise to suggest simple, deterministic mechanisms that might explain cultural tendencies, we can suggest with reasonable assurance that the return of commitment to French cinema can broadly be explained by a coming together of specific cinematic determinants and a broader socio-political context. The French industry's apparent good health and high annual output of films should not distract us from the fact that many small and medium films have to fight to be seen in the face of fierce monopoly pressures, notably at the level of distribution, promotion and exhibition. This struggle to exist would seem to be the best available specifically cinematic explanation for a heightened political awareness among film professionals. At the same time, the return of widespread socio-political dissent in the mid-1990s, the existence of a lively and diverse social movement and the growth of the French counter-globalization movements demonstrate the existence of a climate conducive to the production and reception of a critical cinema. The previous post-1968 wave of committed cinema burst onto the scene when radical socio-political change seemed a genuine possibility: driven by highly elaborated radical leftist ideologies, it was able to draw on a politics that preceded it and set itself, at its most ambitious, the aim of reinventing cinema while helping to remake society. The current wave has emerged in the aftermath of the defeat of the twentieth-century left and in the silence left by the unravelling of a leftist grand narrative of opposition: dependent on the commercial sector and state support mechanisms, it would not seem to be in a position to radically question either its own mode of existence or means of expression.

Some clearly think, as we shall see in the next chapter, that this is pseudo-radical cinema, one that places a veneer of progressive concern over fundamentally conservative political positions and formal choices constrained by the pressing need to bring in an audience in order not to simply vanish from cinema programmes. But others, the current author included, judge it much more positively, believing it should be seen as a positive part of a broader revival of opposition and of critique. Caught between the politics that was but is no more, and an emergent, diverse radicalism, it must work on a new terrain with no overarching framework to give shape and meaning to its interventions. Where once struggle and suffering came to it shaped and made productive by an overarching oppositional vision, they now come to it, one might say, raw and threatened with meaninglessness. Where a discourse of class once served to name oppressions rooted in economic equality, critique now seems to have lost its voice. This is an enormous symbolic shift that will be picked up and developed in chapter 3.

Notes

1. The evolution of some of the collectives is discussed in Gauthier ed. (2004). Specific attention is paid to the evolution of the aims of one group, Les Films Grain de Sable, in Heller (2005). Heller notes how the group's aims shift over time from radical social change to something considerably more anodyne and consensual.
2. Chris Marker's *2084* (1984), produced for the CFDT or Confédération Française Démocratique du Travail, a trade union federation, to mark its centenary, is probably the last piece of film-making sponsored directly by the official left.
3. For a discussion of the different films made in support of the *sans-papiers*, see Agard (2005).
4. It is surely no accident that documentary makers, very much the poor cousins of fiction cinema and people who have to exist in the interstices of the production system with often very difficult access to cinema and television screens, have also led in the production of films critical of globalization.

2

DEBATES

One might say, for the sake of neatness, that there are two kinds of debate. There are those which take place at an agreed time, in a single location, with two clear sides, an explicit question and a set of rules that both agree on. There are also those that take place over time, straddle different media, lack clearly defined protagonists or rules and only loosely converge on an issue or set of questions but nonetheless have sufficient focus to indicate marked disagreement on some topic of concern to a general or more tightly defined public. French cinema is routinely the object of a number of debates of the latter variety. The one discussed here revolves around the way in which one should interpret the return of some sort of commitment to French cinema. Because the debate is diffuse and multi-sided, I have given it an artificial focus, not least by concentrating on only some of the voices that have made themselves heard. This is not a purely arbitrary manoeuvre. The intention is to bring some real fault lines to the surface that can also be made to play a productive role in my own developing argument. The central point of disagreement, as indicated at the end of the previous chapter, is clearly over whether the object of concern here is a pseudo-political cinema or one that represents some sort of genuine and effective return of commitment. Two subsidiary and overlapping questions are whether, given the drastically changed context (chapter 1), one can reasonably apply criteria used to judge the post-1968 wave of committed films to current cinema and whether the realism deployed by the films recycles the conventional and the already known or, rather, shows a genuine capacity to open onto contemporary reality, to bring underlying violences to the surface and to drive us back towards a politics. While I seek to explain what divides defenders and critics of the films, I do not seek fusion between opposing viewpoints. Nonetheless, I take something from each. Although I feel that the critics of the films misjudge them in some important ways, I consider that criteria they develop to gauge the effectiveness of a political cinema have undoubted usefulness and will therefore draw upon them at a later stage. From defenders of the films, I take above all important insights about the films' originality and their capacity to bite upon the real. I turn first to those who broadly defend the films before moving on, in the second half of the chapter, to some of their chief detractors, a group of critics at *Cahiers du Cinéma*.

Supporting Voices

One of the most important voices raised in defence of the political effectiveness of the current wave of French films is that of long-time *Positif* stalwart and now film critic at *Politis*, Jean-Pierre Jeancolas. Jeancolas made his initial intervention after the film-makers' mobilization in support of the *sans-papiers*. Defending their cinema from accusations that it was closed to contemporary issues and detached from the public, Jeancolas suggested, on the contrary, that it is anchored in the present and manifests what he calls, *un réel de proximité* or 'proximate realism'. Developing this line, he suggests that the *cinéastes* are engaging with the fragments of an atomized society that, because we have lost the social and ideological frameworks that were so strongly present in 1968, we now encounter without being able to make full sense of them. He asks rhetorically if this is a political cinema as those of 1968 might have understood it before suggesting that the old categories (to which we shall come), no longer apply. Cinema, he notes, has lost its pedagogic function. It no longer approaches the real with a pre-existing and all-embracing politics whose validity is to be demonstrated. Rather, it narrows its focus to a small section of the real, a *réel de proximité*. Within the framework of this real, the sincerity and freshness of the film-makers' look upon the other or upon variants of the self allows for the irruption into the film of a conflictual present, of shifting social structures and of otherness. Conventional understandings of politics link it to a series of union and party actors armed with programmes. But if, as Jeancolas underlines, these actors are failing, politics must be conceived differently. In the search for a new politics, in their capacity to probe the real, the film-makers may perhaps be a 'reel ahead' (Jeancolas 1997: 58). He later returned to the same issues, linking his conception of a *réel de proximité*, with the need to return to discussions of realism by André Bazin, the great French film theorist of the post-Second World War era (Jeancolas 1999). It is this latter invitation that we will now take up before turning to some analyses that complement that of Jeancolas.

Bazin's key writings on realism are concentrated in his most famous work, *Qu'est-ce que le cinéma?* (1990 [1958–62]). The part of this work of most obvious relevance to Jeancolas's conceptualization of a proximate or immediate realism is the discussion of Italian neo-realism. This is dispersed across general thoughts on cinematic realism and analyses of the work of specific neo-realist directors such as De Sica, Rossellini or Visconti. Bazin associates neo-realism with certain features that are by now part of standard film history: use of non-professional actors and the avoidance of star performers; the move away from the well-made plot to more open and loosely constructed narratives; stories whose basic unit is the 'fact', the raw chunk of social reality, rather than the shot predigested by the needs of the narrative; a preference for long takes and an avoidance of the effects created by montage; a rootedness in the contemporary absent, for example, in the French production of that same period (Bazin 1990). While some of these features also characterize the contemporary French films that we are concerned with here (notably the widespread use of non-professional actors, a shift to loosely constructed narratives and rooting in the present; see chapter 7), of more profound interest is Bazin's core underlying suggestion that neo-realist films refrain from pre-digesting the real. Bazin fascinatingly suggests that neo-realist films are 'pre-revolutionary'; that is, that they signal their refusal of an unjust social reality but refuse to instrumentalize it by subjugating it to the demands of a political ideology that precedes the film (Bazin 1990: 263–65). Thus, in a film like *Bicycle Thieves* (De Sica, 1948), events are not made to be the signs of a pre-existing meaning, but retain their singularity and ambiguity while still being embedded in a social context. Rather than people and events within the narrative being instrumentalized to back up a social thesis, our minds must retrospectively construct the thesis (Bazin 1990: 295–309). It is in this sense of a real that comes unprocessed by a preceding political vision that Bazin and Jeancolas clearly converge. Bazin's analysis suggests how one might begin to assess the political 'use-value' of the current wave of socially engaged French films. Having no ready-made answers or overarching meanings to give us, the films nevertheless drive us urgently to engage with the real, asking us to search for answers and meanings that are lacking. This shift from a cinema that communicates an existing politics to one that pushes us towards a politics yet to be found also supposes a shift in the relation between politics, film and spectator, from what one might call a vertical mode, characterized by pedagogic transmission from a source of knowledge to a receiver, to a horizontal one whereby the spectator is asked to share actively in the production of a politics.

A discussion involving, among others, film-makers Claire Simon and Serge Le Péron, in a book devoted to the encounter between the cinema and *le mouvement social*, moves us in some similar directions although without the reference to Bazin. Simon suggests that after the quiescent 1980s, when French cinema essentially turned in upon itself, asked itself how it was to adapt pre-existing fictional vehicles to a French setting and turned its back on the social, the 1990s saw a return to the real led primarily by documentary. This return freed films from ready-made narratives and allowed directors to draw upon what Simon calls, *les fictions du monde réel*, or 'real-world fictions' (Breton et al. 2000: 142–43). Contrasting post-1968 militant cinema with current socially engaged film, she remarks, 'We've gone from militant cinema to "What's going on here, down from where I live?"' (Breton et al. 2000: 144).[1] This implied retreat from a cinema that approaches the world with a ready-made politics to one that asks questions of an immediate real has clear resonances with our discussion above of Bazin and Jeancolas. But it also points towards one of the key criticisms – of engaging with social realities but of failing to be political – that is addressed towards those film-makers who merely seek to interrogate the real.

An answer is perhaps provided by Le Péron, who adds a new theoretical dimension to the discussion so far. To begin with, Le Péron partially disagrees with Simon about the entire self-absorption of the French cinema of the 1980s, noting how the then emergent *banlieue* or outer-city cinema (see chapter 4) had already opened the way towards a return of the social. He notes too that, since the 1970s, we have witnessed the collapse of the leftist social imaginary and thus, implicitly, of what used to provide a grounding for a committed cinema, but nonetheless suggests a consistent concern among worthwhile directors to go beyond reality to what, drawing on Lacan, he calls the real. Akin to the Lacanian symbolic order, reality is that which elicits the comment, 'things are like that', a reflection of the status quo and of the surface appearance of the social world. The real is precisely that which one does not ordinarily see and that the film-maker must make apparent by work upon the world. It is thus equated, in Le Péron's version of Lacan, with the underlying dynamics of relationships (between father and son or boss and worker), that hidden part of them which causes suffering. Le Péron draws a clear demarcation between what he pejoratively labels 'tele-films' with their banal and predictable sociological content and those genuinely creative films that work upon the real (Breton et al. 2000: 144–45). His comments suggest how a cinema with a purely interrogative relation to the world might still be a committed one with its commitment lying not in its explicit message but in its effort to render hidden violences visible. They also begin to provide an answer to those critics, whose analyses we will shortly consider, who equate realism as a whole with conservative representation of the status quo.

A recent article by Patricia Osganian in the progressive review *Mouvements* moves out beyond the confines of French cinema to suggest that a group of contemporary European directors share a concern with social exclusion as an extreme form of class domination. Although her main focus is the Dardenne brothers, Belgian film-makers discussed at length in this volume, Osganian also refers to the work of British directors such as Mike Leigh and Ken Loach, some French directors, as well as representatives of the originally Danish Dogme 95 group. She suggests that what unites these directors is an aesthetic of the fragment as opposed to a totalizing, epic aesthetic able to locate the foreground action as part of a meaning-giving whole. Whether anti-naturalist or realist, these directors all seek to pin down the real through the collision of a hard core of exploitation and the struggles of an individual moved by his or her desire for autonomy. Osganian clearly converges with Le Péron and others in her implied differentiation between a cinema of the real and a naturalist cinema and in her equation of the former with the bringing to visibility of underlying social conflicts.[2] She adds to Le Péron by suggesting that this cinema is one that shows the evacuation of the social so that what is left is the un-cushioned conflict between individuals. The kind of collective values that might provide both a reassuringly stabilizing and ultimately conservative background to the action and a totalizing sense of the social, are precisely that which can no longer be called upon. What is now shown, through the aesthetic of the fragment, is the absolute non-reconciliation of individual and society, so that what one might call a social cinema in fact shows the deconstruction of the social (Osganian 2003).

Osganian's discussion of a cinema of fragments chimes with Jeancolas's description of a cinema of fragmentary social facts that was in turn inspired by Bazin's account of Italian neo-realism. Implicit in all three is a sense of the loss of a totalizing vision that could make sense of and tame a real that therefore comes to us with a new rawness, challenging us to make sense of what we see. This book develops the notion of an aesthetic of the fragment to make it a core part of its own argument. It firstly elaborates upon its emergence, tying it explicitly to the withdrawal of a leftist politics that once gave shape, meaning and a language to local struggles by locating them within a broader dramaturgy of class struggle (chapter 3). It develops, secondly, its central characteristics, notably the raw, quasi-mute corporeality that ensues from the individualization of social struggle and the loss of a collective voice (chapter 6). It considers, thirdly, the essentially melodramatic strategies deployed by the films to restore some eloquence to the fragment (chapter 7). If, as Osganian notes, part of the originality of the films discussed is their capacity to underline the lack of a stabilizing sense of a social whole, the notion of an aesthetic of the fragment is not simply synonymous with social fragmentation. Intrinsic to it also is a symbolic lack, a withdrawal of a voice and meaning. It is only the latter that, as we shall later see, can explain some of its key features.

A Return to the *Fiction de Gauche*?

In sharp contrast to the favourable accounts we have just considered, some of the critics at *Cahiers du Cinéma*, one of the great bastions of French cinema criticism, generated a sharp critique of the films with which we are concerned here.[3] They essential saw them as a return of the superficially progressive but fundamentally conservative *fiction de gauche* or 'civic' cinema that became an object of great scorn in the years following the great student and worker rebellions of 1968. The year 1968 witnessed not just an upsurge in the production of politically committed films but also sustained attempts to develop a complex critical apparatus that would provide sophisticated tools for assessing the political work done by films and the broader machinery of production and reception within which they took their place. A core part of this effort, in which *Cahiers du Cinéma* played a central role, was the drawing of lines between genuinely and only apparently progressive films.[4] Over time, and at the risk of simplification, one might say that a tripartite typology developed, consisting of a good object, the properly political cinema, a not-so-good but still useful object, militant cinema, and a decidedly bad object, the *fiction de gauche*, the film that appeared to have a progressive content but that in its production, reception and form in fact reinforced the status quo. Typically associated by *Cahiers* with the name of Jean-Luc Godard and with the Dziga-Vertov collective of which he was a founder member, a properly political cinema sought, at its most radical, simultaneous breaks with commercial production and reception and conventional narrative strategies that amounted to a self-reflexive rethinking of all of the stages of cinema. Thus, collective, anonymous production was to replace the conventional centrality of the director as *auteur* and its fetishized celebration of individual creativity. Reception was to take place in contexts that allowed for the address of spectators as a politically active collectivity rather than a passive mass. Mainstream narrative was to be disrupted in ways that enabled or enforced an interrogative relationship with the film that was to become a vehicle for both a critique of conventional cinematic representation and a broader ideological questioning. Militant cinema, a distinctly poor cousin, was simply the production of films for immediate use by leftist organizations and trade unions in their meetings. Its essential inferiority was felt to lie in its lack of self-questioning and in its top-down transmission of an already established line. Rather than problematizing film form and the spectator's relationship with the image, it simply sought to get a message across, and was thus, at worst, akin to propaganda of right or left. The *fiction de gauche* was a film that contented itself with putting an apparently progressive content (a critique of state repression, the story of a strike) into the same forms as conventional narrative cinema. As a result, the necessarily collective and systemic political dimension was dissolved by focus on star images, positively or negatively connoted individual protagonists and narrowly framed social issues that targeted the surface problems of the status quo and not the status quo itself. Moreover, instead of sending an actively questioning audience back to real world struggle, the *fiction de gauche* sucked them into the passive consumption of the pleasures of fictional narrative and genre codes within established circuits of film exhibition. If the *fiction* was explicitly realist, and this was usually the assumption, it presented the spectator with an immobilizing reproduction of the already familiar, failing thus to problematize the real or to show it in movement.

Cahiers' analyses might seem to belong to a specific historical moment when radical change seemed a real possibility and when sharp political dividing lines could be drawn in ways that made a similar demarcation of the cinematic terrain a reasonable and necessary proposition. They posed a series of questions about the relationship between a progressive politics and film production, reception and form that should, one might imagine, receive different answers today, even if the questions themselves retain their validity. Yet, a reading of relatively recent numbers of the journal suggests that it has courageously, stubbornly, perhaps perversely returned to the same or similar categories, notably in its response to the wave of socially engaged films that concern us here and that tend to be seen as a continuation of the *fiction de gauche* with all its faults and thus as a pseudo-political cinema. Thus, the continued validity of the old categories was affirmed as recently as April 2003 in companion pieces from critics Patrice Blouin and Stéphane Delorme. Delorme's piece reveals a growing nostalgia for the old *cinéma militant* because of its capacity to immerse itself in a struggle, its typically collective mode of production and its ability to bring together cultural producers and political actors (Delorme 2003).[5] Blouin's companion piece evidences a determination to maintain the core distinction between a self-reflexive and actively questioning political cinema and the *fiction de gauche* that, failing to operate a shift in the spectator's outlook, gives them back what they already know (Blouin 2003).

A more rounded working through of *Cahiers'* positions is provided by the special number the journal brought out on the thirtieth anniversary of 1968. While the division between the authentic *film politique* and the *fiction de gauche* is not explicitly featured, it nevertheless runs through key articles by critics François Ramone and Emmanuel Burdeau. Both largely dismiss the political credentials of those current French fiction films with which we are concerned here, essentially by re-enacting some of the core criticisms of the *fiction de gauche*, notably its subordination of the political to the disabling conventions of conventional narrative fiction and its frequent recourse to a naturalism that immobilizes the social. Ramone's text focuses on the cinematic representation of the common people. He begins with an evocation of May 1968 that, in a way clearly indebted to Badiou, is presented as a political event that, exceeding all pre-existing determinations, allowed for an opening up of liberatory and transformatory possibilities. The 'people' of 1968 was not a static sociological category with an established identity but a self-creating and creative political actor,

co-emergent with the event itself.[6] Building from this conception of the
political people as one characterized by self-invention, Ramone suggests
that French cinema has historically chosen the fixity of identity and the
inertia of representation (the reproduction of what is) against the radical,
political mobility of the event. Thus, during its classical period in the 1930s,
far from denying workers access to the screen, it gave them a solid presence
in what was its predominant populist strand. Their identity was positively
valued precisely because their very fixity allowed them to be associated with
reliability and moral uprightness. Their heavy body, as typified by the
dominant male star of the time, the robust Jean Gabin, resisted liberatory
metamorphosis, while their sociability, so often present on the screen,
locked them into static groups within which change could only be
negatively figured as disruption.[7] Renoir's committed cinema at the time of
the left-of-centre, anti-fascist Popular Front represented only a partial
exception to this regressive representation. If, unlike the rest of the cinema
of the period, it showed a common people capable of leading social
transformation, it did so by locking historical leadership into a still fixed
identity without ultimately freeing this identity for a more truly radical self-
definition.[8] The *cinéma vérité* of the 1960s escaped from this immobilizing
and objectifying representation of the people to record the masses' self-
expression but only succeeded, according to Ramone, in locking them into
their depoliticized everyday experience. Unless, of course, it escaped from
this entrapment by recording, not their immobilized identities, but their
imaginings – as in Jean Rouch's *Moi, un noir* (1958) – or if it miraculously
captured, as in 1968, the moment when the transformatory event ruptured
the continuity of the everyday (Ramone 1998).

Caught between the immobilizing fictional representation of the masses,
and the depoliticized, documentary recording of their everyday life, a
putatively political cinema might thus seem to have had few positive choices
to make outside those moments like the Popular Front and 1968 when the
transformatory people made their presence felt. One choice was to take a
Jansenist, ascetic turn and to show the absence of the political people, along
lines described by Deleuze with reference to the films of Alain Resnais and
the Straubs (Deleuze 1985: 281–91). Another more positive choice, learning
from the 1968 slogan *l'imagination au pouvoir* or 'power to the
imagination', was to turn to a cinema of creativity and theatrical play,
which, refusing to root characters in a fixed social location and cultural
identity, allowed them the possibility of constant self-reinvention. Thus,
Godard's Michel Poiccard (*A Bout de souffle*, 1959), a protean, depthless
character, anticipated 1968. But instead of creating more Poiccards and
despite its break with the advertising aesthetic of the 1980s and its return
of the common people to the screen, recent French social cinema has
essentially resurrected old errors. Like *cinéma vérité*, it has turned to the
everyday and away from the political. Like the populist French cinema of

the past, it has chosen the defensive representation of community over social reinvention. When it figures leftist politics, notably in the films of Guédiguian, it shows it as something that has gone before and which is thus dissolved into a nostalgic celebration of folkloric cultural identity with the same status as pastis drinking. Or, imitating the more contemporary vices of tame multiculturalism, it has espoused a defensive and consensual anti-fascism that locks minorities into established identities. In sum, it has preferred the concrete to the possible and an immobilizing realism to the play of form. In this it has mirrored the vices of contemporary British social realist films that represent the people exhaustively, weigh them down so they cannot move and fill the spaces that should be held open for the political people yet to come.

Ramone's colleague Burdeau also rejects the example of the British cinema of Ken Loach and Mike Leigh and of *The Full Monty* (Cattaneo 1996) and other similar films. His rejection has two strands. The first is that British cinema produces its effects by adding colour (the famous striptease of *The Full Monty*, for example) to a grey, naturalist and quasi-obscene depiction of the working class. The second is that the realism of this cinema is one produced through a clichéd accumulation of signs (of ugliness, poverty or distress). Doubly condemned by this miserabilism and formal conventionality, British cinema is decidedly not a model to follow. Rather counter-intuitively, Burdeau then suggests that French cinema has rather more to learn from Hollywood cinema that, because it ties the individual into the national epic, produces stories that are simultaneously and inextricably local and international, personal and political. Yet, working within a different tradition, French cinema cannot simply call upon this intrinsic connection of levels and must thus constantly reinvent the marriage of the fictional and of the political, in (good) ways which set the political dimension in motion, or in (bad) ways that block its development. Recent French cinema has generally made the wrong choices. Some films (Masson's *En avoir (ou pas)*, 1995; Guédiguian's *Marius et Jeannette*, 1996) initially seem to promise an engagement in contemporary issues only to allow them to be swallowed by conventional love stories. Others have made the *banlieue*, that epicentre of contemporary social malaise, *watchable*, creating in the process a new genre, the *film de banlieue*. The films concerned, notably Kassovitz's *La Haine* (1994), are locked into the closed interplay of generic motifs so that, instead of opening onto political questions, they only engage with other films. Referring back to 1968 or to extreme leftist militantism, another group of films similarly dissolve the political into genre convention and cliché. Thus, for example, Cédric Klapisch's *Le Péril jeune* (1993) narrates 1968's inheritance through the biographical form, turning its massive socio-political disruption into a phase in growing up, while Guédiguian's cinema reduces politics to folklore and memory. In sum, contemporary social cinema is repeating the depoliticizing vices of the *fiction de gauche*. Politics is absorbed by the fiction or a prelude or an inert, unquestioned background to it (Burdeau 1998).

Burdeau however concedes exceptions where the political, instead of being an adjunct to the fiction, is placed at its heart and becomes its motor, allowing for mutually supportive interaction of the sort routinely found in Hollywood cinema. For example, Chabrol's *La Cérémonie* (1995) and Poirier's *Marion* (1996) (chapter 4) are driven throughout by class conflict and are thus truly political films and not simply films that have political themes or backdrop. Instead of reassuring us about the unity of society and our immobilizing connectivity to others, they signal the return of an authentic politics, along lines laid down by Badiou and Rancière, as movement, disruption and the breaking of those links that tie us to the existing social order. These films are, however, exceptions in a group that broadly fails to be political. However, Burdeau holds out considerably more hope for a different strand of film-making, one that signals the return of a psychoanalytical cinema. Rather than fixing characters to an established social identity, this latter strand, by its turn to the irrational and the insane, destabilizes characters, freeing them to change places and roles, demonstrating in the process the ultimately arbitrary and contingent nature of the social order. Instead of being immobilized, the social thus loses its reassuring solidity while the social bond takes on the status of a hypothesis, a way people might be connected, not one that ties them into their existing social roles (Burdeau 1998).

Ramone and Burdeau show a desire to update an understanding of political cinema while remaining faithful to the core divisions laid down in the post-1968 period. While their critique of current French social realist films clearly reworks certain criticisms of the old bad object, the *fiction de gauche*, it is also decidedly contemporary in its ideological grounding. One of the key political topics of the 1990s has been that of social exclusion or what President Chirac called *la fracture sociale* and the need, in a spirit of inclusiveness, for all to pull together, making sacrifices where necessary. The *Cahiers* critics' pointed refusal of those films that celebrate a pacifying social link is thus clearly a polemical intervention in current politics and a reminder that a radical politics implies a break. So also is their connection of a long-established critique of representation to a more specifically contemporary critique of anti-fascist consensus politics that, by equating political justice with the representation of minority groups' existing social identity, locks each group in its place and pacifies social interaction. So too is their refusal of those films which, taking note of the historical defeat of the left, seem to consign political revolt to a fondly remembered past. Moreover, their formal preferences have moved away from the Brechtian alienation, narrative disruption and explicit political questioning that post-1968 criticism associated with a genuinely political cinema. They instead celebrate either a cinema of creativity and theatrical self-invention or one that undermines the current allocation of places and the fixed links that hold them in place. By thus refusing the fixity of current identities and social relationships, they are, one might say, holding open the space, not so much of the political people, but of politics itself. This stance might seem particularly apposite for a period when systematically oppositional politics is conspicuously lacking but it does also point to the potential weakness in their argument. At the more abstract level, it is hard to see why creativity, self-invention or non-fixity of social roles are inherently progressive when detached from any even vaguely specific political project or social critique. At a more concrete level, their examples might also cause one to question their position. For example, Jean-Luc Godard's Michel Poiccard, a key figure for Ramone, is undoubtedly a mobile, entirely superficial character but it surely makes as much sense to link these qualities to the massified mobility and consumption and mass-mediation that were such an explosive force in the France of the era as to connect them to the outburst of radical creativity of 1968. Burdeau's examples might also cause one to question at least part of his core argument. Although one could hardly argue against his general disqualification of films that allow the political to be absorbed by the sterile interplay of genre conventions, it is far from obvious from his examples that a turn to genre is necessarily counter-productive. *La Cérémonie* is in many ways a typical Chabrol suspense, while it would seem hard not to categorise *Marion* as a family melodrama (chapter 7). It is unclear why some genre fictions (*La Haine*) are to be condemned for generic self-enclosure while others are seen as politically productive. Taking a very different line, this book will argue for the political productiveness of some of the typical generic motifs of the *banlieue* films as deployed in specific cases (including *La Haine*). It will also make a more general case for the productiveness of melodrama and the capacity of its generic repertoire and some of its typical themes to restore eloquence and visibility to socio-political struggle (chapter 7).

The general dismissal by Burdeau and Ramone of the films under discussion is echoed by another regular columnist in *Cahiers*, political philosopher Jacques Rancière, who in his own way holds the line separating a properly political cinema from the latest avatar of the *fiction de gauche* which, perhaps confusingly, but illustrating the inevitable variability of terms, he labels *film militant*. Rancière grounds his argument in the distinction he makes between 'the real of fiction' and 'fictions of the real' (Rancière 2000). Associated with political fictions but also with realist representation in general, the former seeks to ground itself in the real by calling on two complementary mechanisms. Firstly, a documentary-like 'real of recognition' that gives us back what we already know about the social and which is thus inert and clichéd. Secondly, the 'real of surprise' which feeds off the unpredictability of fiction and the apparently spontaneous existence of its characters to bring representations to life. This leads to the paradox that the dead, unmoving part of political fictions is what roots them in life, while their life can only come from the fiction.

Rancière takes particular exception to one *film militant* to which we shall later return in more detail, *Nadia et les hippopotames* (Cabrera 1998).[9] This film narrates the encounter, at the time of the 1995 strikes, between striking railway workers (the hippopotamuses of the title) and Nadia, an impoverished single mother. Rancière uses the discourse of the former to exemplify his first real: the real of recognition. The railway workers, the film's 'documentary' element, appear to speak an inert language of political cliché while it is left to Nadia, the fictional Mother Courage figure, to provide the spontaneous life, the real of surprise, that brings the film to life. Formally, this interdependence no longer works because the combination of the clichés of fiction with a clichéd view of the real can no longer convince. Politically, it is untenable because, giving us back the already known, it cannot but play a conservative role. Thus the inert realism that *Nadia* brings to bear on 1995 chimes with accusations that, seeking to refuse necessary modernization, the 1995 strikers were attempting to cling onto a fossilized vision of justice and social struggle. More broadly, by immobilizing the social and the political through the real of recognition, realist fictions inadvertently connive in the contemporary evacuation of political conflict and its consignment to history (Rancière 2000).

Rancière's positive counterparts to the 'real of fiction' are, as we noted, the 'fictions of the real', his equivalent of the *film politique* or *properly political film*. These latter find a new, radical combination of the document (what we already know) and fictional inventiveness. Because they are essentially documentaries, albeit ones that refuse the usual pretence at objectivity, they have no need to demonstrate their grounding in the real and can thus devote themselves to the politically far more productive task of questioning and destabilizing what we think we know to create or invent new objects, new 'fictions' of the real. Rancière's examples are Claude Lanzmann's *Shoah* (1985), Godard's *Histoire(s) du cinema* (1989), Marker's *Level Five* (1996) and Le Roux's *Reprise*. The last mentioned, one to which we shall return at length in the next chapter, is a retrospective search for a rebellious woman worker seen by Le Roux in a legendary piece of 1968 *cinéma direct*. Rancière notes that because Le Roux does not have to convince us of the reality of the woman (she is there on the 1968 footage), he can bring her to us in her ambiguity (is her voice that of raw revolt or is she an activist?), while asking what circumstances created and then dissolved the possibility of the encounter between her revolt and a broader history. At a deeper level and through a self-conscious use of form, the film, like the others mentioned, is also asking questions about how truths are produced (Rancière 2000).

Rancière's analysis of film feeds off his broader defence of a polemical understanding of the political as expressed notably in his key book, *La Mésentente* (1995), where he expressly rejects any model whereby politics is equated with the representation of people's established social identities. Because the existing identities of dominated groups inevitably reflect their subordination, a politics based on them can only reinforce the status quo. In contrast, an authentically radical politics is one tied to disidentification and the refusal of allocated social places and roles. It is thus unsurprising that Rancière prefers cinematic works that destabilize what we think we know to essentially conservative films that give us back the already familiar and lock us into what is. Along with the analyses from his fellow *Cahiers* contributors, his work suggests a determination to patrol the line drawn after 1968 that divides an authentically political cinema from ersatz versions that immobilize the social and pacify history and politics. The interventions in *Cahiers* thus collectively oppose a broader pacification of the social and emptying out of the political and are thus decidedly of their time. What would be ironic, however, is if, in their anxiety to keep the space of the political open and to reassert certain core divisions, they were turning their back on a cinema that was making an important political intervention in the present. Rather perversely perhaps, this book will draw at key moments upon Rancière's political philosophy to argue just that point. It will nevertheless retain insights from him and the *Cahiers* critics concerning the dangers of an immobilizing realism. While these insights reach back to 1968 and earlier, there is no reason to think that they have lost their validity. It is indeed hard to think how a radical cinema could do other than challenge the existing distribution of places, roles and of the right to public speech in the strong sense that Rancière gives to it. If I am to argue, as I will, that the films are politically significant, I will need to show that they define those at the bottom not by their identities but by their recalcitrant agency, by their non-coincidence with their allocated roles and by their determination to resist immobilization.

Conclusion

My own argument, as developed in this book, is broadly sympathetic with those who read contemporary French social-realist fiction positively for its ability to bite upon the real. I find the notion of the shift from an aesthetic of the totality to an aesthetic of the fragment a particularly productive one for reasons that I have introduced here and will develop further as the book progresses. I also concur broadly with the suggestion that the films concerned show a capacity to bring underlying socio-economic violences to the surface – I explore this idea particularly through a discussion of their class dimension (chapters 4 and 5) but also through a consideration of the new, raw appearance of social struggle (chapter 6). The *Cahiers* critics are undoubtedly right to point to the dangers of folkloric, identitarian and immobilizing representations of class that consign struggle to the past. I will argue however that, while the films discussed may not be entirely innocent on this score, they nonetheless put class to politically productive use. Again in broad disagreement with *Cahiers*, I will further argue (chapter 7) that, rather than allowing cinematic convention to neuter their politics, the films turn productively to the conventions of melodrama as a way to restore eloquence to social struggle deprived of a voice. Despite these disagreements with the *Cahiers* critics, I will retain and develop some of their core criteria for the evaluation of the effectiveness of a political cinema, notably its ability to refuse the fixity of identity, the immobilization of social structure and the reassuring solidity of the already known.

Notes

1. '*Du film militant, on est passé à: "Qu'est-ce qui se passe ici, en bas de chez moi?"'*.
2. The Dogme group's original 'Vow of Chastity' stresses the importance of the kind of work upon the real that will force 'truth' to the surface (Dogme 1995).
3. While *Cahiers* was one of the chief locations for a progressive critique of the films, it was neither the only one nor uniform in its stance. *Cahiers*' (now ex-)editor Serge Toubiana was, for example, more nuanced in his judgement than some of his colleagues. Writing in 1997, he defended the film-makers against accusations that their stance in support of the *sans-papiers* found no productive prolongation in their filmic output, by identifying a real openness to the other and to the elsewhere as well as a refusal of majoritarian moral positions in their works (Toubiana 1997b). Outside of Cahiers, one of the most robust, stimulating and challenging if less formally sophisticated critiques of the films concerned was provided by Jean-Pierre Garnier in the sociological journal *L'Homme et la Société*. Garnier suggests that a series of films produced typically by *petit-bourgeois* directors bring exploitation, racism, urban violence and social class back to the screens, only to treat them in an actively depoliticizing way. Thus, class struggle is dissolved into a formulaic critique of the bourgeoisie, engagement with the workplace is rendered anodyne by a focus on emotions, the causes of unemployment are evaded, exclusion is shown but in a way that allows the excluders to remain unseen and social questions are largely framed through individual narratives. A vigorous example of ideological critique, Garnier's piece is interesting not least for its convergence with the established critique of the *fiction de gauche* explored in this chapter (Garnier 2001).
4. For a full account of post-1968 debates over cinema's political role see Harvey (1978).
5. While the old militant cinema may indeed have disappeared around the beginning of the 1980s, the current wave of anti-globalization documentaries would seem to suggest a revival and renewal of the form (Marie 2005).
6. Interviewed in the same special number of *Cahiers*, and drawing explicitly on the memory of 1968, Badiou stresses that a true politics only emerges when people (students, workers, peasants) start to move away from the place that they are meant to occupy. It is this movement that allows a broader reshaping of the social order to become thinkable (Burdeau and Ramone 1998: 13).

7. The best account of Gabin's star image is provided by Gauteur and Vincendeau (1993).
8. I am far from convinced that this judgement does justice to the Renoir of the pre-war years. As I have discussed in my own work on him, his films of that period repeatedly figure a history whose ultimate shape is yet to be decided and historical actors whose ultimate role cannot therefore be fixed (O'Shaughnessy 2000: 101–54).
9. The film was also released in a shorter television version entitled *Retiens la nuit*. It is to this latter version that my own subsequent analyses apply, the longer cut of the film being unobtainable at the time of writing.

3

A GENEALOGY OF CONTEMPORARY OPPOSITIONAL CINEMA

As noted in the last chapter, the notion of a general collapse of emancipatory grand narratives is of no specific concern to this book. What it is profoundly interested in, however, is the consequences for a political cinema of the specific undoing of a leftist grand narrative of opposition. It initially turns to two classic post-1968 films, Marin Karmitz's *Coup pour coup* (1971) and Jean-Luc Godard's and Jean-Pierre Gorin's *Tout va bien* (1972), placing some emphasis on the contrasts between them, but concentrating above all on the totalizing socio-political dramaturgy that both are able to deploy and which is precisely what contemporary committed cinema has lost. The chapter's main energies are devoted to an exploration of the nature and consequences of this loss as developed, firstly, through an analysis of Le Roux's seminal documentary, *Reprise* and, secondly, through an exploration of the Dardenne brothers' early films as they move from recording politically articulated conflict to the kind of raw resistances so typical of their later and better known works. If these films by Le Roux and the Dardennes are above all of interest because of the genealogical investigation they enable, they are also significant for the different ways in which they seek to resist the defeat that they so eloquently explore. The tactics that they deploy point the way to those mobilized on a broader front by other contemporary films as later chapters will underline.

Tout va bien and Coup pour coup

The action of *Coup pour coup* involves a garment factory in a French industrial town. It has a predictable cast for the period: a wealthy owner, tyrannical foremen and women, oppressed women workers and trade union delegates who operate within the status quo rather than challenging it. The film's early stages show the oppressive working conditions in the factory: heat, noise, bullying surveillance, sexual harassment and overdemanding cadences. The factory's grim routine begins to break down when a woman worker cracks up, when some workers begin to sabotage the line and the management in response sacks those whom it identifies as ringleaders. The women walk out, bringing a timid intervention from their union which seeks to bring about a return to work in exchange for minor gains for elements of the workforce and without reinstatement of the sacked women. The women reject the union line, occupy the factory and sequestrate the owner, effectively taking control where once they had no say. Despite police pressure, the union's attempt to disarm the situation and violent attacks organized by management, they hold firm and are backed by other workers in the town as well as by peasant farmers. The prefect, the state's representative in the *département*, tells the owner that the government will not back him and he must negotiate. The women, by implication, have won the day. The situation at the heart of *Tout va bien* is similar. Workers again occupy a factory – this time a meat processing plant with a mixed workforce – and sequestrate the boss. Oppressive working conditions (noise, dirt and smell) and unbearable cadences are again evoked. The union – in this case clearly identified as the communist-dominated CGT – again works to contain and depoliticize the situation by turning a radical challenge to the social order back into a conventional dispute over pay and conditions. But the film is wider in its scope than *Coup pour coup*. It introduces a journalist and a film-maker – famously played by Jane Fonda and Yves Montand respectively – into the factory occupation forcing a questioning of their position both as individuals and as a couple in relation to broader events. Moreover, unlike *Coup pour coup*, it does not confine itself to a single chain of events worked through to a conclusion in a specific locale. Rather, it carries on beyond the end of the strike to engage with the state's wider repression of workers' actions and the continuation of the film-maker and the journalist's relationship and careers, thus questioning how each should evolve as a result of what has been experienced.

Tout va bien's ability to generate something apparently much broader from a very similar core story is intrinsically tied to its deliberate refusal of realist film-making, a quality that is signalled from the start by the self-conscious presentation of its narrative as narrative and by the transparently theatrical artificiality of its main set. It is this anti-realism that frees it from the restrictive demands of a cause-effect narrative and spatial coherence and allows it to introduce emblematic characters, locations and actions which in turn permit a more thorough and nuanced exploration of the then state of class struggle in France. It is the same anti-realism that lies at the heart of the overwhelming preference that *Cahiers du Cinéma* expressed for it. *Cahiers* give *Coup pour coup* credit for its engagement with class conflict and recognize that it breaks with conventional commercial practice by calling on real workers to participate in the development of the script and provide the bulk of the cast. Yet the journal maintains that it ultimately fails to break with cinematic convention and thus cannot succeed as political cinema. It allows itself to be tied into a cause-effect narrative and to narrate the blows and the counter blows (the *coups*) of class struggle rather than engaging with its underlying dynamics. Moreover, its espousal of naturalism condemns it to reflect the familiar surface of experience and generate effects of recognition ('yes, it is like that'), rather than analyzing the real and asking political questions of the audience. These formal 'mistakes' spring from the ideological errors of the film-makers, notably their espousal of a spontaneist workerism, a naïve belief in the rightness of the workers' spontaneous action and consciousness that grounds an equally naïve belief that it is sufficient to give them a voice and to unreflexively reproduce their words and actions in a realist drama (Groupe Lou Sin d'intervention idéologique 1972). Although the *Cahiers* text does not mobilise the term *fiction de gauche*, it is clear that something akin to the opposition between the authentic political film and the *fiction de gauche* (see chapter 2) lies behind it. Whilst this opposition works well to underscore the differences between the two films, it may blind us to what they share, something which one might term a common dramaturgy of the socio-political.

What might this common dramaturgy involve? Firstly, both films have an epic dimension, that is, they show collective class actors engaged in apparently decisive struggle. Secondly, both are able to insert their actions into a longer-term history that meaningfully connects the present to what has gone before and will come after. *Coup pour coup*, for example, links the memory of an old woman worker from the Popular Front strikes of 1936 to current experience while at the same time portraying its strike as part of a wider and ongoing process. *Tout va bien* looks back to anti-colonial struggles as well as to Soviet repression in Eastern Europe while at the same time showing its protagonists learning lessons for the future. Thirdly, both also connect to a broader spatial frame. This is most obvious for *Tout va bien* which is overtly national and international in its spatial reach – the film self-consciously presents its action as an interrogation of the state of class relations in the France of the period while the presence of Fonda as a journalist for an American press agency and references to the Vietnam war and to the Soviet bloc tie the national struggle into a broader context. The explicit spatial frame of *Coup pour coup* is much more restricted. It is, as we have noted, about one industrial town in France. Yet, because it mobilizes emblematic class and institutional actors (the workers, the owner, the union, the police, the media, the prefect), it is intrinsically rooted in a national context. Fourthly, both films are totalizing in their scope, not simply because of their spatio-temporal reach, but because they tie the personal into their broader, epic frame. Thus, for example, the women in *Coup pour coup* are driven to challenge the organization of their home and family life by the needs of the struggle, while the Fonda-Montand couple in *Tout va bien* learn to rethink their relationship within the historical unfolding of the class struggle rather than allowing it to constitute a depoliticized private arena.

Because the political articulation of embodied struggle is a key issue for this book, it is worth paying attention to how each film deals with the corporeal. As we noted, oppressive physical conditions and cadences are foregrounded in both works. In both, the workers' control that results from factory occupation is accompanied by the constraint exercised upon the boss's body through his sequestration and notably on his access to toilet facilities. If suffering and struggle are thus clearly embodied, they are also clearly taken in hand by an elaborated politics. Early in *Coup pour coup*, one of the women can no longer bear the heat and the strain of the line and has a hysterical attack, a moment when the individual body and emotions enter into simultaneous crisis. However, this personal suffering is immediately followed by collective resistance (the sabotage of the line) while being ultimately redeemed by the occupation's overturning of the status quo. Embodied suffering is thus rendered public and meaningful by articulation within the film's broader political frame. The same is true of *Tout va bien*, but Godard's and Gorin's film is characteristically more reflexive and subtle in dealing with this issue. The workers at one stage describe the unpleasant bodily experiences associated with their job before stopping themselves and noting that this is how the CGT representative would have put things as a way of grounding claims for improved conditions within the status quo. What is more important they note, implicitly rejecting an immobilizing realism in the process, is not merely to describe how things are but to show how they are changing or can be changed. While connecting bodily suffering to the political, *Tout va bien* shows the contingency of this connection, the fact that it can be made in different ways. Both films' articulation of the corporeal within an established leftist politics again underlines what they share despite obvious contrasts.

A succinct discursive expression of the kind of totalizing dramaturgy mobilized by the films can be found in one of the classic analyses of political cinema from the same period, Christian Zimmer's *Cinéma et politique* (1974). In a chapter tellingly entitled 'Décolonisations', Zimmer notes that, since 1968, all that was condemned to silence around the world by a *universally recognized* order has begun to speak. Being opposed to the same order, expressions of resistance are also universal. Zimmer writes:

> This 'taking of voice' is general, universal, because all struggles are connected, because there is only one self-same oppressed party, only one oppressor. The Third World is everywhere. It is within us. Remember what Che Guevara said

and that Godard took up in his own name in his contribution to the collective film *Loin du Vietnam*: we must multiply the number of Vietnams, create one, two, three Vietnams around the world (Zimmer 1974: 182).[1]

Zimmer's totalizing vision would seem to be a perfect illustration of the process analyzed by Chantal Mouffe and Ernesto Laclau by which specific anatagonisms are articulated within a broad counter-hegemonic movement (Laclau and Mouffe 2001: 134–45). Laclau and Mouffe's theoretical starting point is the work of Antonio Gramsci and his recognition that political struggles are not spontaneously generated by social antagonisms but depend upon their contingent articulation within civil society in the context of a broader struggle for hegemony. They stress that a specific grievance, over wages for example, has to be articulated with a more general wrong, done to a class or a colonized group, say, before it becomes a truly political struggle. In this process, of course, both the specific grievance and the universalizing instance of the general wrong are transformed, the former by its articulation within a politics, the latter by its connection to a specific content which simultaneously grounds and 'contaminates' its universality. Political articulation, they underline, depends on the establishment of equivalences between different causes so that each is raised from particularity and made available to the universalizing claims of a broad counter-hegemonic movement. It also depends, crucially, on the prior positing of a fundamental social antagonism, the identification of a common enemy being a necessary moment in the establishment of the chain of equivalences that can pull together a set of diverse struggles. At the time when Zimmer was writing, it was routinely possible to establish such an equivalence chain between so many 'decolonizations,' so many 'Vietnams,' essentially through the positing of such a tight connection between state, capitalist and imperialist dominations that they became identified as a single enemy. However, at the present moment, as Laclau notes, no such totalizing unification of struggles is possible. Endorsing Badiou's account of a collapse of an overarching leftist oppositionality (chapter 1), he suggests that the left's traditional imaginaries have been shattered so that there is an urgent need to develop a totalizing oppositional discourse to enable the translation of individual to general claims and to mount a counter-hegemonic challenge to ascendant neo-liberalism (Butler, Laclau and Žižek 2000: 211).

The films with which we are concerned in this volume operate, one might say, in the space where such a radical left-wing voice used to be. That is, they point with great urgency to fragmentary local suffering and struggle that cry out for a political taking in hand that would give them meaning and reconnect them to the totalizing explanatory level of the systemic. Operating between the old totalizing leftist dramaturgy and this new face of the social, the particular films to which we shall now turn underline the profundity of the change that has taken place and reveal its roots whilst pointing towards new forms that resistance may take.

Reprise and the Shifting Articulation of Struggle

When explaining why he had made *Reprise*, Le Roux said that he had been obsessed by a still he had seen in *Cahiers du Cinéma* of a woman from a classic piece of 1968 *cinéma direct*, *La Reprise du travail aux usines Wonder*, made as the events began to wind down by Pierre Bonneau and Jacques Willemont, two students from the state cinema school, the IDHEC (Institut des Hautes Etudes Cinématographiques).[2] With normal activities and systems of management suspended at the school as in many other educational institutions and factories, the young film-makers had had to seek permission from the school's general assembly to make their film, a project suggested to them by a *gauchiste* (radical leftist) contact in the Wonder factory at Saint-Ouen in the Parisian *banlieue*. Having received this collective endorsement for a project deemed to be of use to the broader struggle and in conditions of extreme urgency, the film-makers had driven their equipment to the factory gates, arriving just in time to capture the moment when, following an allegedly rigged vote to resume work, the strikers re-entered the factory doors.

Their film, predominantly a single eight minute shot, was thus able to capture, by an astonishing stroke of luck, the debate between key actors of the period that accompanied this moment. On one side were the management, predictably calling for an orderly return to work and to a status quo that the upheavals and factory occupations of 1968 had so dramatically threatened. In the middle were the representatives of the institutional left, primarily the Communists and the CGT, but also the rival union organisation the CFDT (Confédération Française Démocratique du Travail). On the other side were two voices that opposed the return to work with so little gained and so little changed. These latter voices came, firstly, from a young *gauchiste*, quietly arguing with the institutional left and, secondly, more vocally and emotionally, from a young woman worker, expressing her outrage both at the return to work and at the acceptance of horrendous working conditions that it implied. As various commentators have noted, the film had miraculously condensed the dramaturgy of 1968, the dramaturgy that of course also underlay *Coup pour coup* and *Tout va bien*. It had assembled representatives of the key forces in play (the bosses, the institutional left, the leftists and, as stereotypically embodied by the woman, a hitherto unorganized and voiceless proletariat) and it had shown them working through what then seemed the fundamental choice between slow, negotiated reform and a continuation and radicalization of 1968. It was undoubtedly this fortuitous crystallization of the drama of 1968 that allowed prominent critics Serge Daney and Serge Le Péron to describe the film as the 'primal scene', the *scène primitive*, of committed cinema, something which it would forever try to rediscover but with no success.[3] As 1968 receded, the possibility of the coming together of its actors around a moment of decision also faded away.[4]

Like the original 1968 film, Le Roux's documentary fortuitously managed to capture more than it intended. The director set out, as he said, to give a second chance, or another take (*une re-prise*), to the protesting woman. More broadly, he sought to track down all the main players of the original film to allow them to explain their role on that day. This he did by building painstakingly from one contact to another, and expanding to bring in other testimony from those who had worked at the Wonder factories in Paris or elsewhere. Deliberately refraining from the kind of instrumentalization whereby witness testimony is used to illustrate a truth that a documentary already claims to possess, the film grew to allow each contributor to talk more broadly about their own trajectory and the interweaving of their own story with a bigger history. It is essentially because of this openness that it did not simply limit itself to providing an explanation of people's behaviour that day outside the Wonder factory gates. By allowing union and party activists, leftists and ordinary workers to tell their own stories, the film effectively narrated the history of the French working class, the popular suburbs of Paris (the celebrated *banlieue rouge*), the French left, and the evolution of capitalism.

The story that emerges is a complex one. We learn of grim working conditions and repetitive, mindless tasks. We hear of women taken out of school at fourteen, obliged to work in the factory and often to hand over their wages to their families, yet still finding this a form of independence in comparison to the domestic service that might otherwise have been their lot. We are told, more positively, of a working class sociability that overspilled the workplace into the bars and cafés around the factory. We learn the story of a family company, feudal in some eyes, paternalistic in others, that provided batteries for French colonies in Africa and later for colonial wars in Indochina and Algeria. Witnesses recount trade unionists' stubborn fight for support and recognition and subsequent struggles over hygiene, the availability of soap and the right to go to the toilet when the need was felt. And, most importantly, perhaps, the film's assembled voices provides a complex, polyphonic account of what happened in 1968 when, along with so many other workers, the women of the Wonder factory went on strike and occupied their factory, challenging, if only briefly, the existing social order and its distribution of roles, powers and the right to public self-expression. It is with respect to this latter story that disagreement is most strong. Representatives of the Communist left and the CGT still justify the decision to persuade the workers to return to work in return for union recognition and small gains in conditions and wages. The leftists recall the CGT's muscular approach to opposition and a seemingly rigged vote to return to work. Two right-wing women workers say that they were forced to follow the strike call, reminding us that, like the left, the working class itself has never achieved anything approaching unity.

However, the story does not end in 1968. It carries on to describe the demolition of the *banlieue rouge* and of the sociabilities and solidarities that were so deeply embedded in its fabric. The buildings may still be there, but the mass redundancies and factory closures of the 1970s and 1980s have undone the old working class. Exposed to global competition, Wonder ceased to be a family company. Bernard Tapie, celebrated in the 1980s as an entrepreneur but now infamous, bought it up and was seen as a saviour until a wave of redundancies opened the workers' eyes. The company was then sold on to an American multinational, Ralston, with large parts of it being shut down. The short Tapie period was one where resistance still seemed possible if doomed but the Ralston takeover and the ultimate dismantling of the old company firm is registered as taken for granted, unopposed process. The drama that was played out in 1968 is no longer possible – not in the same way, not in the same place and not with the same actors.

Radical Theatre Loses its Stage

It is a commonplace to suggest that politics is a form of theatre, especially in these days of neo-liberal hegemony where, with the evacuation of alternatives, presentation and image seem to replace substantive disagreement. Yet, as Rancière convincingly argues, a truly radical politics, one that mounts a general challenge to the established order in the name of equality, is also of necessity theatrical. The status quo – what Rancière calls the 'police order' – allocates set roles and identities to people and, crucially, regulates access to the *logos*, to meaningful intervention in public debates over the distribution of the commons. It draws lines, at the same time, between what is and is not an area of public concern, ruling, for example, that what happens in the factory or in the home are purely private issues. The 'police order' is challenged when, refusing both their allotted places and their silencing, an oppressed group takes public voice and challenges the ordering of the commons, speaking not from the subaltern identity allotted to them but in the name of the wrong done to them constituted as a general wrong. This public challenge is, as Rancière notes, essentially theatrical in nature. It has to create a new dramaturgy, a new collective actor and a new public stage while at the same time rejecting the old script and the names and roles it gave to people and places (Rancière 1995: especially 126–27; Hallward 2006). The year 1968 was a moment when just such a radical dramaturgy was proposed, when roles and hierarchies in factories, universities and homes were opened to public challenge, and when students and workers refused the roles and places allotted to them. The original Wonder film catches the last act of this theatre, showing leftists, trade unionists and workers engaged in public debate about the next step that should be taken before the workers were again swallowed up by the factory door, disappearing once again into a privatized space of fixed, hierarchical roles where they were effectively silenced.[5]

What could not be foreseen then, but what Le Roux's films eloquently demonstrates, is that the dramaturgy of 1968 can now no longer be enacted for a number of essential reasons. Firstly, its cast is dispersed. The capitalist owners are now a disembodied, multinational corporation, little more than a name mentioned in the film, whilst the working class as a visible public actor is gone. The union and party militants are, to some extent, still active, but they are no longer major players on the public stage, a fact which Le Roux underlines by choosing to interview many of them in their homes, where their private identities as individuals come to the fore. Secondly, the drama's stage has gone. The *banlieue* of course remains – it is there as a backdrop to the film – but it is no longer the *banlieue rouge*, the red suburb, the space where the strength of the organized working class could be seen and felt by itself and others. Thirdly, the script has been lost, or perhaps more accurately, it has lost the spatio-temporal frame that gave it meaning and direction and has become dislocated and disembodied. If, in the short term, reform seemed to have won out over radical change, in the longer term reformism was also undone as capital's offensive reversed post-war gains and dismantled the security of the working class. What was lost, as a result, was any sense of a future that could continue earlier struggles, consolidate gains and atone for past injustices, thus giving sense and direction to the present by inserting it into a still unfolding collective history. Lost too was the ability to connect each local struggle to a broader national and international frame. Such a frame is implicitly present in the 1968 film – what is happening outside the factory door in Saint-Ouen only makes sense because of the ability we have already noted to condense that broader event. It is more explicitly present in *Reprise*, notably through such testimony as that of Pierre Guyot, a communist, and Poulou, the *gauchiste*, both activists engaged in much broader political struggles underpinned by leftist internationalism.[6] Their stories, anecdotal as they might seem, help underline the broad symmetry of scope of radical leftism and the capitalist and imperialist forces it ranged itself against. This symmetry has now been lost, for even as capital has increased and intensified its global reach the left has lost its capacity to connect different national and international struggles within an overarching narrative of emancipation (chapter 1). The management at Wonder could be physically confronted up to the time of Tapie but the American multinational that ultimately dismantles the company figures only as an absent cause, as something that has local effects but which cannot itself be seen or be opposed. Taken in conjunction, these shifts amount to the traumatic collapse of the leftist dramaturgy that was once available to mediate and make sense of local sufferings and struggles.

The transformation can be productively approached from a different angle. In his discussion of *Reprise*, Laurent Marie mobilizes the Saussurian terms of *langue* (the general linguistic code of a language) and *parole* (each individual instance of language use) to describe the language of the union and political actors on the one hand and the revolt of the woman worker on the other (Marie 2000). The language of the former works at a general level, connecting to broader issues of union recognition and the long-term struggle for rights and conditions. The language of the latter is tied to the immediate – it evokes the dirty, disgusting conditions that the woman must endure as she and her fellow workers process the black manganese. It also expresses her visceral disgust at the return to work with so little changed. As long as the two types of language, the *langue* of political and institutional mediation and the *parole* of embodied affectivity, work in tandem or in tension, the link is maintained between the general and the specific, the abstract and the embodied, the code and its enactment. But, if the two become separated, then the *langue* of leftist politics risks becoming a hollow shell that can no longer connect to embodied experience, while the *parole* of individual refusal risks losing its access to the universal, its ability to connect local and immediate suffering to a general, public frame. It is precisely such a coming apart that Le Roux's film points towards. This coming apart also connects back to Rancière's analytical framework. *Langue*, as Marie uses it, is not unlike Rancière's concept of the *logos*, of the language of public deliberation about the distribution of the commons. When people are denied access to the *logos*, or when domains of experience such as work are removed from public debate, protesting voices are condemned to the status of animal noises or irritated bodies (Rancière 1995: 44–46, 81–82). The protesting woman in *Reprise* is caught as she resists the condemnation of her embodied revolt to the domain of animal noise, still possessing a public stage but about to lose it.

As the film's more than three hours come to an end, the woman that Le Roux had set out to find has still not been located. His film obsessively replays her image, burning her angry gestures, beautiful face and indignant words into our memory so that she becomes the incarnation of raw, untheorized revolt.[7] While all the other faces from 1968 are pushed back into personal and collective memory by their present selves, she floats free. Voicing raw refusal, her voice is far less tied to a specific moment than the other voices of that time and is thus free to connect to our present. Just as she felt that those who were meant to represent her were failing her, so now there is a social suffering that seems to call out for adequate political articulation and does not find it. This is precisely what the film itself suggests, discretely but pointedly, as it begins its second half. Le Roux is shown in his car as he seeks out the now dispersed actors of 1968. We hear, apparently over his car radio, that the workers at a small factory in Quimperlé have gone on strike due to the management's attempt to regulate the times when they are allowed to use the toilet. This echoes comments about difficult access to toilet facilities at the Wonder factory and reminds us that workers still face an oppression that passes through the body and which denies their dignity. But whereas the earlier revolt could once be articulated within an overarching oppositionality, it is now condemned to be local and immediate and has to struggle for a public stage.

In the article we examined more fully in the first chapter, *Cahiers du Cinéma* critic Ramone also suggests that the 1968 film shows the radical separation of the woman from those around her. For Ramone, this separation has its roots in the ontological difference of the voice of refusal. Whereas all those around her – the trade unionists, the management, even the Maoist – represent a pre-existing, scripted position, the woman embodies a people that only comes into existence through its refusal of any such thing. She cannot subsequently be found because, unlike the others, she only came into existence because of 1968 and thus inevitably disappeared as the transformatory possibilities unleashed by that event faded away (Ramone 1998: 25). It is thus fruitless to try to find her or the people, not in their immobilizing sociological or cultural incarnations, but as a transforming political force. Outside moments such as 1968, the people can only usefully be represented as an absence. While agreeing that the film creates a radical separation between the woman and all those around her, I consider this analysis to be too Manichaean in that it fails to recognize the extent that the stage upon which the woman was able to declare her revolt was a collective production. The union and political actors who surrounded her may have been radically different to her in their attachment to something already existing and may, to a considerable degree, have betrayed her, but they were also crucial in giving her voice its resonance, in providing, along the lines I have described, the dramaturgy which allowed it to transcend its immediate location and become that of the political people. Because of this divergence, I also consider it more useful, rather than simply condemning the woman to exile from contemporary representations, to use *Reprise* in general and her in particular as keys to understanding what happens to revolt when denied adequate political mediation. This, after all, is what the film itself invites us to do, when it brings reference to a bitter but purely local contemporary strike within its frame.

Catching raw revolt and an elaborated left-wing politics as they come apart, *Reprise* looks ahead to all those contemporary French films that figure a rebellion deprived of adequate political articulation and helps provide us with a way to understand its genealogy and the modes of its current appearance. The revolt that features in many recent films can only fully be appreciated if one considers how its rawness is an inevitable consequence of the loss of an overarching political frame to give it meaning and direction by connecting it to other struggles in the past and present and by promising it justice in the future.[8] The same rawness also inevitably has roots in the dismantling, which *Reprise* tracks, of the collective strengths and socio-political visibility of the working class, a process that points towards the current fragmentary and local nature of social struggles. This genealogy is explicitly evoked in some of the films we shall consider while only implicitly present in others. The corporeality, emotional intensity and melodramatic self-presentation which the woman has to call upon when she feels that she is no longer being represented is also something that runs through the films that we will look at, films where individuals or small groups face the uncushioned impact of social disintegration and economic oppression with few if any symbolic resources upon which to call. The same films' spatio-temporal coordinates are also foreshadowed by the coming apart of local, immediate refusal from a broader frame. More specifically, the asymmetry that *Reprise* announces between revolts condemned to be local and causes that are increasingly global is something that runs through current production.

Reprise helps explain the present appearance of socio-political struggle by painstakingly recording the systematic and traumatic dismantling of an epic dramaturgy of class. However, its own political commitment does not reside simply in this genealogical labour but in the fact that it resists the very processes it traces, making a memory of struggle available to a new generation, refusing the erasure of unrealized historical possibilities and painfully tracking down its dispersed witnesses so as to retain some sense of a totalizing picture even as it shows why the old, totalizing dramaturgy can no longer be enacted.[9] It acknowledges that revolt has lost its voice, cast and stage, but at the same time makes it available for future re-articulation by allowing the woman who embodies it to break free from those who once accompanied her, speaking the old, fading script. As Rancière (2000) notes, the film never seeks to fix the past by providing an ultimate resolution to the conflict between competing voices, but its refusal of dogmatic certainties or leftist mythology does not prevent it from being driven by the desire to find the lost face of revolt. Its multi-layered complexity is in sharp contrast to the clear, polarized choices and immediate intervention that seemed possible at the time of the 1968 film that inspired it.[10] The Dardenne brothers' films, to which we will now turn, work on a similar terrain, between the apparently clear choices and battle-lines of the past and the opacity of the present. They complement *Reprise* by finding their own way to express and to resist the traumatic changes that have taken place.

The Dardenne Brothers and the Emergence of Raw Revolt

The Dardennes are film-makers from the French speaking part of Belgium. They came to international attention when they released *La Promesse* in 1997 and have seen their reputation grow enormously with Cannes prize-winners *Rosetta* (1999) and *L'Enfant* (2004) as well as the critically acclaimed *Le Fils* (2002). These four films trace the intense struggles of characters who have neither group solidarities nor symbolic resources upon which to draw and that are thus, to a degree, typical of the strand of film-making of concern to this volume. The brothers' earlier work serves as a prelude to and explanation of their own more recent output, for if their earlier documentaries record the crisis of traditional leftist mobilizations, *Je pense à vous* (1992), the little known feature that followed them, records the passage from collective, mediated opposition to the raw, individualized revolts of the present. In an interview, Luc Dardenne notes this evolution in the nature of the resistance that has been the brothers' constant concern:

> We began with the Spanish civil war … then we did anti-Nazi resistance in our region, and then the workers' movement in the 50s, 60s and 70s. We were always interested in those who had said 'no' when everyone was saying 'yes' … It [resistance] is no longer collective, no longer political … It becomes something more individual, thus a moral issue (Houba 2003: 147–48).[11]

Based in Belgium, the brothers are engaged in a history that has strong convergences with events and evolutions elsewhere but which nonetheless has its own moments of crisis. Thus, the first two of the three documentaries that we will look at relate the period around the great Belgian general strike of 1960, an event without direct parallel in the France of the same period and which culminated in a march on Brussels that briefly seemed to challenge the central power of the state. The first, *Lorsque le bateau de Léon M. descendit la Meuse pour la première fois* (1979), centres on one particular leftist militant, the Léon of the title who, as a skilled metal worker, is one of the traditional industrial elite. The film notes how the gestures and movements he carried out throughout his professional life intersected with the history of an industrial region that they helped to build, with Second World War resistance and with more recent worker militancy. As it is being made, however, this intense connectivity between embodied individual experience and collective history is effectively absent. Detached from collective dynamics, Léon's gestures are now put to work building the small motor boat that he intends to sail down the Meuse. The brothers accompany him, using his journey as a pretext to return to the sites of the strike-wave of 1960, interweaving his testimony with those of the other militants summoned up, as if by magic, by the boat's horn. Each witness is filmed in the spaces where the actions they describe took place, with newsreel from the period being intercut with the present. This interplay of history and memory, of collective event and individual recall, means that, as in *Reprise*, the past is both restored to us and kept at a distance, reminding us of an insurrectional possibility, but underlining its absence from the present. So, while the newsreel bears images of surging crowds, the militants are shown as lonely figures in either empty industrial sites or in streets now only peopled by the routine, everyday circulation of cars and shoppers. The militants may still answer the call, but the spaces where the political people once were found now testify only to their absence. The epic has, for the moment, been lost. Picking up where the first film leaves off, the second, *Pour que la guerre s'achève, les murs devaient s'écrouler (Le Journal)* (1980) recounts the activities of a group of leftists in the aftermath of the 1960s strike. It focuses specifically on Edmond, a self-educated steelworker, and his memories of how distribution of an autonomous newspaper was organized from his home so that his domestic space became involved, for a time, in historical struggle. Although the film refuses the erasure of the memory of this struggle and specifically of how, through their newspaper and self-education, the workers acquired the knowledge and public self-expression usually denied to them, it also underlines how history has now absented itself and how narrow domesticity has reclaimed Edmond's house. The steelworks to which the militants had sought to lay siege is now an empty shell that, like *Reprise*, points to the disbandment of the industrial working class and the hollowing out of its spaces.

The first of the two films is deliberately narrated in an interrogative rather than an affirmative mode. Léon's boat journey is not simply a search for a past that is to be restored and frozen. It is also used to question where the left is going and thus to leave the past and its aspirations open and incomplete. Not without a deal of humour, the brothers develop a poetic, allegorical dimension to their film, drawing on the different natural elements at their disposal, the river and its banks, a seagull, the sun's rays and, out of sight, the sea. If the river's banks suggest the power of the real to constrain and canalize the flow of history, the seagull, a symbol of free movement, reminds us of the promise of the possible. The sea may be an infinite space with nowhere for a left-wing journey to end but may still contain an island of utopia. The sun's rays may represent the dying glow of the revolutionary sun or may be the light of the future. By developing an allegory whose different terms lack fixed meaning, the brothers refuse to endorse either the definitive triumph of capital or leftist historical optimism. The shape of history is left open. While clearly strongly drawn to their witnesses, the brothers also use the humour of their narrative and the ironic contrasts between the epic of the past and decidedly humdrum elements in the present (the small motor boat, the seagull, the lonely militants), to hold left-wing mythology at a distance. A similar refusal of mythologization is found in the second film. The brothers refuse to over rely on archive footage to tell this story. With clear echoes of Marker's legendary *Le Fond de l'air est rouge* (1977), they note that such footage would simply reproduce revolutionary mythology and thus, ultimately, false images which would obscure the present. Instead their film is built from the memories of the militants with ironic contrasts again keeping mythology at a distance. Thus, for example, Edmond's reabsorption into the banality of the everyday emphasizes the absence of the epic while a chess set is used to recount how the militants lost the battle if not the war.

Edmond notes that he is now without most of his pieces and that those few that remain are dispersed. While Léon's little boat was used to suggest an unfinished journey, the chess allegory is here used to point towards a major setback if not yet a definitive defeat.

The third of the three films, *Regarde Jonathan, Jean Louvet, son oeuvre* (1983) leaves no room for hope. It is devoted to Jean Louvet, the radical Belgian playwright and cofounder, in the years following the 1960 strike, of a worker's theatre. If it bears clear formal echoes of the two other films, it is also more complex. It intersperses the testimony of Louvet, an isolated figure in a railway carriage, with scenes and readings from his plays, images of empty and decaying factories and shots of a clearly allegorical shadow-boxer. The boxer, we are told, was once called *la locomotive*, a nickname he has long since lost. At the same time, one of the plays involves characters that await 'the good god's train', that is, a politically untheorized utopia. More generally, the theatrical extracts recall proletarian history with its struggles, hopes and disillusionments. Thus, the voice of the ghost of an assassinated communist leader reminds us of unrealized emancipatory aspirations even as another voice evokes the oppressions of Stalinism and the Gulag. Freed from the chronological limitations of the other films by this montage of elements from Louvet's work, *Regarde Jonathan* is able to take a wider historical sweep and to become a summation of class struggle as the twentieth century knew it. But whereas the other films, especially the first, viewed that struggle interrogatively, holding its future at least partly open, this film seems to consign it to the past, thus marking a key stage in the brothers' evolution. The boxer now only fights shadows. The train of history has mutated into the banal carriage that transports Louvet through what was once one of the world's industrial heartlands but which is now an empty landscape.

Within this overarching context, the playwright's questioning of his own position and of the possibilities that remain open to the cultural producer is also an interrogation of the path to be followed by the film-makers themselves. Having been part of a collective oppositional culture, Louvet is now aware that he has come to an impasse. He notes the loss of a totalizing leftist ideology with its promise of a better life for the masses and finds that, because History as a meaning-giving general framework has been lost, it is no longer possible to write even little stories. All that remains, as an invisible hand writes across the screen, are solitary words waiting for a story/history (*histoire*), fragments of language that are no longer tied into a meaningful whole. The only way forward that Louvet can see is a return to the self, the body, desire and mortality, framed not in a narrow, egocentric way, but as a quasi-anthropological programme to assess what humanity remains to us. This testing of the limits of the human and the turn to an elemental dramaturgy no longer contained by an over-arching sense of the social or the historical is precisely the programme that the Dardennes' later films will implicitly set themselves. *Je pense à vous* shows this programme at its birth.

The film begins in a familiar epic landscape in the historical steel-manufacturing town of Seraing. The leading male is a confident, skilled worker. We first see him as his family holds a party to christen a handsome new house away from the more traditional terraces, thus seeming to complete a social integration that began when his father came to Belgium as an immigrant worker. We also hear him discuss plans for a trip to England to broaden his specialist knowledge. His wife is learning English. As a family, they seem confidently installed in the modern world, part of a tradition, yet confident about the future and their own place in it. This state of affairs is short-lived. The film shows a brief, collective struggle by the steelworkers and the town more broadly to keep their factory open. A demonstration, complete with banners and speeches, is held in the square, making working-class solidarity and apparent strength visible. Manipulators of fire and matter, the steelworkers collectively seem of suitably heroic and promethean stuff to sustain an epic battle. Politicians are reported to have given assurances about the future. Yet, as we soon discover and in decidedly anti-climactic fashion, the factory is closed due to decisions taken elsewhere and because of global competition and overproduction of steel. The epic does not come to a climax. It is evacuated as causality migrates out of story space while the working class and its story dissolve into fragments. As if to underline this, the central character's social being disintegrates, as he first turns to obsessive surveillance of his wife's perfectly innocent friendship with her English teacher and later disappears from the town, confirming and making visible by his own self-erasure the deliberate social cleansing that has taken place.

We next find him living in a shabby hotel by a roadside, seemingly having surrendered all social dignity and earning a living by labouring within the black economy. Only a crisis will rescue him from this state. It comes as, part of a straggling group of workers, he finds himself standing opposite the caravan that serves as a base to their gangmaster. The latter calls over a worker, unceremoniously sacks him and, when threatened by him with exposure as an illegal employer, assaults him and starts to duck his head in a water barrel. Passive spectators, the other labourers look on. The hero however revolts and intervenes, fighting and rolling in the mud with the gang-master before the two are pulled apart. In the subsequent sequence, we see him bind his fellow worker's wounded hand in a mute gesture of solidarity and care. This, at an embryonic stage, and not yet having found a suitable style, is the world of the Dardenne brothers' later films. The collective epic with a past and future, familiar, grandiose locations and an established dramaturgy has mutated in front of our eyes into a raw, essentially mute drama characterized by useless suffering and violence detached from liberatory possibility. Not content to simply register this desolation, as a certain brute naturalism might, the film resists it by forcing the hero to choose between mere animal self-preservation and the most basic of solidarities. This choice is expressed not in an elaborated language, for the old language can no longer be spoken, but through the corporeal and the gestural. The setting where it is enacted, in front of a caravan, next to a field, is one suitably marked by impermanence and an absence of signs of shared tradition. The drama is now purely local. It no longer has the capacity to name or figure causes which come before it or lie outside its scope or to connect to struggles elsewhere. It may still have witnesses, for the ragged line of labourers forms a kind of audience, but there is no longer an organized collectivity that can bring grievances to a shared public stage. Nonetheless, and this is undoubtedly the root of its power, the drama retains a certain universal quality. By taking its central character outside of his social frame and by placing him in front of raw brutality inflicted upon another, it begins to ask the kind of fundamental questions about our remaining humanity put by Louvet in *Regarde Jonathan*.

Je pense à vous starts to rebuild from the ground up. Occupying a space from which all collective values and meanings have been traumatically erased, it poses a stark ethical choice between human solidarity and resistance on the one hand and naked exploitation and domination on the other. The posing of this choice allows the simultaneous return of value and meaning, rescuing the central character as an ethical being while at the same time restoring some sense to his actions.[12] But is 'rescuing', with its suggestion of a passive victim, a misleading term, and does 'ethical' imply the absence of the political? Firstly, it is important to note that values are rebuilt by the characters themselves so that their return simultaneously signals the revival of agency. Secondly, if an ethics is characterized above all by one's responsibility before the other, the choice faced by the central character is not simply ethical. Despite the paring away of the film's cast in its second phase, the hero's commitment to the other does not take place in a neutral context but is decisively shaped by the presence of an oppressive third party. If, as Laclau and Mouffe argue along lines described earlier in this chapter, the building of a counter-hegemonic politics involves the drawing together of different social struggles in the face of a common enemy, *Je pense à vous* suggests what such a politics reduced to an absolute bare minimum, a core cast of three, might look like. Despite the fact that the Dardenne brothers often come close to disowning it, it is a key stage in their development, marking as it does the transition from the documentaries' interrogation and transmission of a fading oppositional dramaturgy to the mature fictions' attempts to build something new in the empty space where the old politics used to be. However, as we noted, it also has a much wider resonance in that it points towards and helps explains the raw, voiceless and corporeal appearance of social struggle across a range of contemporary films. It can be seen in some ways as a failure, an uneasy hybrid of two distinct dramaturgies, one public with a collective voice, a past and a future, the other, raw, voiceless and locked in the present. Yet it is precisely the co-presence of these two dramaturgies that is so instructive, with the traumatic destruction of the former so clearly serving as an explanation of the latter.

Conclusion

Hervé Le Roux's *Reprise* and the Dardenne brothers' earlier films can be seen to provide a genealogy of the current wave of socially engaged cinema and signposts to its originality. By showing the undoing of the organized working class, the demobilization of those who structured its mobilization and the silencing of its public voice they look forward to and explain the raw, fragmentary and often voiceless mode of appearance of social struggle in current cinema as well as some of the core challenges that that cinema faces. Imitating *Reprise* and the Dardennes' documentaries, some contemporary films work in the space of a traumatic defeat but nonetheless refuse the complete erasure of a tradition of left-wing struggle by putting the shattered pieces of the old dramaturgy of class struggle to productive work (chapters 4 and 5). Other films follow in the footsteps of *Je pense à vous* and engage frontally with the current raw face of a social struggle denied a collective voice, a past and a future and thus condemned to be mute, corporeal and local (chapter 6). Working where an overarching leftist dramaturgy of the socio-political used to be, both groups of films must deal with the fading or complete absence of the collective values and totalizing, explanatory frame that used to give meaning to struggle and suffering. If they simply reflect this situation, they risk inadvertent complicity with it. However, taking their lesson from the gesticulating, shouting woman in *Reprise*, or from the engineered ethical collision of *Je pense à vous*, they can seek, as we will see, to restore eloquence and transparency to a social struggle and suffering threatened with meaninglessness. If *Reprise* points above all to the capacity of the gestural and of a heightened language to resist silencing and invisibility, *Je pense à vous* shows how a sense of value and agency can be brought to the surface to restore some meaning to the world. Chapter 7 will show how other contemporary films draw on similar, essentially melodramatic strategies to make social suffering and struggle again speak to us. At an earlier moment in political cinema, films such as *Coup pour coup* or *Tout va bien* seemed unproblematically able to connect the level of embodied affectivity to the systemic. The two levels now seem to have come asunder. When films chose to inhabit the former level, as those discussed overwhelmingly do, they risk profoundly disabling consequences for, if they are not to become politically impotent, they must discover ways to connect struggles condemned to be local with causes that have become disembodied and moved out of story space (chapter 8).

Notes

1. '*Cette "prise de parole" est générale, universelle, parce que toutes les luttes sont liées, qu'il n'y a qu'un seul et même opprimé, un seul oppresseur. Le tiers monde est partout. Il est en nous. Souvenons-nous de ce que disait Che Guevara, et que Godard reprenait à son compte dans sa contribution au film collectif* Loin du Vietnam: *il faut multiplier les Vietnam, créer un, deux, trois Vietnam à travers le monde.*'

2. See www.artmag.com/autresnouvelles/reprise/reprise5.html. Consulted 26 October 2001.

3. See www.artmag.com/autresnouvelles/reprise/reprise5.html. Consulted 26 October 2001.

4. *Reprise* underscores some of the shifts that have taken place in the relationship between film and politics at the level of film practice and specifically of production and reception (chapter 1). The short film that inspired it was a collectively generated and authorised production springing from the suspension of 'normal' activities in the IDHEC and relying on commandeered equipment to go ahead. It was a film whose politics, the radical leftism of 1968, one might say, preceded it. Made in conditions of extreme urgency, it fed directly back into the struggle, notably accompanying Karmitz's *Camarades* (1969) on the exhibition circuit and helping it underline the importance of resisting the recapture of the radicalism of 1968 by the institutional left. Le Roux's film is very different. It was made with the independent production company, Les Films d'Ici, which is a much more conventional continuation of the radical 1968 film collective Cinélutte and received funds from the CNC (Centre National de la Cinématographie) and the Ministry of Work. It was neither produced nor circulated in urgency and was a decidedly individual initiative compared to the earlier film, as Le Roux's persistent on-screen presence and the foregrounding of his personal obsession with the woman constantly remind us.

5. Le Roux's comments on the earlier film are telling in this respect: 'the set-up is very theatrical ... all the characters of May '68 are there, as if by miracle ... All the theatre of '68 is present' ('*le dispositif est très théâtral ... il y a, comme par miracle, tous les personnages de mai 68 ... Tout le théâtre de 68 y est présent*') (Toubiana 1997a: 50).

6. Guyot was expected to speak of his role in 1968. Instead, in a way permitted by the open nature of the film, he showed more interest in recounting the trauma he experienced at the time of the Algerian independence struggle when he was imprisoned for two years following refusal of military service. Poulou, the *gauchiste*, told how, then a Maoist, his intervention at Wonder was part of a trans-national attempt to bring leftists into contact with the working class.

7. 'It [the woman's image] shows revolt, the incarnation of revolt ... It's not a theorized refusal'. ('*C'est la révolte, la révolte incarnée ... Ce n'est pas un refus théorisé*') (Toubiana 1997a: 50).

8. Le Roux himself says, 'What the film is perhaps pointing to is the political black hole: the lack of a politics' ('*Ce que désigne peut-être le film, c'est le trou noir politique: le manque de politique*') (Toubiana 1997a: 55).

9. Le Roux partly saw his film as a response to the interrupted transmission of a memory of struggle (Toubiana 1997a: 50).

10. The textual complexity of the film is reflected by its reception. The film was on the editing tables as mass political protest re-emerged in France in 1995 and found a

receptive public on its release in 1997. Le Roux records that there were showings accompanied by public debates in Paris, Lille, Bordeaux, Toulouse, Grenoble as well as in a host of smaller towns. He notes too the multifaceted public reception of his film. It became a vector of memory for workers, leftists, trade unionists and communists, creating a public forum for voices otherwise denied such a thing. But he also notes its ability to connect to current debates about work, feeding into arguments both against a life centred on alienating labour and against unemployment in a society where social recognition still depends on salaried work. He records too how young workers used the film to articulate their own experience in supermarkets or fast-food restaurants where they face relentless cadences or the humiliation of being searched when they knock off. More generally, he suggests, his film connects to a widespread feeling of revolt that is accompanied by an awareness of a lack of a framework within which it can become productive. People, he comments, know that they cannot act alone but are at the same time mistrustful of any collective organisation (Le Roux 1998: 182–91).

11. '*On a commencé avec la guerre d'Espagne ... puis on a fait la résistance contre les nazis dans notre région, et puis le mouvement ouvrier dans les années 50–60–70 ... On s'intéressait toujours aux gens qui avaient dit «non» au moment où tout le monde disait «oui» ... Elle [la résistance] n'est plus collective, elle n'est plus politique ... ça devient quelque chose de plus individuel, donc de plus moral*'.

12. As the film ends the father is able to rejoin his family, a happy outcome that coincides with the town carnival. When his son sees him, no words are initially used. Instead the son throws him an orange that he in turn throws to his wife. Gesture thus serves to re-establish the bond between the threesome in a setting that also suggests the father's reintegration into a broader group that, despite its traumatic defeat and loss of a political voice, still retains a coherence manifested through the shared traditions of carnival. If, at a banal level, the father's return might seem to reflect the restoration of the self-respect that he lost with the job that, up to then, formed the core of his social being, at a more profound level his return to the community reflects a rediscovery of agency and value that, rescuing him from mere animal existence, restores him to the human and the social.

4

CLASS IN PIECES

We noted in the previous chapter how a leftist, class-centred dramaturgy has been shattered and dispersed with its actors demobilized, its core sites evacuated, its language silenced and its struggles deprived of meaning. The films that we consider in this chapter and the next are obliged to recognize this cataclysmic shift, but work in their different ways to resist it by holding on to one piece or another of the shattered dramaturgy of class and putting it to productive use. Considering how unfashionable a term class has become, the relatively high number of films that are explicitly or implicitly organized around it bears testimony to some of French cinema's refusal of the consensual order. The number of films also explains the decision to deal with the return of class across two chapters with this chapter dealing with two subgroups and the next four. The first subgroup of films that we will look at here are ones by Guédiguian, Beauvois, Jolivet and Siri that perversely live in the ruins of the old working class, revisiting its abandoned spaces, preserving its traditions and using its language, even while recording the defeat that has taken place. The second group that we will consider is drawn from what has become known as the *film de banlieue*, the *banlieue* being, as *Reprise* underlined, the place where the working class could once be found. We will pay specific attention to films by Kassovitz, Richet and Ameur-Zaïmeche that struggle to frame the revolt of outer-city youth in class-based terms, thus seeking to build some sort of bridge between the *banlieue*'s past and its present while simultaneously underlining the difficulty of so doing. The next chapter will complete the picture by dealing with the four remaining subgroups, one showing class as an unnameable violence beneath the peaceful surface of consensus, another the individualized face of labour in contemporary production, another seeking to move back towards collective, politically articulated struggle, with a final group seeking to track the current victors.

Taken together, the films in the two chapters bear witness to the demolition of an oppositional dramaturgy that once allowed epic class actors and a collective language of struggle to be brought together on a public stage. Fragments of the working class can be found but have been evicted from their old spaces and separated from their enemy. The spaces can still be gone into but are no longer inhabited by a group with a self-conscious socio-political identity. The enemy can be tracked but no longer confronted face to face. The language of resistance may still be heard, but is no longer carried by an epic choir. The old dramaturgy of struggle is shattered, but its individual pieces, as we shall now see, can still be put in the service of resistance and critique, even as they inevitably and simultaneously bear witness to a defeat. Sometimes, indeed, the pieces can be put back together, but the painfulness of the reassembly still bears witness to the shattering that must be undone. If the films in the current chapter put more emphasis on shattering and discontinuity and those in the next on rebuilding, there is no attempt to establish a hierarchy or a progression. All the films are obliged to take note of defeat and failure even as, in their different ways, they seek to resist them.

This account of a resistant cinema will be in clear opposition to that generated in the pages of *Cahiers du Cinéma* where it was suggested that the majority of contemporary 'realist' cinema tends to immobilize the social, consign struggle to the past, or render a culture of working class resistance anodyne by endowing it with a purely folkloric dimension (chapter 2). It will also partially disagree with important analyses by veteran leftist critic and film-maker Jean-Louis Comolli and academic Michel Cadé, probably the leading authority on working-class representation in French cinema. Comolli notes how, with the collapse of the leftist narrative of emancipation of which they were the chief protagonists, the working class has been erased from the cultural world of films, novel and song as well as from political discourse (Comolli 2004: 526–44). Tied to production, they can make no positive appearance in a society of spectacle dominated by consumption and the commodity. Resurgent French documentary film-making has resisted this trend by faithfully recording their struggles against neo-liberalism but, by so doing, it has only been able to accompany a defeat and provide inadvertent confirmation of the situation. Fiction film on the other hand has, with very few exceptions, ignored working-class struggles and, when it has focused on them, has shown itself characteristically less able than documentary to engage with the reality. Cantet's highly successful *Ressources humaines* (1999), a film dealt with in detail in the next chapter, is cited to confirm this point. Comolli notes how, like many other similar films of recent times, it calls on non-professionals, in this case a real trade-unionist and factory manager, to root itself in the social world. But, paradoxically, having nothing real at stake, these characters are forced to overplay their parts and conform to existing stereotypes in order to confirm their 'authenticity'. They can thus generate no fresh insights.[1] However, Cantet's film shows that where fiction does has a clear advantage over documentary is in speaking that which cannot be spoken and in filming that which refuses to be filmed. Thus, although the hero's father is a passive character, his silent and docile working body bears eloquent testimony to the disappearance of working-class consciousness in a way that non-fiction never could. While documentary only captures active witnesses (especially if, like French documentary film, it has predominantly chosen to accompany workers' struggles), *Ressources humaines* is able to film the worker's body as a lack and an impossibility of being heard, its self-effacement being a passive admission that it has no positive role to play in the contemporary social imaginary (Comolli 2004: 535–40).

Cadé suggests initial disagreement with Comolli when he notes that workers are more present in recent French film than ever before. He begins to converge with him nonetheless when he concludes that, despite this cinematic presence, there has been a substantial retreat from the post-1968 critique of the alienating effects of labour that has given way to an affirmation of manual labour's capacity to generate self-realization. Fiction cinema has broadly focused, he notes, on declining, old industries such as mines and textiles, being drawn above all to traditional industrial regions, with the Nord-Pas de Calais area leading the way. Unemployment and the profoundly unequal relationship between those seeking work and those hiring labour are recurrently seen. A militancy signally lacking in the period up to 1998 returns thereafter in films such as *Ressources humaines*, Siri's *Une Minute de silence* (1998) and *Retiens la nuit* but with a focus on defensive actions or those condemned to defeat. Some films such as Richet's *Etat des lieux* (1994) show individual resistances, but these inadvertently serve to underline the inaction of the working class as a whole. At the same time, there is a widespread tendency for the personal and the intimate to take a central role in workers' on-screen lives displacing a broader class solidarity that can no longer be counted upon. The sharp frontier that once so clearly separated screen representation of the workers from that of other social groups has moved on to the *banlieue* whose inhabitants distinguish themselves, as the workers once did, by their combativeness, style of dress and pugnacious language (Cadé 2000).

Cadé's analysis is more nuanced than that of Comolli but both tend to suggest that French cinema has consigned the working class as agent of collective resistance and social transformation to history. While Comolli makes the point more explicitly, Cadé's vision of a largely passive social group that has lost its clear social contours and any overarching group solidarity that it may have had tends to point in a very similar direction. Both are surely right to underline how, returning to the world of work, French cinema must inevitably record the defeat of the old working class.

But it could be that both underestimate the capacity of that cinema to resist that defeat by putting the fragments of the old dramaturgy to productive use. Cadé's comment about the shift of a social fault line from the working class to the *banlieue* will feed into my own analysis of some key *banlieue* films but I will suggest, at the risk of undermining my own argument, that the revolt that the films assert needs inevitably to be held in tension with the failure of working class self-renewal to which they also point.

Resisting in the Ruins: Guédiguian

A number of the film-makers that this book focuses upon chose deliberately to work in what might call the ruins where the working class used to be, examining the consequences of defeat, scouting around to see what, if anything, can be salvaged from the wreckage. Foremost amongst them is Robert Guédiguian who, until very recently, has remained resolutely faithful to the industrial heartland of the L'Estaque area of Marseille. Guédiguian has been making films since the mid-1980s, having taken up directing even as he abandoned political activism, with the former being very deliberately a continuation of the latter by other means (Derobert and Goudet 1997; Powrie 2001). Like many others of working-class origin, he studied and moved on. Yet his film-making has been substantially devoted to the class he left behind, tracing its history, the immigration that helped constitute it and, in more recent times, its undoing. His more recent and better known films – those that will concern us here – are all to a substantial extent political fables. Although their firm rooting in an often grim socio-economic context might tempt one to label them as realist or even naturalist films, they are strongly influenced by Brecht and deliberately draw on a range of anti-realist devices such as overtly pedagogic speeches and character-colour association in *Marius et Jeannette* (1996), parodic imitation of Pagnol's stereotypical Marseille dialogue in *A la vie, à la mort!* (1994), comic musical scenes in *A l'attaque!* (1999) and opera-style multiple deaths in *La Ville est tranquille* (1999). This anti-realism allows for the films' self-conscious presentation as fables of the possible, with some being deliberately, even perversely optimistic (*Marius et Jeannette* and *A l'attaque!*), and others (*La Ville est tranquille*) grimly pessimistic to show us what a world without solidarity would be like. If films like *A la vie, à la mort!* straddle the divide, we must also recognize that the more positive films all clearly have dark undertones beneath a surface lightness.

Marius et Jeannette, Guédiguian's first major success, is a case in point. It is largely centred on two locations, the disused cement works where Marius is a watchman, and the courtyard that Jeannette and her two children share with a retired, male schoolteacher, a lifelong, woman communist and another family. One space, the cement works, is large and mainly empty, and is peopled by the phantoms of a working class that has been dismantled just as the works itself is being demolished. The other, the courtyard, is small, crowded and full of life, a space whose utopian promise lies not so much in any positive project that the characters have to bring forward – they have none – but in an ability to tie together generations, maintain solidarity and generate good humour that suggests that there may still be life in the working class and in the political left, even if they have been evicted from their old industrial bases. The characters who occupy the spaces should be read emblematically rather than in a narrow, realist way. The communist woman with her memories of wartime resistance connects firmly to the past. The teacher who, although retired, still finds time to impart wisdom to the children, looks towards the future (Cohen 1997). The two together – and they are a loose couple in the film – evoke the continuity of leftist tradition and its ability to connect past and future. Significantly, the woman reads *L'Humanité*, the once mighty but now modest Communist Party daily newspaper, while the man is seen with *Le Monde Diplomatique*, the core intellectual focus of the French anti-globalization movement that represents perhaps the best hope for a renewal of the French left. Dédé, the father of the other family in the courtyard, is a worker who has ceased to believe in leftist principles and, in his disillusionment, casts a vote for the racist Front National, an unforgivable lapse that neither his wife nor the other inhabitants of the courtyard will let him forget. His wife reminds him of the importance of striking when necessary, stressing how the 1995 strikes saved the social security system and thus their children's future. The couple thus embody the choice between fidelity to and betrayal of one's political principles. Jeanette, the heroine, is a Mother Courage figure who refuses to bow down to tyranny at work and pushes her children to do well at school. The children are by two different fathers, one white, one African, so that the family becomes a living refusal of the racist divisiveness that threatens society (chapter 7). The black child begins to observe Ramadan strictly during the course of the action, thus allowing the question of fundamentalism, another divisive ideology, to be raised and discussed.

The courtyard is utopian in its capacity to resist division, disillusionment and discontinuity. Yet, it clearly points towards the contours of the dystopia that Guédiguian fears – a shattered working class riven by racism and fundamentalism, unable to connect to its past or prolong itself into the future. The presentation of Marius, the hero, is similarly double-edged. Initially he appears to be lame in one leg. However, a race with Jeannette reveals his agility and elicits the confession that he has faked disability to get his job. His fitness and humorous trickery might suggest a character in control, but one should remember that his fake limp is, paradoxically, a better guide to his true, diminished condition as a worker. It is also a pointer to an inner wound, the fact that he has lost his wife and children in a car accident. This in turn explains why he runs away from his relationship with Jeannette and responsibility for her children until, one evening when he is drunk, his friends tie him to her, so that his attachment becomes literally inescapable. It is telling that, unable to face the future, the central worker figure in the film lives in the ruins of his professional and personal past. It is telling too that the construction of a future for him is a collective not an individual act that is prolonged when the other drunken men noisily proclaim their love for their women in a way that asserts the continued viability of the collective, its ability to hold together and face the future.

Marius et Jeannette is ultimately about the threatened erasure of a social group and its capacity to maintain itself, its culture and values. This story is cast implicitly as a narrative of resistance. The now ageing communist woman tells, for example, of her time in a concentration camp, where, in the face of annihilation, clandestine love-making became a way of refusing defeat and of affirming attachment to life. The theme of resistance is also raised jokingly at the start of the film. Jeannette works at a supermarket checkout and refuses to sit up straight because her chair is so uncomfortable, saying that had the Gestapo used the chair on Resisters, the latter would have cracked and given away their secrets. Behind the comic exaggeration, the character signals her refusal to project the image of contented service that consumption requires and thus, at the same time, maintains a working-class tradition of resistance to domination. In a similar way, her verbal reinstatement of memories of her father and of his death in an industrial accident in the cement works can be seen as a conscious act of symbolic resistance to the erasure of the history of an increasingly invisible social group. Whereas the death might once have been retrospectively redeemed by working-class enfranchisement, it is now made to hang over the present as an unpaid debt to the past. In a more light-hearted vein, the festive meal involving the preparation and consumption of the archetypal southern dish of *aïoli* within the ruins of the factory can be seen as a willed continuation of a subculture despite the demolition of what had seemed to lie at its heart.

The film that preceded *Marius et Jeannette*, *A la vie, à la mort!*, works on a similar terrain. It begins with mobile nocturnal shots of an out-of-town shopping centre and its neon lights before showing us the multiple faces of a politician on a bank of television screens telling us that we must adapt to the new order. This is, of course, an evocation of the way the world might now be seen, as spectacular consumption alongside a purely spectacular politics. But this is not what the film itself is interested in. Instead it takes us into a familiar Guédiguian group, a loose and unconventional working-class family. The oldest member of the family is an ageing Spanish Republican who still promises to kill Franco despite the fact that the dictator has been dead for twenty years. The three males of working age are all unemployed. They are skilled workers who can now, at best, earn some money by unskilled manual labour. One, José, runs a club in which his wife, the main attraction, strips, although she increasingly feels too old to do so. His sister, Marie-Sol, wants a child but her husband, one of the unemployed trio, is infertile. When the film begins things are going from bad to worse. Marie-Sol and her husband are moved out of the little house that went with her cleaning job as the owner wishes to build a swimming pool instead. Faced with the latter's sexual advances, an indignant Marie-Sol in any case resigns, adding herself to the unemployed group. Her adoptive brother has been working on a bourgeois-style house for which he can no longer pay. Its imposed sale points towards the downfall of the skilled workers who once formed the working-class elite. Having gravitated towards a seemingly ever-expanding middle class, they find instead that they are forced back into a vulnerability and marginalization that they appeared to have left behind.

As in *Marius et Jeannette*, the group is able to provide solidarity, support and continued social integration to characters that the broader society seems to have deserted. It is also strong enough to incorporate a beautiful young drug addict and occasional prostitute called Vénus and a teenage boy of North African descent who has been making a living cleaning car windows on the street. José will begin to pass on his mechanic's knowledge to the boy, thus suggesting the possibility of resuming the transmission of manual skills that was a key feature of the working class, a theme which also lies at the heart of the Dardenne brothers films, as well as suggesting the possible establishment of a continuity between the old working class and the children of immigrants, something which, in reality, trade unions and parties of the left signally failed to ensure (Masclet 2003). The film is thus utopian in its use of a small group to reassert the power and value of the core leftist value of solidarity, not only between those of the same age but also between different generations. This solidarity is given a warm human glow by association with popular culinary tradition (the gathering and cooking of sea urchins) and with Pagnolesque bar-side banter. But, even more obviously than with *Marius et Jeannette*, one only has to scratch the surface to find dark undercurrents: the undoing and marginalization of the old working class in a society centred on consumption; the failure to connect new immigrant groups to the indigenous working class; the widespread existence of 'useless' social suffering (drugs, prostitution) no longer promised redemption by an emancipatory politics.

As its title suggests, *A la vie, à la mort!* is essentially about the struggle between life and death, Eros and Thanatos. It is no accident that its central locale is a strip club, a place of sexual desire, nor that the young drug addict, Vénus, bears the name of the goddess of love. It is no accident either that Marie-Sol, the core female protaganist, is desperate for a child. The film revolves around the non-continuity of a social group as encapsulated by the sterility of the erotic drive. José and his wife are too old to have children. His adoptive brother has been abandoned by wife and children. Marie-Sol is young enough but her husband is sterile. Vénus is loved by the young *Beur* but prostitutes herself to others and he, in any case, is too young. The strip club generates desire that has become merely an escape from an unbearable reality rather than a stimulus to renewal. The group thus seems condemned to extinction until Marie-Sol persuades her adopted brother to get her pregnant. Yet her state only makes material needs more pressing. In a tragic conclusion, her husband drowns himself in the sea, knowing that his life insurance policy will free his family from immediate need and provide for the child. This outcome, whereby a group sacrifices one of its number so that its life can continue, has a clear mythological resonance that, while giving an added dimension to the story, might blunt its political edge. Collective struggle for life is, of course, a primordial form of resistance, yet it risks losing sight of any socially embodied enemy, especially once Marie-Sol loses her job and the last direct contact between exploiter and exploited is severed.

The film is aware of this dislocation of a culture of resistance and draws it within the story in the shape of the father with his Spanish Republican past. As we know, he still swears to kill the long-dead Franco. This anti-fascism without an object is clearly close to a working class defiance that can no longer confront capital. Although he is confined to a wheelchair, he struggles to paint a copy of Goya's famous *The Third of May* that, depicting a scene from the Spanish war of independence, refers back to an earlier resistance, this time against Napoleonic occupation. He paints the painting in two halves. Initially, he depicts the dying partisan on the door of the fridge, but eviction from the home that went with the Marie-Sol's job forces him to down his brushes. Once relocated within his son's house he can paint the firing squad on the wall next to the relocated fridge, finally bringing victim and tyrant back together in the same frame. However, the separable nature of the painting and the long, painful effort needed to produce it underline the fragility of oppositional narratives and the determination needed to maintain them. Similarly, while the grim closing singing of the famous Spanish Republican song 'Ay, Carmela!' underlines the group's determination to resist, its forced importation from another conflict underlines a failure of transmission and renewal of oppositional culture.[2] Something similar might be said for the use of the celebrated Italian partisan song 'Bella ciao' in the later *A l'attaque!* The film is also a story of resistance, in its case by another loose family group that is threatened with bankruptcy and the loss of its garage because an international company deliberately withholds payment of its debts. It recounts the kidnapping of the company's manager by the women of the family but acknowledges the profound improbability of this direct confrontation of international capital by presenting it as a fable invented in a discussion between a director and a scriptwriter. When 'Bella ciao' is defiantly sung by the ageing anti-fascist grandfather, it again underlines both the need to feed off a tradition of resistance and the lack of an anthem more specifically relevant to the present conjuncture.

A l'attaque! was written alongside a much darker companion piece, *La Ville est tranquille*. Whereas the former takes as its premise the possibility of politically articulated resistance and of a defiant if fading connection to left-wing tradition, the latter explores what remains when collective resistance no longer seems possible and meaningful connections to the past are severed. The contrast between the films is perhaps best signalled by the treatment it reserves for what was the main anthem of the radical global left, the 'Internationale'. The song is performed not by a group but by a solitary and disillusioned character as a way of underlining its consignment to history. The driver has been a docker and, faced with redundancy, has chosen to take severance pay rather than continue the doomed fight alongside his fellow workers in the name of values that no longer seem to apply. The money has allowed him to become self-employed and to replace solidarity with individual self-reliance. His pointedly ironic performance of the 'Internationale' in different languages in a film that consciously engages with the impact of globalization underlines the fact that there is now no rival to capital at the global level (chapter 8). At a later stage in the film, his father quietly sings it to himself as he works in the kitchen. Because he fought in the Resistance as a young man, the song is still a meaningful part of his culture, but the line of transmission between generations has been broken and the younger characters in the film have few if any political resources upon which to draw. They have lost their collective voice and with it the ability to join with others in struggle and to name their enemy.

As in other films that we will look at such as Poirier's *Marion*, racism is all too ready to step in and fill the void. Having been unemployed for three years, the husband of Michèle, one of the main characters, turns to the Front National (thinly disguised as a group called *Préférence nationale*) as a way to deflect his exclusion onto others. This choice will lead him into a disaster that is far from the mockery reserved for Dédé in the light-hearted *Marius et Jeannette*. He finds himself one of a trio that is putting up racist posters and which kills Abderamane, a young black man from a contrasting multi-racial group that has begun to tear them down. Abderamane has been a lonely, progressive voice in the film, someone who can both resist the retreat of young second or third generation immigrants into exclusionary ethno-religious community and criticize the empty, violent lyrics of a young rap group while warning them that their desire for material success will only lead to the reinforcement of the unjust social structure that they claim to oppose. The threat of social fragmentation that hung over the other Guédiguian films has materialized. Unlike in those other works, there is no small but resilient social unit at the heart of the film that can hold the pieces together while ensuring its own reproduction. The core female character, Michèle, cares for her drug addict daughter and grandchild while holding down a job as a fish-packer. Increasingly desperate, she first prostitutes herself to feed the daughter's habit and then gives her an overdose to ensure the future of the grandchild. As in *A la vie, à la mort!* the sacrifice of a life is needed for life to go on, but here it is no longer the life of a working-class group with a coherent set of values to transmit, it is bare life. Struggling for life, the character is still of course resisting, but this is a resistance made raw, a resistance without a politics.[3] To underline the grimness of a world where there is no collectivist opposition to the brutality of the capitalist economy, the voice that now perversely seems most life affirming is that of a young rightist woman who speaks out against abortion and for the continuity of the race. The love of the female lead's life, split from her by the traumatic memory of a teenage, back-street abortion, has become a hit-man, a decidedly improbable occupation in a broadly social realist film, but one that makes sense emblematically in one where death seems to be triumphing over life.

The film however ends characteristically with a utopian celebration of community. It had opened with a young boy, a Georgian immigrant, playing an electric piano on a grassy hill as he tried to raise money to buy a grand piano. It ends as the instrument is lowered into the courtyard where he lives. As he begins to play, a popular community previously conspicuous only by its absence is brought miraculously back into existence, repopulating the empty landings of the block and embracing and holding together not only the immigrant boy and his neighbours but also, improbably, the racist murderers who happen to deliver the piano. Whereas *A l'attaque!* and *A la vie, à la mort!* ended with groups singing celebrated songs of leftist resistance, *La Ville est tranquille* ends with a purely instrumental piece. There is no song that the community can sing together because there is no longer a shared language or tradition and the community itself is a knowingly unrealistic utopia, one that shows an attachment to popular unity but recognizes that there is currently no political path to such a thing.

Without an overarching progressive politics, the film can only cling to fragments of hope provided by isolated individual gestures and behaviours such as the helping hand that, in a tellingly mute gesture of solidarity, the taxi driver stretches out to a fallen, drunk Michèle, or the work that the bourgeois music teacher does with autistic children. Her smug architect husband, once a socialist, has now become an apologist for the wholesale reshaping of the city in a way that fits it for the globalized economy and opens it up to tourism while leaving no place for those who belonged to the old industrial port. Far less grandiose in her ambitions, the woman simply aspires to help where she can by opening up forms of self-expression to those denied it. Her autistic pupils are in the image of the film's major characters who are similarly shut in upon themselves having been deprived of a collective language and shared values by the violent restructuring of their communities. The other films use the memories, desires and solidarities of small groups to proclaim the continued vitality of left-wing values in perverse defiance of apparently inevitable social evolution. *La Ville est tranquille* resists social evolution in its own way by showing both its disastrous consequences and also the possibility of individual ethical choices and actions which, despite their lack of a political language or a project, nonetheless point back, at a very elemental level, to leftist values of solidarity and commitment to the well-being of others. With its making, Guédiguian moves onto a terrain very similar to that occupied by the Dardenne brothers and which will be explored fully in chapter 6.

Guédiguian's films collectively accompany the dismantling of the old working class, taking us to the decaying spaces where it could once be found, recording its fragmentation, its loss of a collective voice and its current incapacity to confront its traditional capitalist enemy. To this extent, and along lines mapped out by the *Cahiers* critics (chapter 2), they might seem to record a defeat to which they add a comforting, nostalgic glow through the mobilization of humour and folkloric touches. Yet, the films do more than this: they resist that which they show by aligning themselves firmly with the defeated, refusing the erasure of their unredeemed suffering and collective values and underlining the resources that they still retain. A similarly perverse resistance characterizes the work by other directors to which we now turn. All the films choose to focus on the wreckage of the old working class. One, Beauvois's *Selon Matthieu* (2000), is part family history, part perverse romance. Another, Jolivet's *Fred* (1996), is part comedy, part detective story. The last, Siri's *Une Minute de silence* is a buddy movie set amongst a group of miners whose pit is about to close.

Resisting in the Ruins: Beauvois, Jolivet, Siri

Beauvois's *Selon Matthieu* is set on the Normandy coast, in the Nord region. Its opening aerial shots of luxury mansions, heavy industrial plant and a golf course suggest a landscape heavily marked by class divisions. Yet the first sequence – a boar hunt in beautiful woodland that brings boss and workers together – points to a more flexible and open social terrain. Subsequent sequences take us into the high-tech, precision engineering factory where the hero, Matthieu, his brother and father all work. The former, the image of a worker at home in the modern economy, is usually seen in front of a computer screen rather than a machine. The brother is building himself a comfortable detached residence and, as he announces at his wedding, is soon to be a father. The wedding itself is a large and vibrant affair suggesting a family group securely integrated into a broader community. The film thus begins by suggesting a world within which class barriers may still exist but are softened, so that the working class seems to be both secure in its continued existence (with father and sons in the same workplace and a pregnancy greeted with joy) and to have a realistic prospect of complete social integration (as symbolized by inclusion in a modern economy and by the house). Yet the father is an isolated figure at the wedding. Despite lifelong service to the company, he has been sacked for breaking the no-smoking rule. He is henceforward a broken figure, a character who seems fully to fit Comolli's description of the worker whose passivity and silence is testimony to the defeat and erasure of a class. The initial picture of social integration is completely undermined by his humiliation and powerlessness. His subsequent death (suicide?) when he is knocked down when leaving an unemployment office would only seem to confirm the symbolic destruction that occurred when he mutated from elite worker to someone too old to employ.

While all the other characters seem to accept the initial sacking as inevitable, Matthieu refuses to acquiesce. He initially approaches the union delegates, only to find that they are unwilling to act, not least because they feel that the workers on temporary contracts will not follow them. He then harangues his fellow workers reminding each of their responsibility to his father and of what he has done for them or meant to them in the past. He accuses his brother of cowardice and self-interest and confronts the company's head of human resources, describing the company's behaviour as fascist. He thus become an isolated figure, someone whose fidelity to his father, insistence on naming oppressions and refusal to abandon traditions of collective resistance alienates all those who have accommodated to the new order. His intransigence only finds an echo in the priest's reminder at his father's funeral that Christ asks us to change that which is inhuman in this world, an injunction that reasserts an ethico-moral imperative in the vacuum left by class demobilization. Having found himself unable to oppose, as an isolated individual, the inhumanity of what had happened to his father, Matthieu decides to get back at the company by seducing the boss's wife with predictably messy consequences.

The brother is the realist of the two characters, the one whose loyalty is to the future represented by his new wife, unborn child and house. Matthieu is perversely loyal to the past and refuses the current state of the world without having at his command either a developed political language or an oppositional vision.[4] When his mistress tells him that the French working class is condemned due to technological innovation and relocation of production, he simply expresses disgust, a purely emotive intervention that underlines his lack of an overarching political language with which to analyze what has happened, but which, as we will see in chapter 7, may have a certain political effectiveness. One might think that the film condemned him for his destructive opposition to inevitable change. Apart from the hurt he does to the boss's wife who, despite her privilege, is hardly the guilty party, he eventually succeeds only in triggering his own sacking and that of a brother whose future had seemed so assured. Yet what the father's sacking, humiliation and imposed social uselessness showed was that the working class has no dignified future in a neo-liberal order. This is what Matthieu rightly throws in the others' faces by reminding them of the pride and self-assertion that they have surrendered. He does not simply betray the future out of misplaced loyalty to the past. He emphasizes that without some loyalty to past aspirations and some commitment to redeem injustices, the future is simply not one worth living. His experience thus shows, not that he is wrong to resist, but the lack of symbolic and material resources to resist with.

The Fred of Jolivet's eponymous film is likewise someone who refuses to betray the past. A skilled JCB operator, he has led a strike opposing the closure of the factory where he worked. The action has failed, but despite the recriminations of at least one of his ex-comrades, he refuses to disown the stand that he led them in. The factory itself, still bedecked with the tattered remnants of the workers' banners, is to be turned into a leisure and nature centre, part of a new sanitized economy in which not only do industrial workers have no place, but from which the very memory of their struggles will be erased. Yet the past refuses to go away. Following the murder of an ex-workmate, Fred finds himself sucked into a drama that centres on the old works where, it transpires, asbestos panels that ended up in the workers' houses were handled. Part of an ongoing project on Jolivet's part to recreate the kind of cinema centred on the common people that was so successful in the 1930s and the postwar period, *Fred* seeks to reassert a narrative centred on class interaction and a combative popular hero in a recalcitrant physical and social landscape.[5] The hero, a scruffy figure on an ageing racing bike, contrasts comically with the racing cyclists with sportswear who seem more suited to the new world of leisure and consumption. When at the controls of a container lorry or a JCB, he seems to embody the strength that his class once possessed but, when he applies for a new job, he is told that his past militancy will count against him. Workers may still be needed but only when deprived of the socio-political power they once wielded. By struggling against an exploitative capitalist (the dishonest constructor who used the asbestos) and by refusing to disown his previous struggles, Fred, like Beauvois's Matthieu, seeks to resist both class domination and the denial of its existence. It is in this context that the asbestos story takes on its full resonance. In the sanitized world of leisure and nature centres within which workers and bosses no longer directly confront each other, it allows a narrative of class oppression to be reinstated and to suggest that struggle is still valid and necessary. Yet like *Selon Matthieu* and Guédiguian's films, *Fred* also acknowledges the undoing of the working class and its capacity for collective resistance.[6]

Siri's *Une Minute de silence* is a film that, like *Fred*, deliberately chooses to live in the wreckage and to remain perversely faithful to values, a class and its aspirations that seem to have no place in the present world. Drawing directly on the director's family background as the son of a miner, the film is based on real events surrounding the announcement of a pit closure and the violent confrontations that accompanied it in December 1995. Unlike the public sector strike wave of the same month that could be seen as renewing a tradition of action, the miners' action was decidedly the swansong for a group who had traditionally been in the vanguard of worker militancy. The film acknowledges this fact by repeatedly ending the shots of the opening credit sequence with black and white freeze frames, as if consigning the miners to history before the story even begins. This impression is reinforced by the first dialogue between the two heroes, Mimmo and Marek, as they discuss the end of the French mining industry and one of the pair tellingly comments that, in any case, the public already think that there are no more mines in France. They are condemned to public invisibility even before their seemingly inevitable final disappearance. The prevailing nocturnal shooting also suggests a world of phantoms with one character comparing the location to a ghost town. Yet although the film's title, *Une Minute de silence*, implies mourning for the dead, the characters' relish for struggle and the film's ferocious closing battle scene suggests a still live anger rather than the silence of death. This is a film that chooses to live in the ruins and to hold on to the values associated with them in defiance of the passing of time. Mimmo is partly seduced by the lifestyle of a seedy people trafficker who, flourishing in the new amoral order, tells him that one must never look back. However, when driving the trafficker away from the film's final confrontation, he stops the car, violently throws him out and returns to find Marek in pitched battle with the police. He thus rejoins his comrade and the film itself in perverse yet resolute fidelity to the past and its values.

Like *Selon Matthieu*, *Fred* and Guédiguian's films, *Une Minute de silence* deliberately re-inscribes past sufferings and frustrated aspirations in the present. Thus, it shows Marek as he pauses silently before the monument to those who died in a pit collapse and amongst whose names figures his father. It shows too how the aspirations of Mimmo's and Marek's immigrant fathers to integration within France are betrayed by the enforced dismantling of their community. But the miners' collective memory is not only of loss and disappointment. It is also of struggle. Thus, Freddy reminds the younger men of how to fight the riot police with wooden staves, aiming alternately at the knees and at the head to bring the guard down before striking. This stubborn loyalty to the past, a kind of inter-generational solidarity, finds its natural prolongation in the fraternity which is inscribed in the very fabric of the film through its constant *mise-en-scène* of groups in struggle and in play. The film is, as I have already noted, a buddy movie, with the tight ties that bind the two heroes being mirrored in close family solidarities, broader friendship groups and a more general class and professional unity.[7]

Une Minute de silence joins the other films mentioned in not simply registering a defeat but in seeking to resist it. The films' collective resistance is multifaceted. Part of their thrust is to continue to occupy the disappearing spaces where the working class used to be, re-inscribing past suffering and aspirations, recording a violent undoing and condemning a debased present. Part of their thrust is to underline the ethico-political necessity of resistance even when that resistance seems either doomed or not yet to possess the resources to become effective. One could of course read them along lines suggested by Comolli and find in them a tacit admission that the working class is doomed to fragmentation, passivity, silence and invisibility. One could also accuse them, along the lines developed in *Cahiers du Cinéma* (chapter 2), of condemning resistance to the past or of developing an essentially folkloric image of the working class. But this would be to underestimate their willed perversity, their refusal to be realistic and to accept present defeat, and thus their deliberate attachment to combativeness and solidarity despite the lack of collective resources to support them at the current time.

Where the Working Class Used To Be: The *Banlieue*

Despite clear differences, the films we have just considered and the *films de banlieue*, to which we now turn, converge in bearing witness to a radical discontinuity in working-class history while underlining the current absence of a politically self-conscious opponent to capital. The former show working-class groups that even if they are still able to call on a tradition of resistance bear witness to the shattering of the larger social collectivity to which they once belonged. The latter, the *films de banlieue*, focus on the space where that same class was once classically to be found, with its current absence testifying to both its undoing at the hands of global capital and its own failure to renew itself through the integration of immigrant workers and their children. If the *banlieue* films show the kind of vibrant and at times quasi-insurrectional revolt once associated with the working class (Cadé 2000), this revolt seems no longer able to deploy a developed political language or cohere around a self-conscious collective actor. Put simply, a tradition of resistance has not been passed on. This story of discontinuity and non-renewal, the Ur story of the *film de banlieue*, is best encapsulated in Charef's fine film, *Le Thé au harem d'Archimède* (1985), the work that perhaps inaugurates the genre.

Significantly, *Le Thé au harem* begins by tracking two characters, a working mother, and an unemployed young man, following the former to an occupied factory, with inevitable echoes of the radical cinema of the 1970s and a broader working class mythology, and the latter to an eventual meeting with another unemployed young man. By leaving the striking woman to concentrate on the youths – one white, one *Beur* – and their often self-destructive struggles and clashes with authority, the film seems to self-consciously underline a transition from a cinema of class conflict to one depicting an underclass while simultaneously pointing to a paradigm shift in the symbolic resonance of a space, the *banlieue*, once associated with the organized working class. *Le Thé au harem* precedes, however, public recognition of the genre it might retrospectively be seen to have inaugurated. It was not until Kassovitz's *La Haine* burst on the cinematic scene in 1995, along with Richet's *Etat des lieux*, that critics and public felt ready to develop a new generic category, the *film de banlieue*, that was typically associated with troubled, predominantly male youth and their confrontations with authority, against a sterile backdrop of tower blocks and concrete.[8]

When *La Haine* hit cinema screens, the *banlieue* was of course already saturated with symbolic resonances. Constructed in the post-war years of economic boom, its outer-city estates seemed initially to symbolize the successful integration of the working class into a modern consumer economy. However, in more recent times, run down, abandoned by those able to leave, concentrating unemployment and social disadvantages, it has come to encapsulate not simply the failure of the left to renew itself but also the inability of the state fully to integrate either an indigenous working class or immigrant groups whose socio-economic marginalization is exacerbated by racist exclusions. It has now become one of the essential symbolic spaces of contemporary French political and media discourses, serving to condense a series of anxieties around unemployment, criminality, drugs, immigration and radical Islam. Attracting intermittent and sensationalist media coverage, riots in the 1980s and 1990s helped embed these negative stereotypes. The *banlieue*'s nationwide conflagration in 2005 further underlined the sense that it encapsulates the divisions that traverse French society. If more progressive elements of the political establishment tend to underline the need to do more to integrate the *banlieue*, the political right, notably Minister of the Interior Nicholas Sarkozy, has leaned increasingly towards emphasizing repression. Discourses of assistance or repression of course converge in objectifying those to whom they apply and underline the enormous symbolic shift that has taken place in the representation of the dispossessed. Taking the place of a working class recognized as a legitimate if subaltern political interlocutor, there are now the objectified and voiceless underclasses of the *banlieue*. Films like *La Haine* thus intervene on a loaded and overwhelmingly negative symbolic terrain.

La Haine begins by showing a demonstration in Paris against police brutality that has left a young *Beur* in a coma. It makes its sympathies clear by intercutting between shots of peaceful, indeed festive, demonstrators and images of the police's quasi-military apparel. The musical accompaniment, Bob Marley's radical reggae anthem, 'Burnin' and Lootin'', further underlines where its sympathies lie and, even as violence erupts, the order of the shots still lays responsibility at the police's door. However, when the introductory song fades out and gives way to the voice of a newsreader, emphasis shifts to the lawlessness of the rioters and the damage they have done, underlining the distance the film seeks to open up between its own vision and regressive media stereotypes. The film's commitment thus partly lies in a self-conscious espousal of the viewpoint of its *banlieue* characters, a positioning that underscores its attempt to constitute them as subjects and not simply as objects of voyeurist contemplation. This is an issue to which we will return in chapter 7.

Significantly, *La Haine* deliberately presents us with a class-driven narrative of the *banlieue*'s troubles, despite the clearly signalled ethnic origins of its three main protagonists. One is Jewish, another black and the third *Beur*, yet the film situates all three within a transatlantic, essentially hip-hop based cultural mix that gestures simultaneously towards Kassovitz's own influences, among whom leading African-American director Spike Lee is prominent, and to the strength of a hip-hop subculture in France. The shared subcultural identity of the characters both provides resources for resistance in the film – with tagging, scratch music and break-dancing being used to contest the possession of public space with the police – and pushes us to read their social marginalization as that of an underclass or sub-proletariat, rather than of a series of ethnically demarcated groups.[9] Support for a class-based reading of the film is provided when the young men travel from the *banlieue* into the centre of Paris. One sequence in an elegant apartment building underlines the difference in the living conditions of wealthy Parisians and those on society's edge. An elegant, sweeping staircase and vast, high-ceilinged rooms contrast sharply with the claustrophobic interiors and confined basements that we have earlier seen in the suburbs. Another sequence takes the young men into an art exhibition and underscores their shared incomprehension of highbrow culture and their lack of the social skills required to move in bourgeois circles. The film is conscious of the racialized nature of contemporary social marginalization, in a way underscored by a collision between the heroes and a group of skinheads and a painful scene in a police station in which the black and *Beur* characters are tortured, with clear colonial resonances. Yet this awareness qualifies rather than undoes the clear class oppositions that structure the narrative.

The observation that the film is about class needs some further qualification. Firstly, despite their joint mobilization of the resources of hip-hop, the lead characters have no clearly articulated sense of class identity that would give a sense to their rebellion. Secondly, they do not draw on any tradition of class struggle, their lack of historical awareness being underlined by the way in which they fail to respond to the film's clear references to anti-Jewish pogroms and colonial repression. Thirdly, although their world is clearly divided along class lines, their main quarrel is not with the bourgeois they encounter but with an oppressive police force with whom they repeatedly collide with increasingly disastrous consequences. Whereas a class-centred narrative might once have looked to progressive social transformation as its ultimate horizon, *La Haine* presents itself above all as a warning of impending social explosion, not least due to the ominous ticking that accompanies the countdown introduced in its early stages. If the film is driven by class, it would seem condemned only to point to the shrunken expectations associated with that term. The final murderous collision between youths singularly lacking in class consciousness and a racist police force suggests a sterile final closure of a class epic rather than its continued productive capacity. But, despite the absence of a self-conscious collective protagonist and a sense of historical possibility, class as mobilized by the film is perhaps more effective than it might initially appear. It has the virtue of generating a clear sense of social division and of bringing socio-economic disadvantage to the fore. It also serves to highlight how a state that once sought full social integration now turns increasingly to repression of those condemned to social uselessness. Whereas it is all too easy to categorize the *banlieue*'s problems as the local pathologies of a deficient underclass, *La Haine* uses them to generate a message about systemic failings (chapter 8). As the voice-over of Hubert, the black character, concludes, 'it's the story of a society that is falling'.[10]

Richet's *Etat des lieux* produces a more politically developed, class-centred account of the *banlieue* than *La Haine* while at the same time underlining the fragmentation of the working class. A defiant, lone combatant, its white working-class hero defiantly locates himself within a Marxist tradition of class. As a title that one might translate as 'inventory' reveals and as its fragmentary, episodic structure underlines, the film seeks to establish the current state of things rather than showing a developing story. Thus, different sequences show us various dimensions of the hero's existence. Sequences with the more middle-class woman with whom he lives point towards the very different cultural values espoused by different classes. Sequences at work underline friction with management and a residual class solidarity that is undermined by profound disagreements between radical and conservative workers. A dinner scene with the hero's family also suggests a strong class identity that is nonetheless fragmented by generational differences and, amongst the younger generation, by differential responses to social marginalization. A rather dream-like nocturnal sequence on a housing estate walkway brings the hero into lone confrontation with local fascists while a comic, daytime sequence shows him as he is stopped by two policeman for going through a stop sign on the broken-down motorbike that he was trying to start. Another comic scene, this time in an employment office, underlines the profound current inequality between the unemployed and those hiring labour. The film's episodic, stylistically shifting narrative thus provides us with a series of snapshots of the life of a still militant worker. Giving it a broader resonance, the opening documentary-like sequence shows a group of young men as they discuss the choice between alienating labour and social marginalization, a false choice that might seem to provide fertile ground for the kind of politics voiced by the hero. But there is no coming together of the socio-economic frustration of the group and the radical politics of the isolated hero. While the different 'snapshots' of his life underline the profound class divisions that still run through a supposedly post-class society and restate the importance of certain traditional battle lines between the leftist worker and his habitual foes (the boss, the police, the bourgeois, the fascist), the film, like *La Haine*, also inevitably points to the absence of a politically self-aware collective actor in the *banlieue*.

The film's fidelity to a leftist worldview is underscored when it departs from its general preference for extended takes to make stylistic nods towards the dialectical montage of the great Soviet director Eisenstein, notably in a section where images of the hero boxing are intercut into a sequence depicting him at work, thus inviting us to see beneath the surface of the real to the underlying violence of class relations. Eclectic in its influences the film also draws, like *La Haine*, on contemporary hip-hop music and dance, thus suggesting at the stylistic level the possibility of connecting inherited and contemporary oppositional forms. This stylistic bridging of past and present is mirrored within the narrative by sequences that establish the closeness of the white hero and his family to immigrant groups, thus underlining the proximity of the old working class to more newly established groups. But this utopian connectivity between past and present, white worker and immigrant is counterbalanced by the repeated isolation of the hero and the immobilism implied by the film's episodic form (its inability to connect fragments of struggle into a continuing narrative of conflict). Richet cannot, any more than other directors, erase a historical defeat. Nor can he maintain that the traditional left worked sufficiently to integrate immigrant groups into its structures or its struggles when it manifestly failed so to do. All he can do is to refuse to endorse the current situation, reassert the viability of a class-centred account of the social and remain faithful to leftist values while pointing towards alliances that need to be made.

While in *Etat des lieux* he strikes an admirable balance between recognizing the objective limits of a situation and showing how it can and must be opposed, his next film, the less satisfying *Ma 6-T va crack-er* (1996) seemed to underline the danger of political wishful thinking. Beginning as if it were a contemporary American film about turf wars in the ghetto, it ends with a call for an insurrectional coming together of competing gangs. In the retrospective light of the uprising in France's *banlieues* in 2005, its conclusion might begin to seem more a visionary premonition rather than a pipe-dream. However, because its different confrontations are singularly lacking in a politics, it still tends to underline the absence of a self-aware *collective* protagonist in the *banlieue* films. Much more satisfying is Richet's more modest third film, *De l'amour* (2000). Although lacking the formal radicalism and explicit militancy of *Etat des lieux*, it does echo some of the latter's themes by foregrounding police brutality, showing characters caught between marginalization and alienating labour and underlining the durable solidarity of the popular characters. Like its predecessor, it also privileges class over ethnic identity, firstly by figuring a mixed race couple at its heart and secondly by highlighting the identity of its lead characters as workers from its opening scenes. After being raped by a policeman, the heroine initially decides to abort the child that she is expecting, while her lover, the film's hero, is tempted to murder the rapist, two decisions that would seem to lock them into self-destructive violence and an abandonment of the future symbolized by their unborn infant. However, as the film ends, the characters are able to change their decisions, thus refusing to allow the past to shut off the future and death to triumph over life. But, as in Guédiguian's more pessimistic work, what they commit to is not a better life or a brighter future, but life and the future *per se*.

Ameur-Zaïmeche's more recent *Wesh wesh, qu'est-ce qui se passe?* might be situated somewhere between *La Haine* and *Etat des lieux*. It builds to a tragic explosion like the former, yet has some of the explicit political content of the latter. Like *Etat des lieux*, it was made on a shoestring budget.[11] It has a strong documentary feel due to the use of a digital newsreel camera (it was subsequently transferred to 35mm film for cinema exhibition), real locations, non-professional actors, extensive improvisation and a decidedly polemical contemporary theme, the *double peine*. While *La Haine* might be seen as blending the cult of surface of the *cinéma du look* with a social-realist content (Harris 2003), Ameur-Zaïmeche's low-budget piece has a decidedly unpolished feel to its images. Its refusal to aestheticize its subject should not be taken to signify that it is without formal ambition or, indeed, a politics of form. On the contrary, it develops a characteristic style notably marked by a repeated use of vertical pans up the tower blocks where the protagonists live, horizontal tracking shots that move along the front of the dilapidated buildings before finding the characters, and still shots that frame the entrances to the buildings where the young men seem condemned to spend so much of their time. These characteristic shots combine to suggest both the enforced narrowness of the characters' lives and the essentially collective nature of a drama that connects not simply to the individuals concerned but to the inhabitants of the *banlieue* more generally. The film's central character is a victim of the *double peine*, that is he has spent time in prison and then been punished again by expulsion from France to a North African 'homeland' with which he has no acquaintance. The film tracks him as, between his repeated need to avoid a seemingly ever-present police and his failure as a clandestine immigrant to get a job, it moves towards a violent end. But, the story, as suggested, has a much broader resonance. By showing the lives of his parents, brothers and sister and the young men and children of the *banlieue* more generally, it draws a broader picture of police racism, social tension and disintegration. Its impassioned critique of the iniquity of the *double peine* is thus framed within a broader picture of the failures of French society. As in *La Haine*, the omnipresence of the police suggests a nation that no longer integrates and must thus repress its marginalized groups.[12]

While the film's focus on North African immigrants and their children might suggest that it privileges ethnicity over class, one particular episode provides strong support for a class-based reading of the film. It occurs when the hero is sent to seek work from an employer who is also a *Beur*. All goes well, the hero recounts, until he reveals that he has no residence permit. The employer then loses all interest. The hero comments that all bosses are the same and make their money from the sweat of their employees, thus suggesting that class attitudes run deeper than ethnic solidarities. Strong support for such a reading of the film is also provided by the director himself. Asked in an interview if he reads life in the outer-ring housing estates politically, he responds, 'Class struggle is no longer restricted to factories or workplaces. It now takes place in urban space. Nowadays, government policy is to destroy the housing estates although people have taken years to weave social ties. The aim is to prevent people developing a political consciousness that could lead to an oppositional movement'.[13] It is striking that the director of a film centred on opposition to the *double peine*, a racially discriminatory statute, should push us to read it in class terms.

As analysts such as Rancière (1995) and Žižek (Butler, Laclau, Žižek 2000: 321–26) have noted, one face of contemporary consensus politics is a privileging of claims based on the sexual or ethnic identities of different groups to the exclusion of claims based on other criteria, notably class or economic exploitation. The effect of such a diminished politics is to enshrine the economic status quo by only allowing for demands for recognition within the existing order. Despite important differences, the different *banlieue* films considered converge in rejecting such a shrunken politics. By repeatedly calling attention to socio-economic equality through the inscription of a discourse of class, they register their refusal of the current social order. Yet while they reassert the importance of class, they do not fall into the old trap of allowing it to obscure and thus exacerbate discriminations rooted in ethnicity. Rather, by highlighting the combined effects of racism and socio-economic disadvantage, they suggest ways in which class might be reframed in more inclusive ways. If we were to seek a utopian dimension in films that generally show characters trapped in regressive situations, it is here that we might begin to look.

The antecedents of these utopian aspects of the *film de banlieue* can be traced, like so many of its other characteristics, to *Le Thé au harem*. If, by briefly showing us an occupied workplace, that film seemed to say farewell to the old dramaturgy of class, it also suggested how it might be partially renewed through the depiction, at the heart of its narrative, of an admirably resilient inter-ethnic friendship. Running consistently through the *banlieue* films discussed some such inter-ethnic friendship or romance repeatedly appears, opening class up to ethnic diversity while ensuring that ethnicity is connected to socio-economic disadvantage and not simply characterized in identitarian terms. *Le Thé au harem* also points to another connected and potentially utopian dimension of the *banlieue* films; that is, their search for something beyond their own initial frame. Although their revolt is condemned to open onto nothing, *Le Thé au harem*'s heroes are defined not by their situation but by their refusal of it, as notably when they break out of the enclosed territory of the *banlieue* and drive to the open and apparently unconstrained space of the beach. The other *banlieue* films similarly develop a dramatic tension rooted in the contrast between a stultifying socio-spatial frame and the characters' desire for something, albeit undefined, that might lie outside it (chapter 8). If, drawing on Rancière, we might begin to define a progressive cinema as one where characters speak not from a subaltern identity but from their refusal of such a thing, then we can see why the *banlieue* films might be seen as political (chapter 7). While the films speak of the failure to prolong the old working class and of a revolt that, even when it takes on an insurrectional nature, lacks a coherent collective actor, a class politics and any sense of future possibility, they also show a refusal of the fixity of subaltern social locations that finds a suitable prolongation in a renovating opening of class onto ethnic diversity.

Conclusion

We began this chapter by considering Comolli's important comments about how, while documentary was admirably suited to record active resistances, realist fiction could best register the passivity and defeat of the working class. What we have shown through analysis of films by Guédiguian, Beauvois, Jolivet and Siri has been how a series of fictions have indeed registered defeat by showing a working class undone as an epic socio-political actor, evicted from its old bastions, deprived of a collective voice and threatened in its very ability to continue itself. However, registering a profound disagreement with Comolli, we have suggested that the same fictions were also characterized by a still live resistance as evidenced in the refusal of the erasure of a social group and its values and in the defiant use of a discourse of class to reassert the existence of key social fault lines. Arguing along broadly similar lines, we have suggested that those *banlieue* films which self-consciously used class to structure themselves could not but note the failure of the working class to renew itself in some of its old bastions by incorporating immigrant groups and passing on traditions. However, what the *banlieue* films do suggest is that a certain combativeness has passed from the working class to the youth of the outer cities (Cadé 2000). By articulating this combativeness within a class framework while simultaneously underlining the absence of any self-conscious collective actor, the *banlieue* films repeatedly figure a revolt that calls into question a social order and a repressive state that produce and police the marginalization of the outer-city estates. Thus, if the two sets of films converge, it is in noting dislocation and defeat and in resisting them. The four groups of films discussed in the next chapter work within a broadly similar dynamic, being inevitably obliged to occupy the space of a defeat but working to resist it by refusing the consensual face of the contemporary order, rebuilding critique, asserting the continued viability of collective action and tracking the current victors.

Notes

1. Comolli's analysis is clearly reminiscent of Rancière's vision of an immobilizing realism based on recognition of the familiar (chapter 2). For Comolli, this sterile and politically counterproductive recycling of the already known is in sharp contrast to documentary's capacity to access the rich, unfamiliar store of bodily memories and gestures that real witnesses bring with them to the screen.
2. The words to 'Ay, Carmela' date from the Battle of Teruel in 1937 and express determination to triumph over fascism. Yet the tune originates from the Spanish guerrilla struggle against Napoleonic occupation. The song pulls together the two historical resistances to which the film refers thus suggesting that a tradition of resistance can traverse history.
3. In an interview Guédiguian says of Michèle, 'She is an archaic character who has no class consciousness, no religious faith. She is an animal mother who is driven by instinct' ('*C'est un personnage archaïque, qui n'a aucune conscience de classe, aucune foi religieuse. C'est une mère animale qui fonctionne à l'instinct*') (D., I. 2001).
4. For example, we see Matthieu caressing the dead father's ankle in the mortuary and lovingly polishing his tomb. He is also anchored in the history of his region. While walking on the Normandy cliffs with his boss's wife, he shows her a monument and tells her that another had stood there before, that of a fighter pilot who had shot down Hermann Goering in the First World War. Following the fall of France in 1940, the original statue had been knocked down on the orders of the German who wished to erase an unwelcome memory. Characteristically, Matthieu reminds us of what others have sought to remove.
5. Another of Jolivet's recent films, *Ma petite entreprise* (1998), recounts, for example, the struggles of a small joinery business against banks and insurance companies.

6. *Fred*'s focus on a material, asbestos, with a capacity to carry old oppressions into the present, suggests an implicit admission that they are easier to name than the current ones. But with its ability to do silent harm, the asbestos also points emblematically to the hidden violences of a sanitized contemporary world.

7. It is disturbing but perhaps not surprising that the intense male bonding that runs through *Une Minute de silence* is accompanied by undercurrents of both homophobia and misogyny. There is more than a hint, for example, that the distasteful trafficker in women is not simply interested in Mimmo as an assistant in his dealings.

8. For an excellent account of the *cinéma de banlieue* see Tarr (2005).

9. Tarr indeed criticizes *La Haine* for its failure to develop the specificity of the experience of its black and *Beur* characters (2005: 68–71).

10. '*C'est l'histoire d'une société qui tombe*'.

11. The film draws extensively on the director's own family and acquaintances for its cast.

12. Apart from its *banlieue* locale, and its sustained critique of police repression, *Wesh wesh* also shares with *La Haine* and *Etat des lieux* a connection to hip-hop, as evidenced by the presence on the hybrid soundtrack of the prominent group Assassin, also seen performing in *Etat des lieux*. Co-scriptwriter Madjid Benaroudj, a friend of Ameur-Zaïmeche since their university days, is a leading figure on the French hip-hop scene. On the surface, hip-hop has a lower profile in the film than in *La Haine* – characters are not seen break-dancing, scratching or tagging – but one could argue that, through its rootedness in the *banlieue*, its artisanal production and its more explicit political critique, the film, like *Etat des lieux*, is closer to the radical roots of hip-hop than its glossy predecessor. For a discussion of the film along these lines and for a more general discussion of the emergence of a cinema strongly influenced by hip-hop, see Bluher (2005).

13. '*La lutte des classes ne se passe plus uniquement dans les usines ou les lieux de travail. Elle se passe maintenant dans l'espace urbain. Aujourd'hui, la politique gouvernementale consiste à détruire les cités alors que les gens ont mis des dizaines d'années à tisser des liens sociaux. L'objectif est d'empêcher une prise de conscience politique qui pourrait aboutir à un mouvement de contestation*' (Amarger 2003).

5

CLASS REASSEMBLED?

Completing the discussion of the return of class to contemporary French cinema, this chapter considers a further four subgroups of films that seek in their different ways to reinstate a polemical, class-based understanding of the socio-economic terrain. Underlining the films' ability to reassert the centrality of struggle and the meaningfulness of critique, the chapter necessarily pursues its predecessor's partial disagreement with those voices (Comolli 2004, Cadé 2000) that associate the cinematic return of class and the world of work with recognition of defeat. The disagreement is partial because all the films are obliged to recognize defeat even as they seek to move beyond it. The issue of critique will be a central one for the chapter. In chapter 1, we used the work of Boltanski and Chiapello (1999) to underline how an essential part of globalizing capital's victory over opposition had been its ability to counter or turn to its own advantage the different forms of critique that had been addressed to it. What this chapter will show is how, even if the on-screen workplace is no longer the scene of an epic confrontation between capital and labour, it can still be used effectively to generate critique. It will also show how some films move beyond critique to begin to reunite a militant collective actor and an elaborated politics. But the painfulness of the rebuilding that must take place will of course testify to the shattering that has preceded it.

The subgroups of films are as follows. The first, including works by Chabrol and Poirier, shows us an apparently consensual social order in which, stripped of any explicit presence or accompanying language, class struggle can only reappear as an unnameable, subterranean violence. The next, involving films by Zonca, Devers and Masson take us into workplaces that are no longer occupied by a collective protagonist but where individualized struggles can still be mobilized to unmask the oppressive underside of the social order. The third is made up of films by Cantet, Liénard, Charef and Cabrera that work to bring back together a collective actor and the language of class struggle within the frame of the workplace, seeking thus to undo some of the process of silencing and dismantling to which other films bear witness. Recognizing the difficulty of bringing worker and capitalist together within the same narrative frame, the final subgroup, including films by Cantet and Moutout, chooses to track the current victors exploring both asymmetries of power and the alienation of the powerful.

Class as Struggle

La Cérémonie by *nouvelle vague* veteran Chabrol came out in 1995, the year of the great public sector strike wave, and appeared to be remarkably prescient in pointing to the turmoil that lay beneath the surface of an apparently pacified social order. *Marion*, by then up-and-coming director Poirier, hit cinema screens in 1997, the year of the release of *Marius et Jeannette*, helping to confirm a sense that class was making a comeback to the screens.[1] Yet this was class with a difference. No longer associated with the factory, the urban and the collective, it had been evicted from its old spaces and deprived of its language. It seemed to represent the end point of a process – the dismantling of the industrial working class – whose origins we have traced in our analysis of *Reprise* and the Dardennes' early work and whose consequences we followed through in the previous chapter. But, at the same time, and like the films already discussed, it reasserted the continued existence of oppression and resistance rooted in socio-economic inequality. In chapter 2, we noted a distinction made by Le Péron between regressive films which merely reproduce the familiar surface of reality and truly challenging ones which work to make visible the hidden violences beneath the surface of the familiar. The films we turn to here would seem to provide perfect examples of the latter category.

Both Chabrol's and Poirier's films are set in apparently tranquil rural locations. The former shows the arrival of a new female servant in the country retreat of a wealthy and elegant bourgeois family and goes on to narrate the alliance that builds up between her and the local postmistress. The latter film also narrates an arrival, this time of a poor family who come to live in a French village. The father is a skilled craftsmen who finds work repairing old buildings. A wealthy bourgeois couple who have their beautiful second home in the village become his clients. Mirroring their pastoral locations, both films begin in an apparently pacified social world. Chabrol's bourgeois seem kindness itself. They arrange an eye-test for their maid at their own expense not realizing that her apparent short-sightedness is a ploy to hide her illiteracy. Their charitable attitude is mirrored at a wider level by the local Catholic relief agency which gathers secondhand clothes to redistribute to the needy. We seem to be in a context not so much where class struggle is a thing of the past, but in a world where it has never arisen. The maid's illiteracy and her apparent lack of an opinion on any subject – she repeatedly replies 'I don't know' to questions – seem to point back to an era when the poor were effectively voiceless. Moreover, the *château*-like house of the rich family, the rural setting and the active role of the Catholic church all seem to hark back to the world that predated the French Revolution, a world in which the role of the poor was to be silent and to receive thankfully that which their betters gave. Poirier's film is similarly marked by an apparently benevolent, charitable relation between rich and poor. The rich, childless Parisians take an instant liking to the poorer family's daughter, invite her into their home, give her piano lessons and even set up an elegant bedroom for her. The employment they provide to her father gives precious cash to a family that struggles to make ends meet and has difficulty paying for basics such as electricity. The actions take place in the context of a village whose inclusive, egalitarian community is underlined by the annual village fête and its shared meal.

The violence that ruptures the apparent calm seems to spring from almost nowhere in Chabrol's story. We get a sense of smouldering resentment when the postmistress leads her friend in disruption of the Catholic charity, throwing back clothes that she considers rags in the face of the surprised givers, thus challenging both their self-representation as charitably generous and breaking the rule that the humble classes can only receive with gratitude. The underlying exploitative relation between masters and servants is also underlined when the maid is pressured to work on a Sunday for a party, makes the food as required, but does not stay to serve it, much to the indignation of her mistress. The fundamental asymmetry of the relationship is also suggested by the fact that the family feel that they a have a right to uncover the maid's illiteracy but are quick to protest when they feel that the postmistress may be opening their mail. The viewer is nonetheless amazed – as is the wealthy family – when the maid and her friend turn the family's hunting guns on them, massacring them as they smugly confirm their cultural superiority by watching a Mozart opera on the television.[2]

In Poirier's more low-key story there is a slower realization that a subtler but nonetheless horrible violence is being done. The bourgeois woman has a deep longing for a child but cannot have one. It gradually becomes clear that each apparent kindness to Marion is in fact a symbolic humiliation of her family, serving to underline what they are unable to give her. Things culminate when, over an elegant meal, the wealthy couple suggest that Marion return to Paris with them as a way to ensure entry to one of the best Paris *lycées* rather than the run-of-the-mill local school to which she is otherwise destined. It falls to Marion's rebellious elder sister to inform the parents that the former knows perfectly well who her true family is and to Marion's mother to tell the Parisians that, despite their poverty and social powerlessness, they too have a right to have opinions. Up until then, it had seemed that, faced with the cultured charm and social advantages of the wealthy Parisians, the poorer couple, like Chabrol's servant, had no language with which to name and oppose what was being done to them. The husband's rootless and non-conformist brother still gives voice to a familiar leftist language, criticizing for example the pressure to make public service profitable, but the couple seems unable to make any useful connection between the general principles he evokes and their own urgent problems both with the national power supplier EDF (Electricité de France) and with the Parisians. Racism rears its ugly head to suggest another way that they might articulate the wrongs that they feel are being done to them by linking them to a scapegoat. But while it is rejected with scornful anger, no other public language is found to put in its place. The mother's final assertion of the equality of their voice announces a capacity to speak that has yet to find a positive content.

Chabrol's and Poirier's films thus work to reassert the continuation of class struggle in worlds from which it had seemed banished and in which there remains no language with which to name it. They undoubtedly resonate in a social context in which those at the bottom of the pile are increasingly cast as social objects needing help from a charitable state rather than as subjects having rights. The poorer characters in both films refuse such an objectification, in one case through a dignified reassertion of political equality, in the other through a violent refusal to be cases for scrutiny or compassion. It is also worth noting that the workers in both films are essentially in the position of servants, most obviously in *La Cérémonie*, where the leading character is a maid, but also in *Marion*, where the father looks after the house and grounds of the bourgeois. This is class that seems on the point of disappearing into an older-style world of castes. It has no collective identity, folkloric or other, and no archetypal space, in short no sociological density. It is reduced to its political core: to oppression and resistance, in short, to struggle.[3]

Work without Class: Restoring the Grounds for Critique

If the films just considered underline how, even when nameless and voiceless, class can be brought to the surface to disrupt the calm appearance of consensus, they are complemented by another group which likewise refuse the contemporary pacification of the social order by going into the world of production to bring still live oppressions to the surface. The old language of class in general and the workplace in particular used to constitute primary vehicles for bringing exploitation, domination and alienation to public visibility. That language, as I have noted (chapter 1), has been largely silenced even as the working class as collective actor has been undone. Recognizing the consequences of this demolition, the films discussed here figure labour that is increasingly individualized, vulnerable and largely unseen as it encounters oppressions that all are all the more violent because no longer tempered by collective solidarities, traditions of resistance or an inherited language that could name them, explain them and bring them to public visibility.[4] We will return to the films in later chapters to consider their spatiality, their focus on predominantly raw, voiceless and corporeal struggles and the strategies that they mobilize to restore eloquence and visibility to suffering and struggle deprived of a public voice and face. What will interest us at this stage is how they both underline and resist the seismic symbolic shift that has taken place in the representation of class and the world of work.

Zonca's early work is a good starting point. It has repeatedly figured isolated characters who move between precarious employment and unemployment and thus encapsulate the new face of work in French cinema. The highly acclaimed *La Vie rêvée des anges* (1997) follows two young women with neither permanent accommodation nor stable employment as they circulate between constrained labour and sites of consumption such as bars and shopping centres. The action begins when Isa, the film's free spirit, finds employment in a sweatshop but quickly loses her job due to mistakes she has made. Her summary dismissal is accompanied by verbal abuse while her fellow workers look passively on. She later applies for work in a new club but only receives short-term employment giving out promotional leaflets, having to change into her skater's costume on the street, in freezing weather, for the latter task as the naked but hidden domination of the industrial sweatshop gives way to the constrained yet visible 'carefreeness' of work in the world of consumption. As the film ends, we see her again at work, this time on an assembly line producing electronic components. After what seems like minimal training, she is seen apparently happily threading colour-coded wires into a connector plug. The supervisor approvingly tells her that it seems like she has been doing the job all her life. Cadé (2000: 64–65) reads this closing sequence in terms of the satisfaction of manual labour, but it would seem rather to point towards an alienation that has become so total that it can no longer be spoken of. Isa's work threading wires is an almost exact reprise of her sweatshop labour with threads. Both tasks were so unskilled and so repetitive that they could be learned in a matter of minutes. The difference is that, in the first case, the worker's undomesticated body offered some form of material resistance while, in the second, the constraints of alienating labour have been fully internalized. The apparent compliment that she has been doing this all her life points, with desperate irony, to the complete closing in of her life's horizons and to the rendering invisible of her alienation. The same narrative pattern drives Zonca's *Le Petit Voleur* (1998), a made-for-television film that was part of Arte's *Gauche / Droite* series.⁵ Rejecting the boredom and subordination associated with his job in a bakery, its young hero joins a criminal gang only to find that membership of it exposes him to the same tedious tasks and social domination that he had thought to leave behind. The end of the film finds him, now a docile worker, in a large, mechanized bakery. As with Isa, his apparent integration into the modern economy only comes about because he is forced, by the apparent lack of an alternative life, to abandon all resistance to socio-economic constraint. The earlier short *Seule* (1995) provides the first, partial version of the repeated pattern by depicting a young woman who is unceremoniously fired from her job as a trainee waitress because she has shown herself insufficiently willing to reshape her attitude and appearance. By repeatedly figuring the mismatch between recalcitrant subjects and the constraints of labour, Zonca's films work to reinstate a critique of alienation.

Two films by Laetitia Masson similarly explore the alienations generated by contemporary labour and the economy. Perhaps the more conventional of the two, *En avoir (ou pas)* (1995) focuses on a young woman's attempt to escape from a proletarian condition that seems completely unable to satisfy her personal ambitions. As the film begins, she is made redundant from a fish processing plant. An early scene where she obsessively soaps her skin is suggestive of a desire to wash away her proletarian condition as one would the clinging smell of dead fish. A job interview quickly shows the unreality of her desire to be a singer, a profession for which she clearly has insufficient talent, while highlighting the profoundly asymmetrical relation between buyers and sellers of labour. While the hirer can probe in inquisitorial fashion into her capacities, requiring her to humiliate herself by singing if he chooses, she has to pretend to be utterly committed to a job in which she has no personal interest. As in job interviews in some of the other films (*Etat des lieux*, *La Vie rêvée des anges*) alienation and domination are brought simultaneously into view as the worker has to remake his or her desires in the form required by capital in a giving over of the self that is simultaneously an emptying out. By the end of the film, the heroine has predictably had to concede defeat and accept work serving in a café, knowing that she is condemned to remain a proletarian, that promises of individual self-fulfilment are not for those at the bottom of the social pile, but also having underlined, through her aspiration to something other than her allotted role, that her desire and her objective social being do not coincide. The rebellion of the heroine of Masson's more radical companion piece, *A vendre* (1997), is to say the least perverse. Having experienced the pain of interpersonal relations, the young heroine, a daughter of peasant farmers, decides to avoid future suffering by charging for any future relationships. Remaking herself as a commodity, she frees herself from ties, but at the same time inevitably loses herself. This is made clear at a relatively early stage when, having decided to charge a man whose house she was cleaning for the sex he wanted for free, she loses control of the love-making and has to place herself in the position chosen by him, no matter how little it may be to her taste. In the end, her quest for freedom through self-commodification reaches a predictable dead end when she finds that, having posed for a painter to earn some money, she has lost ownership even of her own image. Engaging with a nexus of issues around self-deter-mination, waged labour and increasing commodification, both Masson films highlight the subaltern status, social entrapment and alienation of those at the bottom, particularly women, while simultaneously opening a space between their dominated social being and their subjective desires.

Another film from the *Gauche / Droite* series, the excellent *La Voleuse de Saint-Lubin* (1998) by respected film-maker Claire Devers, complements Zonca and Masson's work by restoring currency to a critique of exploitation. The film shows a single mother who struggles desperately to make ends meet by working as a cleaner in a meat processing factory, tellingly removing traces of her own messy labours and those of her fellow workers to allow a sanitized product to reach the consumer. She can afford to feed her two daughters foods such as pasta that meet their daily energy requirements but not more expensive foods such as meat that would give them the protein for healthy growth. Inevitably, she cracks under the pressure and steals supermarket meat in order to give them a decent meal. Echoing the elemental struggles for group survival and reproduction that run through Guédiguian's films, her fight to feed her children works more specifically to reinstate an account of the social based on an exploitation that is all the more flagrant when the meat producer cannot afford to buy meat.

We used the work of Boltanski and Chiapello in chapter 1 to underline how a central component of capital's victory over the twentieth-century left has been its successful disarming of the chief forms of critique that had been addressed to it. The group of films that we have just considered resist that victory by foregrounding the alienation, domination and exploitation of productive labour and by using the constraints associated with labour to disrupt the utopian claims of consumption. They underline how, even without the presence of collective resistances and a discourse of class exploitation, the workplace – the privileged space of the old class epic – remains a site where the collision between subjective desires and socio-economic constraints can be used to bring oppression into visibility.

Reassembling the Pieces?

We now turn to a cluster of films that might seem to move us forward from the films above by taking us beyond individual alienation to workplace conflicts that still make active use of the old language of class struggle.

These include Bénédicte Liénard's powerful *Une Part du ciel* (2001) and Cantet's highly regarded *Ressources humaines*, both first features, as well as Charef's *Marie-Line* and Cabrera's *Retiens la nuit*, although our main discussion of the latter will be located in the next chapter. The films are significant in that, although they might seem to be the closest contemporary French cinema comes to showing collective political militancy, in each case militancy is something towards which the films have to carefully build rather than something taken for granted.

Une Part du ciel, an austere but defiant film, is a Franco-Belgian co-production set in Belgium. It cross-cuts between essentially two locations, a woman's prison and an industrial bakery, between which a fundamental equivalence is suggested. Both are bare locales with hard cold surfaces, bars at their entrance and a sense of enclosure, which if anything is stronger in the bakery due to the lack of windows and the constant artificial lighting. Both are places of labour, with the folding of maps by the prisoners finding its visual echo in the folding of pastries by the workers. Within one, the prison, we find Joanna, a former bakery worker who, with no backing from her union, has 'cracked up' and acted alone (in a way never precisely explained), and has been imprisoned as a result. Within the other, the bakery, we find the friend who failed to testify at her trial because of the risks involved, but who now regrets her lack of courage. Within both spaces the characters seem largely isolated, a situation accentuated by extended dialogue-free shots featuring them alone in bare spaces. Movement within the prison is false movement leading nowhere. Always enclosed in long, empty corridors, it simply leads to another part of the prison, both for the warders and for the prisoners, with the former tellingly seeming little more free than the latter. Movement to and from the bakery takes place in a train whose windows are always closed and whose carriages thus provide a visual echo of the prison corridors. This is a carceral world in which there seems, in short, to be no outside. The film is thus not, as Liénard herself was at pains to point out, one that sought simply to denounce prison conditions, but rather one that pointed towards the more general unfreedom of societies based on dominated labour (Verhaeghe 2001).

Yet despite this apparently grim vision, the film is defiantly positive. Firstly, both women are able to connect to their fellow inmates or workers, even if the groups established often seem lost in large, empty spaces. Secondly and crucially, both still resist. Joanna, for example, demands to know who makes a profit from what the prisoners do and insists on the right to refuse labour, thus underlining the possibility of self-affirmation and questioning even by those with apparently no freedom of action. Her former workmate is similarly defiant. She opposes both management and the union in her defence of workers' rights to job security and, repenting her earlier inaction, decides to testify in support of her friend's appeal against her conviction. This decision is followed by a sequence on the train when windows that have been closed throughout the film are finally opened and the character leans out, her hair blowing in the wind as, through her public resistance, she breaks out of the world into which she seemed shut. *Une Part du ciel* defiantly maintains a leftist critique of un-free, exploited labour and collaborationist unions that bears clear echoes of the radical post-1968 films that we considered in chapter 3. Yet, whereas leftist opposition was collective and on the offensive in those works, here it is isolated and defiant. *Une Part du ciel* also resembles *Etat des lieux*, another film that, against the odds, maintains a radical leftist position. Yet, despite its grim austerity, it is the more hopeful of the two in that, in contrast to the other film's stasis, it shows progression. Beginning in a world in which opposition is broken or imprisoned, it reinstates its possibility and necessity, showing how its initially isolated protagonists reconnect to each other, begin to involve others in their struggles and assert their own freedom by resisting.

Ressources humaines is a family-centred melodrama (chapter 7) that seems initially to unfold within a fully pacified social order. It begins when its hero arrives in his hometown to begin a work placement in the human resources department of the company where his father has worked for thirty years. He is a sincere believer in the new, apparently consensual regime that seems to prevail in the factory as in the broader society. Despite his working-class origins, he seems destined to a bright future as a manager and thus to a personal trajectory that confirms the fluidity of boundaries. His initial personal contacts suggest the same, as he is able to maintain cordial relationships with both the factory managers and younger and older workers. The task he assumes is to assist with the negotiation of the application of the then very fresh legislation to reduce the working week to thirty-five hours. He convinces the factory manager to put a questionnaire to the workforce, assuring the latter that their opinions count. Only the mature female CGT representative stands out by presenting the management's direct appeal to the workers as a subterfuge to by-pass the unions and suggesting that a struggle is in the offing. She was similarly defiant at an earlier consultative meeting but was a profoundly isolated voice, receiving lukewarm support from the other unions and voicing a language of class struggle that seemed out of place in an apparently pacified order. As she herself notes, people think she is mad. Her words fail to bite upon the real.

However, the film quickly begins to accumulate signs that point towards a different construction of things. Barriers of one sort or another become visible, suggesting that the new social order is less fluid and transparent than it might appear. The hero finds for example that, having been away to Paris and learned the language of the economically powerful, he can no longer relate to old friends. He also finds that certain spaces are closed to him, that there are meetings from which he is excluded and windows where blinds are drawn to prevent observation. This is a world where access to spaces is regulated and where decisions are taken by some while others are held in ignorance. The positive gloss that the hero puts on his questionnaire as a genuine attempt to discover the workers' opinions is undermined when his bosses indicate that it was a good tactic that has successfully divided the trade unions. As these signs accumulate, the world of the fiction shifts to make the words of the CGT delegate seem less mad.

The hero's father knows that he is part of a dominated social group. He believes, for example, that distances must be kept and thus does not expect his son to sit with him at lunchtime in the canteen. After completing the latter's questionnaire he asks him whether he has corrected his *copie* or answer paper, implicitly placing himself in the role of a pupil. His submissiveness is evident at an early stage when he responds with silence when a foreman, with no respect for his years of service, berates him aggressively for slowing the work down. He even fails to react when, at the film's turning point, his son, who has accidentally gained knowledge of management plans, tells him he is to lose his job and that consultation over the thirty-five hours was being used as a cover to push through redundancies. His silence and round-shouldered posture in these moments suggests a character who knows, as Comolli (2004: 538–39) notes, that the working class has been defeated. Yet, this is hardly where the film leaves things. It shows, firstly, that the father's acceptance of the status quo is untenable. He has sought social advancement for his son while submissively bearing the unpleasantness of his work – this stoic perseverance is what the young, black worker on a neighbouring machine so admires him for. Yet perseverance ceases to be a useful strategy when experience counts for less than nothing and when older workers have no job security. At the same time, the son's success places him in the impossible situation of humiliating his father by being his social superior while bearing the shame that the latter has taught him for his own origins. In either case, accommodation to the dominant order seems an increasingly untenable solution. The union delegate, in contrast, seems more reasonable as the film proceeds until, in its latter stages, she becomes the accepted leader of the strike in opposition to the sackings. The moment of transition in her public perception comes when the hero reveals the management's planned redundancies. She is then able to speak a language that bites upon the real and to explain to the workers that, given the company's outstanding orders, they are in a strong position to win a strike. Rather than the film simply making visible a defeat as Comolli suggests, it works to show that the apparently defeated still have resources (languages, practices, knowledges) with which to resist. Marginal and seemingly outdated at the start of the film, class struggle is rendered central, current and meaningful by the end.

Working on a similar terrain, Cabrera's made-for-television *Retiens la nuit* also underlines the resources that workers still possess. As its co-writer

Philippe Corcuff noted in an interview, it was because the 1995 public sector strikers figured in the film were heavy with experience and traditions of struggle that they were able to oppose the government's attempts to weaken their social security and pension entitlements (Homer 2000). Beginning with a situation in which the popular classes seem irremediably split between those, like its railway workers, with stable employment and those, like Nadia, its single mother, who live in a state of permanent precariousness, the film works to again find grounds, as we shall later see, for a common front of the dominated. A key part of this effort is the reinstatement and reinvigoration of an apparently worn out discourse of class struggle. *Retiens la nuit* shows a social terrain where those with the resources to resist have been cowed both by fear of the loss of their relative security and by the suggestion that they are a privileged group compared to the 'excluded'. However, by the end, a common neo-liberal enemy has been identified and the strikers and Nadia have come together in a renewed experience of solidarity. The workers have tellingly seen that their action has forced the government to think again and that, for a moment at least, as one union delegate says, fear has changed sides.

Connecting back to films like Devers's *La Voleuse de Saint-Lubin* as well as those just discussed, Charef's *Marie-Line* (1999) starts from the seemingly irremediable division of those at the bottom as well as the alienation and social invisibility of their labour. The film's eponymous heroine is the forewoman of a team of immigrants and illegal migrants who work to keep a supermarket and the shopping centre around it clean. Their nocturnal toils, like the cleaning work of Devers's heroine, are self-effacing and enable consumption's pristine self-presentation. Finding no satisfaction in what they do, the only path open to them for much of the film is to retreat into private spaces, as evidenced by the cult which Marie-Line dedicates to the dead heart-throb singer, Joe Dassin, to whom she has made a shrine in her basement storage room. But, in the face of pressures from management and the immigration service, this individual flight proves unsustainable. To get and keep her job, the heroine is obliged not only to rule her team with a rod of iron and but also to provide sexual services and join the Front National to keep her racist manager satisfied. As the film progresses, she is increasingly drawn to side with her fellow workers, not least when she finds herself looking after children of African migrants threatened with expulsion. By the end, she has both broken with the Front and upset the company prize-giving ceremony by defiantly playing a tape of North African music belonging to an expelled Algerian woman while her team members look on supportively. The women's solidarity is as yet mute and there is no reason to think that Marie-Line can even understand the Arabic lyrics on the tape. But, while recognizing that there is no available anthem of international solidarity to replace the 'Internationale', a song whose loss of an epic choir was underlined in Guédiguian's *La Ville est tranquille* (chapter 4), the film refuses the debilitating playing-off of indigenous and migrant workers against each other while pointing to the need for a common front of the dominated.

Une Part du ciel, Ressources humaines, Retiens la nuit and *Marie-Line* all bear witness to a defeat yet seek to move beyond it. They start from worlds that bear witness to the shattering of the leftist dramaturgy of class struggle. They show popular classes that are divided, with their radical elements defeated or isolated and a world in which struggle seems condemned to history and a leftist language no longer connects to the real. None can hold out a vision of a rosy future or an imminent victory of a reunited working class. The struggle in *Ressources humaines* is only beginning when the film ends and, even if it seems to have a strong chance of success, is purely defensive. *Retiens la nuit* reunites its divided popular forces but also recounts a defensive struggle. The most austere of the three, *Une Part du ciel*, reinstates the possibility of collective resistance without offering any glimpse of an eventual positive outcome. *Marie-Line* refuses the national and ethnic division of its working class cast, but also points to the silence where leftist internationalism once used to be heard. However, to only see the films in negative terms would be to miss the essential political work that they do in piecing back together the fragments of a leftist dramaturgy of struggle. They collectively strive to show that struggle is both necessary and possible, that a leftist language is still meaningful and that the division and isolation of the dispossessed is not inevitable. However, what none really succeeds in doing is in bringing the current victors into the picture. Either focusing exclusively on the dominated (*Retiens la nuit*) or showing relatively small companies or local branches of larger concerns, none seeks to bring systemic dynamics or real decision makers onto the screen. One might ask if an oppositional cinema that had chosen above all to show the struggles of the dominated had lost the capacity of engaging with the powerful. Cantet's *L'Emploi du temps* (2001) and Moutout's *Violence des échanges en milieu tempéré* (2002), two films to which we will now turn, suggest that this is not entirely the case.

Tracking the Victors

Complementing his *Ressources humaines*, a film partially focused on the alienated labour of an old worker, Cantet's *L'Emploi du temps* traces the alienation of one of today's winners, a man who works for a leading management consultancy company. Moutout's film also complements his early work. His two highly-rated shorts, (*Tout doit disparaître*, 1996; *Electrons statiques*, 1998), looked at the experience of unemployment and at low-paid temporary labour. *Violence des échanges* moves us on by tracing the gradual corruption of a young high-flyer as he adapts to employment with another high-powered management consultancy firm. Although based in similar milieus, the two films have fundamentally different drives. Moutout's film, as its title suggests, is essentially about systemic violences and its hero's failure to resist them. Cantet's film is broader in its scope, using its account of a management consultant who goes off the rails to develop a broad-ranging critique of the contemporary economic order.

Violence des échanges begins when the hero is travelling by underground train to La Défense, the heart of France's financial power and the site of the offices of the international firm for which he works. He sees a middle-aged man sexually harassing a young woman passenger. Nobody else seems to see what is happening. Courageously intervening, the young man challenges the harasser. He will begin a relationship with the young woman whom he has helped but, sucked by his job into conniving in the much broader-scale violences of the capitalist economy, will fail to live up to the initial act of moral courage. Sent by his hierarchical superior to a successful French company that has been taken over by a foreign multinational, he is ostensibly to give advice that will allow the company to become more efficient. His true task, however, is to work out which parts of the company can be pruned in order to turn reasonable profits into handsome ones. Not only is he asked to decide which activities can be amputated, he is also required to observe and interview each individual to gauge who will and will not fit into the new mode of running the firm. His initial reaction, once he realizes the brutal nature of the task, is to refuse, thus seeming to reproduce his opening demonstration of moral courage. However, pressured by his superior and threatened with the loss of his own job, he caves in and conforms like the other young high-flyers whom his company dispatches around the world to lubricate the workings of the global free-market economy.

The film's hero, a subaltern member of the dominant group, participates in the exercise of power if not in the directions that it chooses to follow. All the people in the provincial company, from senior managers to canteen workers, have the decisions of others visited upon them. Some, the film shows, suspect at an early stage what is really going on but feel bound by their role to remain silent. Others, not so well placed, are less aware. Once things become clear to all, the reaction is angry but there is no sense that effective collective opposition is possible. This is perhaps the political weakness of Moutout's film, its failure to join some sense of political possibility to its dissection of systemic violences. Nonetheless, and in contrast to other films in this chapter which essentially focus on the wreckage and the local resistances left behind once globalization has passed through the social terrain, *Violence des échanges* figures globalization as ongoing process. By choosing to focus on the victors, it is able to come much closer to the system's heart than those films that (understandably) choose to accompany those excluded from circuits of power. It mounts a telling critique of the neo-liberal order by focusing on the extreme inequalities of power which it generates and the violences that inevitably ensue from the valuing of profit before people.

L'Emploi du temps is a more subtle, complex and ambitious film. Vincent, its hero, is, as we slowly discover, a fake who takes on different masks in an attempt to escape from a world of work that offers him no satisfaction or autonomy. It is these masks that allow his story to attain such breadth and to engage with multiple aspects of a global economy that a more conventional framed fiction would struggle to embrace. We initially pick him up in his car, apparently between appointments. He phones his wife to explain that he and his colleagues have to deal with some tricky redundancies and he will thus not be home when expected. As the story unfolds, we learn that he has in fact lost his job, but is carrying on as if he still had it. Because the initial fiction becomes hard to sustain, he invents himself a new post in Switzerland with a UN agency specializing in international investment and development. This buys him time, as well as admiration for both the global power he now seems to wield and the humanitarian cause (African development) to which he seems devoted. But money, of course, soon proves a problem. Vincent invents a scam. Contacting old business friends, he tells them that his UN role allows him to move currency across borders without it being declared. He promises them rich returns if they allow him to invest their savings in Eastern Europe. As he is selling this deal to people all too willing to make easy if illicit gains, he is observed by another character, Jean-Michel, who makes his own living by shipping counterfeit designer goods into France, also with astonishing rates of return. The latter tells him that his money placement scheme will inevitably crash and offers him a job transporting the fake goods. At this stage, Vincent seems able to square the circle. His fictions seemed to liberate him, but his liberty was inevitably constrained by the real (his need for money). As he moves to selling fake goods, fiction and reality converge and merge. The fiction – that the goods are genuine – now provides *real* rewards. However, another face of the real will trip him up more decisively. His family discover his subterfuge, thus making his position untenable. He is forced to return to a more conventional, constrained life. The end of the film shows him as he is interviewed for a high-ranking job in which he has to pretend to be interested. As long as he was the author of his own fictions, he could achieve some kind of freedom. Now that he has to return to playing the role that others – his family, the business world – thrust upon him, he has to abandon his desire for autonomy while pretending to be content.

Based on an intriguing but exceptional real-life story of a high-flyer who hid the loss of his job, defrauded his friends and went on to murder his family, the film manages to mount a powerful multi-pronged attack on contemporary capital, even while showing a world where neo-liberalism seems to rule unchallenged and unquestioned. The central prong of the attack concerns alienation. This is most evident in the case of Vincent but is also seen to affect other characters. Late in the film Vincent explains to Jean-Michel that he was happiest when driving to the different companies where he had appointments. Things began to go wrong when, instead of turning off where required, he carried on, missing the turning and the appointment. If driving might seem to symbolize freedom and self-determination, the need to turn off and stop against one's will underlines the lack of true self-determination even amongst those apparently part of the contemporary elite. The hero's perverse continuation of his journeys is a revolt against social constraint and an affirmation of freedom. A critique of alienation also underlies the central contrast between the liberatory fictions that the hero mobilizes to free himself and the fictions that socio-economic constraints oblige him to act out. In the director's earlier *Ressources humaines*, the creativity and individual self-expression of the manual worker were similarly relegated to the private sphere in a way underlined by the contrast between the deskilled repetitiveness of the hero's father's labour in the factory and the autonomy and creativity developed in his workshop at home. With *L'Emploi du temps*, Cantet rounds out his critique of alienated labour by extending it to the dominant group.

L'Emploi du temps's exploration of the alienation of individuals is accompanied by related critiques of domination, exploitation and inauthenticity. Domination is evoked throughout the film. It is seen most transparently when Vincent applauds his eldest son's triumph in a judo match where he throws and pins his opponent. Personal triumph and the recognition it brings come at the inevitable cost of the subjugation of others. It is evoked more obliquely when Vincent refers to the (invented) redundancies that he is involved in managing: while some people have powers of decision, those that they dominate are expendable. More broadly, the admiration Vincent wins from his friends is tied to the fact that he is perceived as a winner, someone who has the power to decide what others will do. Vincent makes much of the developmental and humanitarian benefits that accrue from his supposed work for the UN, while admitting at the same time that he is ashamed at the contrast between the lush building in Geneva, where he supposedly works, and the complete lack of infrastructure in the African countries that they are helping. If the film had limited itself to this banal contrast between rich and poor it would simply have stated the obvious but, because it maintains a constant attention to the mechanisms of domination, it invites us to see that the obscene underside of humanitarian concern is a sadistic pleasure taken in mastery of the other and one's own resultant self-image as a winner. Vincent's apparent power as a *décideur* is directly dependent upon the powerlessness of those he is supposed to be helping. That, of course, was the point of the judo match.

Vincent is not simply a winner, of course. He is also clearly a loser. He has been sacked, runs short of money and finds himself moved on from places, just as a homeless person might be. If his ejection from the UN building is polite, his expulsion from a hotel car park where he has been asleep in his vehicle is unceremonious and threatening. Because of his double nature as winner and loser, insider and outsider, we are able to see what it means to be both at the top and at the bottom of the pile. And because he is winner and loser, two stories that are normally kept apart are brought together and held in tension so that their interconnectivity becomes clear. Being on the inside only means what it does because there are people on the outside. Being on top is only possible when others are on the bottom.

While pretending to work for the UN, Vincent studies dossiers relating to its developmental work in Africa. He also eavesdrops, at one stage, on a meeting on the same topic. In narrative terms, what he learns is of course necessary to allow him to develop his persona as a UN employee. Its political use-value lies in how it allows the film to show how development has become a euphemism for marketization and exploitation. As the hero underlines to his friends, the UN's development wing works hand in hand with the private sector so that development in reality implies incorporation into a profoundly unequal, globalized economy. One of the more telling things that Vincent reads out from official documents is a list of privatizations in Southern Africa. Another is a list of foreign investments in African countries. In a film about pretence, it would seem that humanitarianism and development serve as masks for exploitation. What might initially have seemed an opposition between reality and fiction, truth and lie, mutates into an interplay of fictions, with Vincent's little fiction providing the key that opens a whole series of bigger ones.

A productive interplay of fictions is also at work when the film turns its attention to authenticity. Inviting himself to dinner at Vincent's house, Jean-Michel, the 'manager' of the small but highly profitable concern that deals with counterfeit designer goods, poses as a UN worker whose job is to fight the counterfeit industry. Vincent's son remarks that he has friends who have bought fake sports goods that are just as good as expensive, authentic ones. Playing his role to the full, Jean-Michel argues that the fake goods are, on the contrary, shoddy ones. Muddying the waters, however, he then suggests that factories where they are produced cannot simply be shut down because they alternate between producing legal and illicit goods. It seems that the line between a legitimate economy with authentic goods and a dishonest one with fakes cannot be clearly drawn. If, as Vincent's son suggests, expensive, designer goods are no better in reality than cheaper fakes, then the problem is no longer the fakeness of the fakes but the pseudo-authenticity of the legal goods, their false promise to deliver something better. Rather than falling back on a traditional leftist opposition between an authentic existence outside the market and an inauthentic one within it (a critique which, relying on dubious notions of authenticity, is almost impossible to sustain), it uses one fake to unmask another.

L'Emploi du temps is a remarkable film. Although, like other works considered here, it remains broadly within the framework of realist cinema, tracking a socially located protagonist through a linear narrative with understandable causes and effects, it frees itself from some of the limitations of realism by placing a fantasist at its core. It can thus mount a critique of the dynamics of contemporary capitalism that is wider in its reach than any of the other films considered, taking in both winners and losers and exploring power dynamics and systemic logics while mounting a critique of inauthenticity, alienation and domination. One could use it purely negatively to point to the inability of most of the other films to register anything beyond the local consequences of systemic dynamics that resist representation in spatially circumscribed realist narratives tied to a handful of broadly working-class protagonists. But this would be to fail to recognize the extent to which those other films succeed in looking beyond their own story space (chapter 8). It would also be to fail to see how much *L'Emploi du temps* is part of a broader, collective attempt to rebuild the grounds for critique and opposition.

Conclusion

We began the previous chapter by drawing on Jean-Louis Comolli's view that recent French fiction film had largely turned its back on class and, where it did show it, was able at best to reveal the demoralization of a working class condemned to silence and invisibility. The films we have examined in the last two chapters could be used to provide support for Comolli's harsh judgement in that they bear witness to the defeat of a class evicted from its old spaces and stripped of its collective prominence in the social imaginary. Yet such a judgement would clearly be partial. If all the films effectively do show the shattering of the old leftist dramaturgy, they also make it clear that the pieces can be put to positive use. Even when voiceless and nameless, class struggle can be brought back to the surface to refuse the consensual face of the contemporary social order. Even when emptied of an epic protagonist, the workplace can still be used to restore grounds for critique and to disrupt consumption's smooth appeal. The *Cahiers'* critics that I considered in chapter 2 suggested that many of the films discussed gave the working class a fixed and immobilizing social identity that helped confirm its place in the current social order. This chapter and the last have led me to some very different conclusions. In almost all the films considered, rather than being simply a question of identity, class is intrinsically tied to struggle. Although the films show that this struggle is constantly threatened with the loss of its own grounds (a shared language, a collective protagonist, a future), they use its very existence to reassert a polemical account of the current order and to bring underlying violences back to the surface. They struggle to make struggle itself once again visible, possible and meaningful. In some cases, they only seem able to justify it negatively, by showing, in films like *Selon Matthieu*, that accommodation with the existing order is effectively impossible even if there are no available tools with which to fight it. In other cases, they begin to put the pieces back together: going back into the workplace, reassembling an oppositional cast, giving the cast back a voice, each painstaking step bearing witness to the shattering that has taken place but also to the re-emergent possibility of moving beyond it. Films in the next chapter move us beyond even the remnants of a dramaturgy of class.

Notes

1. Poirier, Guédiguian, Jolivet and Klapisch can collectively be seen as having sought to reinstitute a popular cinema in which class issues were brought back to the forefront.
2. The murder is simultaneously and almost inextricably an act of class revenge and of arbitrary savagery, with the film leaving the possibility of both interpretations open. Its intent to cultivate a fundamental ambiguity is signalled at an earlier stage when the two working-class characters discuss their violent pasts. We learn that the postmistress has killed her handicapped child, apparently by accident, but has had to defend herself against murder charges in court. The servant on the other hand has been exonerated, at least publicly, from responsibility for her father's death in a house fire, with suspicion hanging over the property developer who made money from the land. The people at the bottom of the pile seem to be either monsters, or victims (of the rich, of the courts), or both.
3. A similar analysis could be applied to Klapisch's *Un Air de famille* (1995). As its title indicates, it recounts the story of a family. The eldest son is near the top of the hierarchy of a large capitalist company. His less successful brother runs a bar. His barman, another recalcitrant quasi-servant, is the sister's secret lover. The film begins as the elder brother is to appear on television to discuss the company. When the family meet, it is he who is the centre of discussion, the only one who, being both socially successful and publicly visible, seems to merit attention. His wife is treated as a passive object without opinions of her own, her brother as a failure (he has not modernized his bar) and his sister as a petulant child. Even lower in the pecking order, the barman is treated with high-handed scorn until he loses his temper, manhandles the elder brother and opens the way for a broader revolt and taking of voice by the dominated. Like the other two films, *Un Air de famille* shows an apparently pacified world whose public face is entirely monopolized by the values of the dominant group and in which the subordinate, denied a voice, cannot name that which is done to them. Like the films by Chabrol and Poirier, Klapisch's work resists that regime by restoring visibility to class and validity to struggle.
4. If the Dardenne brothers' *Je pense à vous* is the film that perhaps best illustrates the shift in the representation of labour, one could also cite Tavernier's *Ça commence aujourd'hui* (1998). The film is set in a former mining town whose monumental old infrastructures serve to underline the public visibility once enjoyed by one of the most prominent groups of industrial workers. But the pits are now empty. The new

face of labour is represented by the lorry driver father of one of the pupils from the primary school at the film's centre. He is only sometimes employed and, when working, is away from home, his labour thus effectively invisible. Tellingly, the head teacher hero has to bring him to the school with his lorry to teach the children what a worker can do. A class once central to the social imaginary has to be forced back into visibility.

5. Zonca initially planned that the stories of *Le Petit Voleur* and of *La Vie rêvée des anges* should form two parallel narrative strands within one three hour film. In the light of this, their narrative parallelism is unsurprising. The Arte series *Gauche / Droite* was produced by Pierre Chevalier as a self-conscious interrogation of the continuing validity of the core dividing line of modern politics.

6

AN AESTHETIC OF THE FRAGMENT

Referring particularly to works by Zonca, Poirier, Dumont, Vincent and the Dardenne brothers, this chapter develops the idea of the cinematic fragment introduced in chapter 2. It will be argued that the appearance of an aesthetic of the fragment signals a paradigm shift in the mode of appearance of social struggle in French cinema. Focusing on Hervé Le Roux's *Reprise* and the Dardenne brothers' early work, chapter 3 provided a genealogy of this shift by locating its main cause in the separation of social struggle from the established leftist dramaturgy that had once accompanied it. Losing its voice and its stage, becoming detached from a tradition, a future and from combats elsewhere, struggle shifted to become raw, immediate and local, passing through the body while at the same time losing its voice and being threatened with meaninglessness. One would do scant justice to the radical nature of this shift if one were to label what emerged from it simply a cinema of social fragmentation. Social disintegration is clearly somewhere near its core, but the multi-facetted nature of the transformation in the appearance of struggle in terms, for example, of spatio-temporal relations or the place of the body and the voice suggests that it is more suitable to talk of an aesthetic shift, a transformation at the level of representation and not simply of the represented.

If one wishes to suggest that what is being described is a paradigm shift in the cinematic appearance of social struggle, one should be able to find evidence for it across a broad range of films and not just some carefully selected examples. For this reason, I will return briefly to some of the films discussed in chapters 4 and 5 to show that the shift described is indeed operative within them although not as fully developed as in those films that form the main meat of this chapter. Put simply, one might say that fragmentation was emergent in the films discussed earlier. If the cinema of the fragment is characterized by the absence of an explicit politics and social connectivity and the presence of unmediated, corporeal collisions and raw struggles, the emergent fragment is one where an explicit politics is falling silent or becoming disembodied, where individuals and groups are becoming detached and where struggles are becoming raw and corporeal. This convergence between a cinema where fragmentation has already happened and one where it is incipient should not lead one to assume their equivalence. The films that formed the principal focus of the last two chapters could all still call productively on the pieces of a shattered leftist dramaturgy to make sense of struggle, to resist silencing and erasure and to name and reveal oppressions. Where fragmentation is complete however, there can be no recourse to even the remnants of an elaborated politics. The films have to find ways to make political sense from within the fragment itself.

The paradigm shift described above poses a challenge to our understanding of a social or a political cinema. It is here that the work of Jeancolas and Osganian to which we referred in chapter 2 comes in particularly useful. A social cinema is conventionally taken to be one that, in one way or another, is grounded in a society taken as a rounded whole, even if only part of that whole is ever figured. But as Osganian and Jeancolas point out, this is a cinema in which a sense of overarching social connectivity is precisely what is lacking. The films' main characters, whether they be the discarded fragments of the old working class, or individuals at the margin of the world of work, are characterized by their non-belonging. Society, to the extent that some such thing is still seen to exist, is that which has no place for them and with which they are inevitably in active or passive dispute. The critique, emanating from the *Cahiers du Cinéma*, that the films lock characters into their existing identities and thus immobilize the social order (chapter 2) risks missing the key point that, far from figuring social immobilization, the films show characters in violent struggle with what remains of a society on a terrain where the kind of shared values and understandings that might make human interactions meaningful are precisely what is lacking. If the films cannot therefore be seen as a social cinema, can they be seen instead as a political one? If by the term one means a cinema that presents a situation or a struggle that is predigested by an existing, elaborated politics, the answer is again no. A politics – an established language, a pre-set dramaturgy of social relations – is, as Jeancolas (1997) notes, what is lacking in films whose usefulness lies rather in driving us back towards a politics through an intense exploration of the dynamics of the social fragment.

However, the question that remains open is what sort of politics the films push us towards. Social fragmentation, suffering bodies and meaningless violences are commonplaces of contemporary media and political discourses that, rather than opening onto a progressive politics, are overwhelmingly used to shut down the space for such a thing. As Rancière and others have noted (chapter 1), the term exclusion, broadly synonymous with social fragmentation, is routinely used in a profoundly disabling way that opposes those in work to those without it. Television screens, as Luc Dardenne notes, routinely bear pictures of suffering bodies, almost always framed within a depoliticizing, humanitarian discourse that casts the suffering as voiceless objects while obscuring systemic processes.[1] 'Mindless', self-destructive violences are routinely evoked to justify the depoliticizing penalization of social pathologies.[2] If films simply return these clichés to us they are less than politically useful. The challenge is to make the screen representation of suffering bodies, apparently useless violences and social fragmentation productive. Rancière (1995) can prove helpful here in seeing how this might be done.

As we have seen, Rancière draws a sharp dividing line between a true politics and what he calls the 'police order'. The 'police order' is the existing allocation of social roles and places and, crucially, of the right of access to the *logos*. The latter concept, with its roots in classical Greek political philosophy, delineates a foundational political division between those whose voice carries the power of decision and those who, denied access to the dignity of public speech (the *logos*), are granted a purely *animal* presence in the social body and whose voices can only express pleasure of pain. A true politics begins when, in the name of equality, the latter demand a say in the distribution of the commons, thus challenging their silencing and their relegation to the realm of mere animal existence (Rancière 1995: 43–49). This conceptualization of the political offers a privileged way into the cinema with which we are concerned here and which exists, one might say, on the faultline that divides access to the *logos* from the realm of animal suffering and mere bodies in collision. It notably provides a way to begin to evaluate the political usefulness of a cinema that may seem to lack a politics. As long as it contents itself with merely registering contemporary suffering and violences and fails to challenge the current allocation of the right to a say in the social order, it is not in a proper sense political. At best, it is essentially humanitarian in its thrust, drawing attention to suffering without challenging the system that generates it or which denies a voice to those that suffer. At worst it is voyeuristic, offering up the struggles of the victims of oppression or exploitation for our contemplation, reprobation or horror. This is why it is vital to consider not just what face of the social is shown by contemporary film but how, despite the lack of an overarching language of political opposition, it attempts to restore some semblance of a political voice to struggle. Put differently, one might say that the political value of current cinema lies in its ability to challenge the relegation of the voices of the oppressed to the domain of meaningless violence and animal pleasure and pain. This chapter and the next will explore how it might be seen to achieve this.

Embodied Social Struggle and the Loss of Language

Zonca's early work provides an ideal way into a discussion of the cinematic fragment as I define it above, underlining its raw corporeality but also showing how cinema can resist the depoliticizing framing of the suffering and violence of the margins. The three films that we will consider – the well known, *La Vie rêvée des anges*, the made-for-television *Le Petit Voleur*, and the short *Seule* – all narrate the trajectories of socially isolated individuals as they struggle to survive and fight marginalization while at the same time proving resistant to the kind of low skilled, precarious employment intermittently available to them (chapter 5). Because they have no political voice, they might seem condemned, in Rancière's terms, to the domain of animal pain and pleasure. None of them can be defined, however, by their social beings or their milieus. Rather, their strongest shared trait seems to be refusal of their allotted place and role, a refusal which opens a space between their desiring subjectivities and the alienating labour, social marginalization and humble acceptance that seems required of them.

La Vie rêvée des anges has two heroines, Isa, a warm, empathetic character, and Marie, a hardened, rebellious one. As the film opens, Isa arrives in the Northern town of Roubaix where some of the action is set. It is winter. A handheld camera tracks her with obsessive closeness so that her body and its movements dominate the frame even as a microphone picks up both the sound of her movement and her breathing to make her a forceful, physical presence. She is on the road, as her rucksack signals. She has come to seek out a friend who she hopes will lodge her. But the latter has had to go to seek work elsewhere and Isa is reduced to breaking into his van to seek shelter from the night and the cold. With great narrative economy, the film has indicated its starting point in its treatment of the social. Picking up an isolated, disconnected character, it confronts us, not with injustice in an abstract or discursively mediated form, but with a social suffering that operates directly on a body that thus becomes a privileged source of meaning. Beginning from this situation of social atomization, the rest of the film might be seen as an interrogation of the possibility of social reconnection and an attempt to create space and time for reflection in a cinema that seems otherwise condemned to the breathless tracking of struggling individuals. As if to indicate this, Zonca shifts increasingly away from a mobile handheld camera to a fixed one as the film progresses, at the same time drawing back from obsessive proximity to a single character in order to focus more on the characters in their social interaction (Zonca 1998). The corporeal nonetheless remains a key vector of expressivity for characters who have no shared social language to give sense to their struggles or, indeed, to express the local solidarities that they manage to establish. Thus, for example, when Isa obtains her first job in a sweatshop, the women workers establish an initial bond with her by giving her food rather than through the evocation of shared values. Likewise, the other female lead, Marie, expresses somewhat reluctant solidarity with Isa, firstly by giving her a roof and then by sharing food. A residual class solidarity may remain but it tends towards the elemental, working at the level of food, shelter and warmth. Significantly, when Isa is fired from her first job, her fellow workers look mutely on.

Marie, as we noted, is a rebellious character. Her refusal of social subordination is primarily expressed through bodily gestures. She recounts to Isa, for example, how she fell out with the manager of the bar where she had once worked and left her mark upon his face. Her initial disastrous encounter with Chris, the young bourgeois man who will become her boyfriend, is sealed when she smashes the rear light of his car. A first drink together in a bar ends when he grabs and kisses her and she throws a drink in his face. Their subsequent love-making shows a mute struggle for domination after which Chris ends up on top. It is in sharp contrast to the tender scene where she is shown in bed with Charlie, a nightclub bouncer, where the couple lie peacefully side by side, gently stroking each other. When Marie does rise above the corporeal to speak a language of class, it takes the form of isolated, emotively charged insults – usually the word *bourge* (bourgeois) accompanied by obscenities. These scraps of a discourse of class are thus subordinated to the action and not part of an elaborated reflection upon the social. Thus, after Chris has walked arrogantly out of Marie's flat leaving the door wide open, she calls after him, 'dirty bourgeois cunt'[3] with her words serving only to name the class enemy and not to analyze her situation and communicate with others. It would seem that, no longer mediated by collective instances or a shared language, class struggle takes on a new brutality and passes directly through individual bodies without the characters having the space, time or words to reflect upon what they are doing. This suffocating denial of reflexivity is encapsulated in a sequence where Isa seeks to prevent Marie from going self-destructively to meet Chris. As she blocks the door with her body, Marie struggles with her and hits her. Despairingly, Isa begs Marie to reflect upon what she is doing. But this kind of self-reflexive gesture is precisely something of which Marie is incapable. The focus on bodily struggle and suffering in socio-politically engaged cinema is not of course new. We noted in chapter 3, with reference to emblematic films by Godard and Karmitz, how class struggle was grounded in the violence done to individual bodies and in the physically oppressive and restrictive nature of factory labour. However, as we stressed, that bodily suffering was immediately connected to a universalizing politics and an elaborated language of struggle that gave it meaning and promised it redemption. The novelty of embodied struggle in the works of Zonca and other contemporary film-makers lies not in its mere presence but in its disconnection from an overarching language of opposition and from its incipient meaninglessness.

The characters of Zonca's other early films inhabit a similar universe of unmediated and unreflexive embodiment. As we noted, the early short *Seule* recounts the story of a young woman who improbably loses her job and her lodgings on the same day, and thus finds herself on the street, exposed to the same pressing need for shelter and food as Isa in *La Vie rêvée*. The film adds a further improbable element to the situation when a gun put on a window ledge in the course of a police raid entirely tangential to the narrative, falls beside the heroine as she squats upon the ground. Initially she does nothing with it. However, when another, more streetwise, homeless young woman steals her remaining possessions, it becomes her only resource. Initially she tries to sell it and thus enter back into the economy of exchange from which she was violently expelled when sacked from her job. The gun shop owner predictably refuses to buy it. The young woman then uses the weapon in an abortive attempt to rob a taxi driver. Having fled the scene, she goes into a bar, orders a coffee and lays the gun upon the table, just as a more conventional customer might place a payment. The police enter quietly and arrest her. If the improbable combination of events and circumstances seems on the surface to belie the film's apparently gritty realism, it again points, at a deeper level, to a sharp shift in the appearance of social struggle, a move to a world where, no longer mediated by collective resources nor indeed by the pacifying, depersonalizing instance of money, individual desires and bodily needs collide directly with that which resists them. This collision, as the gun so eloquently indicates, is inevitably violent.

Zonca's television film *Le Petit Voleur* leads us towards some similar conclusions. Following a familiar pattern of social isolation, it begins with a young man's unceremonious dismissal from a job in a bakery and continues when, breaking the last link of solidarity that bound him to other people, he steals from his girlfriend and begins a life in a criminal gang. Within the gang he finds that his role is essentially unchanged in that he still has to do as he is told and is still right at the bottom of the pile, sometimes being required to do menial, domestic tasks for an old lady, sometimes being asked to stand guard as a prostitute does business. The social domination to which he is exposed has become more evident and more immediate. When he was fired, he commented metaphorically on the social domination present in the world of work by saying that the boss would get his replacement to 'suck him off'. But later, as a low-level criminal, he finds that he is actually obliged to perform oral sex on a gang leader. What has changed is that, while language once mediated between him and social domination, it is now practiced directly on his body. In an effort to harden himself up, the young man practises intensely in a boxing gym. The boxing, like the gun in *Seule*, points towards a social context in which, without the intervening presence of reflexive thought or of collective solidarities, individual bodies directly collide.

Through this tracking of embodied collisions, Zonca's cinema might seem merely to reflect a broader rise of a useless violence that can no longer be productively inserted within a narrative of progressive social evolution and has, as a consequence, become meaningless (chapter 1). However, rather than simply registering this loss of meaning, Zonca's films and others we will come to work actively to resist it. They do this essentially by reconnecting the raw violences of the margins to the hidden violences of the centre and by using the former to unmask the latter. Brute, 'animal' violences are recuperated and rescued for meaning by their reinsertion into the films' symbolic economy. Thus, in *Seule*, the young woman's turn to the threat of violence is only a despairing response to the violence done to her when she is thrown out of her job and physically ejected from her flat. More broadly, the brutality of her life on the street is directly continuous with what preceded it rather than being radically different. This is underlined with great economy in the scene where she lays the gun on the café table in place of the expected money, thus implicitly establishing an at least partial equivalence between the circulation of violence and that of cash. Something similar happens in *Le Petit Voleur* where parallels are deliberately drawn between the obvious domination and violence of the criminal world and the less obvious, symbolically mediated domination of the 'respectable' world. The combative individualism of the boxing ring is not an aberration, but a more direct expression of an underlying social logic that connects the criminal world and the legal economy. Within Zonca's films, the violence of the margins and that of the centre are neither completely the same nor absolutely different. Both are brutal, but one is economically mediated and the other raw. This combination of difference and similarity allows one to stand in for the other, bringing its hidden features into visibility. Within the normal scheme of things, the margins function as a conflictual and radically different outside, a place of useless suffering and mindless violence that confirms the apparently consensual peacefulness of the inside. What the films by Zonca and others do is to refuse this apparent normality by configuring marginalization and the suffering it generates as a centrally driven process and by connecting the violences of the margins to the violence of the centre. Embodied pain and conflict are thus rescued for meaning. This is an essential part of the films' politics.

Despite its considerably lighter tone, Poirier's *Western* (1996) points in some similar directions to the work of Zonca. A decidedly off-beat road movie, the film recounts the very local journey of two immigrants, Nino, a Russian, and Paco, a Spaniard, in the western French region of Brittany. As the film begins, Paco, a travelling shoe salesman, stops his car to pick up an attractive young woman hitch-hiker, only to find that Nino gets in his car instead, and adding injury to insult steals it, along with its load of shoes. Paco is unceremoniously fired over the telephone by his boss, an unseen, distant figure whose disembodiment underlines how the violence of the legal economy works in a way that places an insulating distance between perpetrator and victim. In contrast, the violence done by Paco to the Russian when he catches up with him is directly to the body as images of the latter in his hospital bed eloquently demonstrate. The penitent Spaniard visits him and the two agree to take to the road together.

When in his car Paco was an active if distinctly subaltern part of a modern economy based on the circulation of goods and money. Power over the latter enabled him to keep unwelcome aspects of the real at a distance in a way symbolized eloquently by his ability to choose whom to pick up from the roadside. Even after becoming unemployed, he is initially insulated from the fragility of his new condition by his smart appearance and financial solvency. However, as the film progresses, he becomes an increasingly vulnerable figure who can no longer keep the world at a distance. The turning point comes when, in an effort to earn some cash, he and Nino offer to prune some trees with a chainsaw for a farmer. Predictably an accident occurs. Paco's leg is badly cut. Knowing he has not employed the men legally, the farmer sends them quickly on their way and, in his desire to destroy evidence of their presence, burns Paco's case with his clothes and money inside. Dishevelled and wounded, no longer able to buy himself food, drink or shelter, Paco now finds himself in the same economy of unmediated physical need and harm as Nino. However, having been freed, albeit painfully, from the money economy, he is able to experience a new way of relating to others based not on exchange but on sharing and giving. He is initiated into this world when a disabled black Breton takes him and Nino into the house he shares with his white French partner. He later sees Nino go out of his way, in an act of disinterested kindness, to reunite a homeless young man with his estranged father. Finally, as the film comes to a close, he sees how the apparently valueless Russian becomes a highly valued partner in the house of a single mother due to his abilities as cook, entertainer and surrogate father. Although the French woman chooses the Russian as a partner in preference to him, he is still welcomed within the group. Thus, in a low-key way, and despite the absence within it of anything approaching an elaborated political discourse, the film reasserts the possibility of an alternative to the mediated violences of the capitalist economy and the immediate, physical sufferings of those on its edges.

Initially best known for the sharply critical bourgeois comedy of manners, *La Discrète* (1990), Vincent signalled a sharp shift in his film-making with *Sauve-moi* (1999), a film produced by Guédiguian's film-making collective Agat Films. Set in the now rundown industrial heartland of Roubaix, the film grew out of a writing project set up amongst some of the unemployed of the town by novelist Ricardo Montserrat. The writer wished to help restore a voice and a sense of self-expression to a group seemingly condemned to social silence and passivity (De Bourbon 1999).

Although an offshoot of the novel rather than a direct adaptation, *Sauve-moi* can be seen as a prolongation of its intentions. It begins when Mehdi, a *Beur* who drives an unlicensed taxicab, picks up Agatha, a Romanian woman who has come to find a French doctor she had met when translating at a conference. Clearly dismayed to see her again, the doctor is happy to give her money to be rid of her, not without suggesting that they might again make love. The ability of the well off to mediate social encounters with cash contrasts to the warm solidarity of Mehdi and his friends who are all either at the bottom end of the legal economy (in the service sector), in the black economy or unemployed. Nonetheless, one of the group is defiantly building his own house with the help of the others. Although the house is unfinished and unfurnished, Agatha is put up in it and provided with light, water and food. She in turn begins to contribute to a construction that becomes both a direct physical manifestation of a solidarity that no longer has a language to name itself and a way to reassert the capacity of the popular characters to be creative political subjects. Although they have no voice, they can still build something that asserts values in sharp contradiction to those that prevail around them.

The film has a darker side that makes a newly raw socio-economic violence sharply felt. It becomes apparent when, in a bid to earn more money, Mehdi starts to work for a local debt collector. He is initially silent as he sees how the latter inserts himself into the houses of the desperate, pries into their personal circumstances and extracts payments that they cannot afford. Silence, a minimalist, passive resistance, turns to clandestine action when, having seen how the debt collector extracts sexual services from a mother, Mehdi vandalizes his car. Finally, seeing how a woman whose son has died owing money for medical tests is pressurized into assuming his debts, he speaks up and enters into overt opposition. A scuffle ensues, provoking a brief intervention of the woman's neighbours that drives the debt collector from the street. What is again striking is the extent to which oppression and resistance have become individualized and are transmitted directly through bodies and things, whether it be the body of the woman forced to provide sex, the damaged car or the struggling men in the street. A similar process is seen in another, less prominent narrative strand involving the secondary characters. One of them has been behaving erratically. It transpires that he has to repay his boss half his salary in order to keep his job. He cracks and is fired. His friend confronts the boss who in turn attacks him. In the ensuing struggle the boss knocks his head and is apparently killed. As in *Western*, the physical harm that is done would seem to be not an aberration but a direct prolongation of the extreme economic violence operant within the clandestine economy or hidden behind the closed doors of privatized misery. One might again see it less as something qualitatively different and more as a figuring forth of that which could no longer be shown or named.

The films that I have discussed by Zonca, Poirier and Vincent provide examples of what I have termed a cinema of fragments, allowing me to underline some of its key characteristics and to begin to elaborate upon the nature of its political intervention. What the different films have in common is to track the unmediated, often corporeal impact of newly brutal socio-economic relationships on isolated individuals. Certainly there are residual social solidarities in all of the films, most notably in Poirier's *Western* where still vibrant Breton communities are seen to exist and in Vincent's *Sauve-moi* where strong mutual support operates amongst those at the bottom. But these solidarities are local and residual and cannot mask the failure of the broader national society to integrate both existing citizens and newcomers. Crucially, those groups that do remain can no longer transmit a common understanding of the world framed in a shared language that would allow them to name and account for what happens to them and to oppose it in the name of publicly recognized values. Unable to connect to a broader social framework that might map out their lives, with no sense of a tradition of class struggle or of a better future, characters are condemned to live in the present. And because their struggles and sufferings are no longer mediated by a shared language or values, they are threatened with meaninglessness. A clear part of the films' common commitment is to resist this threat by connecting the violence of the margins with systemic violences as a way of restoring sense to it. But, perhaps more importantly, they refuse to treat their characters as social objects by framing them through the eyes of a more empowered individual or group. Rather, they commit themselves to a close accompaniment of their movements and gestures as they encounter social others and come up against socio-economic and physical barriers to integration. It is this attention to the friction of interactions that allows the films to constitute the characters as recalcitrant subjectivities who have no language to express their rejection of their situation, but who nonetheless signal their refusal of their marginalization and political silencing. We will now come to the Dardenne brothers whose work follows a similar pattern to that we have just described, but who explore it with unparalleled intensity.

Eloquent Fragments: the Colliding Bodies of the Dardenne Brothers

I suggested in the third chapter that the brothers' cinematic trajectory was emblematic of the broader transition from the depiction of social conflict articulated within a universalizing language of opposition to a focus on raw violences and resistances. We noted how that transition was found in condensed form in their *Je pense à vous*, a film that moved from the collective action of steelworkers to the mute, individual revolt of the hero against the violences of the black economy. The shift indicated by that film is confirmed in the brothers' subsequent work that operates on a similar social terrain to the films discussed above but pushes exploration of it to the limit by focusing with unparalleled intensity on bodily struggle and by seeking with single-minded determination to restore ethical transparency to a world apparently deprived of values. Like the films of Poirier, Zonca and Vincent, the Dardennes crucially carry out their ethico-political work through an intense attention to the trajectories of their popular characters and not through recourse to more 'enlightened', more politically 'progressive' third parties. Committing themselves fully to characters who lack symbolic resources to make sense of their situations, they have to free themselves of any pre-elaborated discourse of value. What values can be found must be found with the characters. The latter are thus doubly subjects: firstly, because the films track their refusals and collisions and, secondly, because they are effectively the authors of the values that re-emerge within the fragments in which they move.

La Promesse (1995), the brothers' next project after *Je pense à vous*, is still located in the industrial landscape of Seraing. But the old working class has gone, as the empty factories silently testify. The film instead chooses to focus on the present drama of characters who are, one might say, living in the ruins, not just of the buildings, but also of the collective values and traditions which once inhabited them. The two chief protagonists are a father, Roger, and his son, Igor. Roger makes a living by exploiting the illegal immigrants that he brings into the country, accommodates, puts to work and denounces to the police when it is expedient. Igor is torn between helping his father and an apprenticeship in a garage that would allow him, despite the broader circumstances, to learn a trade and thus prolong, on a small scale, the otherwise devastated tradition of skilled manual labour of the region. But his father keeps pulling him out of his job to help with his illegal and ultra-exploitative activities. The frustrated garage owner is forced to end the apprenticeship.

Although the story might seem a relatively banal and indeed predictable piece of social realism, it is far more than that. What is at stake is something that goes to the heart of the social. The film has two father figures. One, the garage owner, attempts to give Igor something solid to carry forward that would enable him to situate himself in the world by knowing who he is and how he can be of use. The other, his natural father, transmits nothing to him that will identify him positively or connect him usefully to others. Instead, he locks him into destructive relations in the present. Luc Dardenne describes the monstrosity of this behaviour eloquently by suggesting that we now live in an age where the fathers devour the sons (Houba 2003: 146). One of the tasks to which Roger puts the migrant labourers is the building of a house for himself and Igor. In the brothers' own *Je pense à vous* (and in films like Vincent's *Sauve-moi* and Beauvois' *Selon Matthieu*), house construction suggested a proud or desperate working class attempt to claim a place in society. Here, it suggests something of the same, but has lost its egalitarian drive. Confirming the monstrosity of the current order, the film shows that the inclusion of some now comes at the price of the radical exclusion and exploitation of others. One can only become part of the social by denying the very responsibility towards others on which social connectivity is founded.

The drama crystallizes when one of the migrant workers falls off some scaffolding. Rather than taking the man to hospital and risking legal repercussions, Roger allows him to bleed to death on the ground and then entombs the body in the house upon which they are working. Igor is made party to what is effectively a murder that, rather than representing a break with what has gone before, takes it to its logical limit. When the other becomes a mere instrument of one's own needs and desires, he or she is denied any properly human status and is thus destroyed at the symbolic level. Bodily destruction and the elimination of its traces merely makes explicit what has already taken place implicitly, in the same way as in the films by Zonca and Vincent that we considered, raw, physical violence continued a less manifest violence that was already present in the economy. However, before the migrant dies, he speaks to Igor, making him promise to take care of the wife, Assita, and the child that he leaves behind. Assita's presence means that Igor is now faced with the constant reminder of what he and Roger have done and the promise that he has made. The device of the promise goes to the heart of what is at stake in the film. Constituting a relationship to the other based on trust and responsibility, it is the polar opposite of the debased, antisocial relationships that otherwise structure the film. Connecting past to future and, by proxy, the dying father to his child, it offers the possibility of rescuing, *in extremis*, a positive continuity between generations. Giving a weight back to a language which otherwise only seems to serve to deceive, it also offers to restore the capacity for communication between individuals. Igor keeps his promise at the end of the film and thus, at a purely individual level, re-enters the domain of language and the social. But up to that stage, neither he nor Roger can draw on values that can make sense of what they do. They live in enforced proximity to what befalls them and are confronted with their denial of the other's worth, not in the abstract terms of a political or moral discourse, but in the brute form of a dying and bloody body. Similarly, their responsibility to the person they have harmed and to those who depended on him is materialized through the physical presence of two more unwelcome bodies, his wife and child, and their immediate needs for food, warmth and shelter.

Rosetta works with the same raw materials as *La Promesse* but is even more suffocating in its denial of anything beyond the confines of the intense foreground drama at its centre. Although much of the camera work in *La Promesse* places us in close proximity to the bodies of the narrow cast of characters, it does at times pull back to locate its action in the broader context of a deindustrialized region and as such provides at least some mute explanation of the roots of what we see, thereby giving us access to something it denies its characters. *Rosetta* denies us even this distance and places us in constant, claustrophobic proximity to the struggles of its eponymous heroine. The bravura opening sequence sets the tone. A series of heroic tracking shots follow from impossibly near the back of a woman's body as it plunges through corridors and under machines. There is no music, so the only sounds are footsteps and laboured breathing. Another body appears in pursuit and a third person, a woman, comes into frame. Voices are heard. We begin to make sense of what we are seeing. The heroine has been fired from her job not, as alleged, because she has come late but rather because she has come to the end of her short-term contract and thus is the most disposable person. Rather than accept her fate passively, she confronts those who have decided to dispense with her and physically attacks the supervisor who has been pursuing her. This dramatic beginning is not a stylistic flourish nor a mere attempt to grab the spectator's attention. Its instability, collisions and violence tell us something essential about the world of the film. Like the Dardenne brothers' other works and like other films discussed in this chapter, *Rosetta* begins not with the social – a sense that we form part of a connected whole – but with its lack (Osganian 2003). It does not give us a stable world with a shared set of values but instead shows an isolated and driven social atom moving through space, encountering obstacles and colliding with others. Sense does slowly emerge from this, as we have seen, but it is not where we start from. The base of the narrative is a desiring body and its encounter with a physical and social context from which meaning and a common language that might mediate it have been withdrawn.

Rosetta's social exclusion is signalled above all by the bus journey that she has to take to return to the caravan park where she lives on the edge of the town. It is further underlined by the change that she has to make into wellington boots to walk through the woods to the caravan park and reinforced by the impermanence of the mobile homes. Indeed one of the things that she fights about with her mother is when the latter begins to plant things around their caravan, thus suggesting that she accepts their situation as permanent. Tellingly, their difference of attitude is expressed first through the relation to things and only subsequently in words. In a similar way, Rosetta opposes her mother's acceptance of charity by grabbing the food she has been given from her hand and running away with it. When she finds her drinking with the site supervisor, a man who demands sex in return for feeding her alcohol habit, she grabs the bottle, runs outside and smashes it. Even more than in Zonca's films, relationships to others are expressed through movement and action with words playing a secondary role.

Rosetta's only durable relationship with someone outside her family is with Riquet, a young man who, in a way that clearly baffles her, deliberately and repeatedly tried to help her. When he comes to the site to tell her that she is being offered a job by his boss, for example, she attacks him before he can speak, enraged, one assumes, that he has discovered where she lives. Their movements together, rolling in the muddy grass, seem a grotesque parody of love-making. They serve to underline how Rosetta has been made savage and apparently incapable of connecting positively to others. This impression is underlined when, invited to dance by Riquet, she has to be taught by him how to coordinate her movements with his. Her stiffness suggests a body formed only for struggle. As in Guédiguian's *A la vie, à la mort!*, although with far greater intensity, a primordial struggle between life and death drives is played out across the characters' bodies. The key turning point in the film comes when Riquet falls in a fishing pond on the site and she hesitates between saving him and letting him drown because the latter possibility would allow her to take his job. She eventually chooses correctly, with her decision being worked through entirely at the bodily level, as she first seems to run away into the woods, but then returns, branch in hand, to pull him out. Finally, when, she is exhausted by her struggles, resigns from her job, and is ready to kill herself, Riquet arrives in time to help her carry the gas canister that she cannot manage alone. Having accepted help and recognized, at the most basic, physical level her connection to others, she is then able to cry in front of him, finally releasing the tension that had characterized her gestures up to then. The relationship is not without words, but it is carried by bodies and gestures. One is unsurprised therefore to learn that the Dardennes worked obsessively on Rosetta's bodily movement before shooting began. Similarly, it is entirely logical that the starting point of their *mise-en-scène* was not the camera set-up or the framing but Rosetta's movements that the cinematographer was then asked to track (Benoliel and Toubiana 1999: 50–52).

The priority accorded to the corporeal makes sense within what one might term the elemental dramaturgy of the film as a whole. This is most clear during those sequences that are located in the caravan site, a place effectively outside the broader society. Rosetta's journeys to it through the wood imply a move away from the social world to a more primitive state. Similarly, the fish traps that she puts in the pond suggest a reversion to hunter-gathering. Most strikingly, the two near drownings that take place (Rosetta is also left struggling in the pond by her mother), underscore the savagery to which interactions have shrunk. But one should emphasize that the site, rather than being radically different to what is seen elsewhere, merely serves to render more self-evident the generally regressive nature of interactions. The first violence that we see is not in the woods or by the pond but in the decidedly hygienic factory of the opening when Rosetta first confronts those responsible for her brutal sacking and is then pursued by those wishing to expel her from the premises. As the film progresses, she is 'socialized' into a world in which one person can only take his or her place by displacing another. Each job she loses or gains is because another has been replaced. Her near murder of Riquet is thus a concentration of a violence that takes place routinely in a world that produces exclusion through the systematic rationing of the useful employment that is still the chief route to social integration (Castel 1995). Similarly, when she resigns from her job, having implicitly decided that it comes at too high a price (the social death of the person she replaces), she is committing a symbolic suicide. The real suicide attempt that follows simply renders concrete a social erasure that has already taken place. It thus evidences a rigorous working through of the violence of the contemporary world similar to that found in Zonca's films. Like the films discussed earlier in this chapter, *Rosetta* refuses the marginalization of the margins and the uselessness of its violences by depicting exclusion as a systemic process and by using the obvious violences of murder and suicide to bring to the surface the hidden violences that take place elsewhere. Crucially, it also works through its characters' embodied interaction to open a window in its harsh reality onto something radically different: an alternative reality founded on cooperation and respect for the other's existence instead of a primitive struggle of all against all.

Registering but resisting the implosion of the social, *Rosetta* clearly works on the same devastated ground as *La Promesse*. When parents have nothing positive to transmit to children and civilized human inter-connectivity has been replaced by brutal or exploitative relationships with the other, ethical values are not a given but something that has to be rediscovered from within situations by the characters themselves, reinvented *ex nihilo* as a way to restore some meaning in the social ruins. The brothers' next film, *Le Fils*, squarely occupies the same terrain. Intergenerational continuity and thus the ability of the social to regenerate itself lies at its heart, as again does the choice between violent destruction of the other and cooperative coexistence. The story is simple. Olivier, a carpenter, works in a centre that equips young ex-offenders with a range of skills. Francis, a young man, joins his small class. We learn that he is the person who murdered the carpenter's son when the boy attempted to stop him stealing their car radio. The carpenter is placed before a choice equally as stark as that faced by Rosetta by the pond: will he take the young murderer under his wing and train him, thus simultaneously retying a broken bond between generations and allowing Francis to re-enter the social order, or will he take revenge, thus confirming its implosion?

Le Fils is stylistically very close to *Rosetta* with a camera that again obsessively tracks the bodily movements and attitudes that are the main vehicle of the action. As in *Rosetta*, the main character is filmed for much of the time from close behind in a way that privileges the bodily exterior over the interiority often implied by close-ups of the face. This underlines Olivier's strength and thus his capacity to destroy. Yet, for much of the time, we see him constructing things and training others to do the same. An elemental tug of war between competing human capacities is thus played out across his body. Fittingly, as if to underline the austerity of the drama, and to avoid distraction from embodied interaction, much of it takes place in bare, sparsely furnished interiors. Fittingly too, and in a way again reminiscent of *Rosetta*, the climax takes place in a wood, a place outside society. The older man drives the younger into the countryside to select timber. It is there that he comes to the verge of strangling him for his son's murder. He draws back and the two begin work loading planks into a trailer. A fundamental, pre-social choice appears between destroying the other or working together to garner the products of the earth.

The relationship between people and things plays a central role in the film. Although we only learn about it once the film is well under way, the car radio is, in story order, the first object of concern. We learn that Francis has broken into the car not realizing that Olivier's son is on the back seat. His only wish is to obtain the object and he is surprised when grabbed by someone who will not let go of him. This situation encapsulates, in heightened terms, a social order in which the commodity takes precedence over the human. Preference for the thing over the other, although never presented as such, is a form of symbolic assassination that the world normally holds at a distance. When the son grabs Francis this distance is abolished, making a direct choice between thing and person unavoidable. In contrast, what Francis learns from Olivier through shared manual labour is a connection to the world of things that involves cooperation with others and not their destruction. While the radio was an already made technological object, the wood that they work upon together is a raw material that re-roots their activity in the physical world, giving it an essential anthropological dimension: to be human is to cooperate to transform nature. Working on similar ground *L'Enfant* (2004) shows a young father who, seeing his own son as a replaceable commodity, sells him for adoption with no notion of the gravity of what he has done until the child's mother collapses in shock at the horror of what has happened. Having believed that, in the same way as commodities are produced in multiple versions of the same, they could simply make another equivalent child, he is forced to recognize the irreplaceability and thus the non-exchangeability of the human.

The films from the Dardenne brothers later period have a tight unity. All work in the space where the organized working class once was but is no more, focusing on interpersonal interactions that have taken on a new violence due to the brutality of the economy and the falling away of the solidarities and institutions that used to mediate between individuals and the systemic. All also show a world where values are no longer transmitted between generations, so that the young are left to find their place and to deal with others without symbolic resources or inherited values. The consequence of this situation is that rather than being a 'social' cinema that conservatively reflects an existing social order, their work is what one might term a post-social cinema, a cinema of fragments that works in a world where the very connectivity between people that might have allowed one to speak of a society has become problematic. The virtue of the brothers is not simply to have explored a devastated social terrain with unparalleled intensity, but to have sought to restore meaning and ethical transparency to situations by pushing them to the point where they recover a lost eloquence and again start to speak to us. This is something that we will pick up again in chapter 7 where we will show that, although in a less systematic and concentrated manner, other film-makers also have repeated recourse to such knowingly contrived moments. However, returning again to the Dardennes, we will also suggest that not all such moments are politically equivalent, that some open productively onto an antagonistic construction of the social terrain by allowing, despite their minimalist cast, the identification of a common enemy, while others, whose cast is even more refined, only open onto a radicalized humanitarian commitment to the other.

Bringing Salvation to the Fragment: Tavernier, Dumont and Alnoy

Despite variations between them, all the films discussed so far in this chapter share an egalitarian politics of form. Refusing themselves access to discourses or viewpoints unavailable to their popular and excluded characters, they accompany them through a devastated social terrain as they seek to find ways to live within it. Because the characters themselves are the agents of whatever salvation can be found and the creators of whatever values can be reclaimed, the films refrain, in a way examined by Beugnet (2000: 59) from treating them as objects of compassion, horror or voyeurism. The same cannot be said for the films by Tavernier and Dumont that we will now consider. Sharing the essential features associated thus far with a cinema of fragments, both directors can be considered to work on the same ground as the other film-makers discussed. But both bring into their films viewpoints and values denied their popular characters, implicitly or explicitly distancing themselves from them, thus casting them, at least at times, as objects. Moreover, despite a sharp critique of the contemporary period, Dumont tends to naturalize the suffering and brutality he depicts. Rather than generating politically productive connections between the violences of the margins and those at the centre, he tends to naturalize both. While characters in other films find some form of socio-political salvation from within the fragment, those of Dumont aspire to a quasi-religious transcendence. A similar tendency, but deployed more progressively, can be found in Siegrid Alnoy's striking first film, *Elle est des nôtres* (2002), to which we will shortly come.

Daniel, the hero of Tavernier's *Ça commence aujourd'hui* (1998) is in the director's own activist image.[4] A primary school head in a community destroyed by the closure of the mining industry, he leads the fight of a small group of people (the woman he lives with, a committed social worker, the teachers and classroom assistants) to provide care, protection and a semblance of a future for the children in the school. The film begins by presenting some of its key elements: starting with Daniel as he drives before daylight to work, it then shows the children in the playground, picking out signs of social distress. An activist hero is thus to be confronted with a series of social problems that he will bring to the surface and attempt to address. Contrasting strongly with the social fragmentation outside the gates, his school in general and his classroom in particular is a place of caring community, a place where each child is valued and nurtured. The end of the day brings the first crisis. A mother who has come late to pick up her child collapses, gets up and runs off, leaving not just the child she should have collected, but a baby in a pram. Daniel first runs to help the mother and then, following her dramatic exit, takes charge of the children. Faced with a lack of response from social services, refusing to hand the children over to the police, he takes them to their home. He finds the mother in a dark, cold flat where the electricity has been cut off. The husband, an intermittently employed lorry driver, is away. A neighbour takes the children in. Daniel will later bring their mother food. In the face of the immediate bodily need of the vulnerable, social solidarity expresses itself, not in abstract terms, nor through an elaborated politics, but through urgent physical intervention and the provision of the basics of life. These early scenes set the tone for what is to come.

The world of the film is one where the social itself seems on the verge of disintegration due to the shattering of group connectivity and the crisis of intergenerational continuity. The former is suggested by the isolated suffering that the film repeatedly underlines. Where the local miners were once the bearers of a proud tradition of class solidarity, only social fragments now remain. Significantly, and in a way that is reminiscent of the symbolic use of the autistic children in *La Ville est tranquille*, some of the children refuse to speak or cannot hear or see properly. They are thus threatened not only with educational failure but with an inability to connect to others or to their surroundings. Daniel's fight, alongside others, to open these children to the world suggests a defiant refusal to accept either the collapse of social connectivity or the abandonment of sectors of society. Social disintegration is signalled also, as one might expect in a school-centred film, by the inability of one generation to secure the future of the next. One unemployed couple have given up hope and are unable to make the effort to get up to take their children to school. Other parents cannot afford to buy their children school meals. In another home, the father beats his partner's child, suggesting that class struggle has been replaced by self-destructive violence and a monstrous failure to nurture the young. Older children, including the head's partner's son, break into the school and vandalize it. But, most dramatically of all, the mother who had fallen down drunk kills herself and the children for whom she can no longer provide the basics of life. As in Guédiguian, what is left of a class is threatened not merely in its material well-being but in its very physical continuation and its ability to project itself into the future.

School is traditionally a place of socialization, a place where, rising above the particular and the local, children are inducted into the forms of abstract, universal knowledge required for participation in the modern world. The school in Tavernier's film reverses the normal order of things, dragging the teachers into the struggle against embodied, local need (see also chapter 8). School too is conventionally a place where values and knowledge are transmitted, opening the young onto the past whilst preparing them for their future. But the school in the film is sucked into dealing with immediate crises. Like the other films considered here, *Ça commence aujourd'hui* thus points towards a paradigm shift in the mode of appearance of the social. One might be tempted to see it simply as about social decay. But this would be to underestimate the profundity of the crisis it signals: an evacuation of the social, a disconnection from past and future and from any sense of totality leading to imprisonment in the immediate, the corporeal and the elemental and the presence of useless suffering and senseless violence. The film's strength is to use the school as the place whose symbolic associations with collective solidarity, republican integration and an ethic of care can make this shift resonate to maximum effect.[5] But its weakness is to give too strong and too predictable a pedagogic role to its activist hero and to middle-class professionals more broadly. Although Daniel, the hero, is not without support from his colleagues, classroom assistants, a social worker, relevant therapists and, at times, the parents, it is he who drives most of the initiatives and, in a film not loathe to preach, who draws the lessons from events and intervenes where necessary. As the film comes to a close, devastated by the suicide of the mother and her killing of her children, he becomes discouraged. It is then that his sculptor partner steps in to lead the school community in the organization of a fête that transforms the grey playground into a multicoloured space of ludic creativity. Mobilizing professionals, parents and children alike, the fête points towards a different world within which a restored community can rediscover the capacity to shape its environment. The problem is that, as throughout, the popular characters need to be organized from outside for things to happen. So, despite its admirable energy and commitment and a highly informed, semi-documentary anchoring in the social terrain, the film falls into the trap that the other films considered above avoided by their unrelenting proximity to their protagonists. Aligning itself with people who do and understand more than its popular characters, it casts the latter as victims and thus, inevitably, as social objects. Something not entirely dissimilar, if a good deal more complex, happens in the work of Dumont.

Dumont came to public attention with a remarkable first feature *La Vie de Jésus* (1996), a film followed by Cannes prize-winner *L'Humanité* (1998). These films helped establish him as one of the leading new directors in the France of the 1990s. Both were shot in his native Bailleul, a rundown, northern French industrial town, inviting obvious comparisons with the Dardennes who also keep returning to the old Belgian industrial heartland area of Seraing where they grew up. *La Vie de Jésus* figures Freddy, an epileptic, unemployed young man who lives with his bar-owning mother. His time is split between home, his supermarket checkout assistant girlfriend and his unemployed young male friends as they hang out, fix an old car or circulate aimlessly and repetitively on local byroads. The boring routine is punctuated by a series of events: a visit to a hospital by the young men to comfort a friend dying of Aids; a collective escape to the seaside; a sexual assault by the young men on a plump young girl; a rather absurd parade around the area with the local brass band; finally, shockingly, the brutal murder by the young men of a young *Beur* who has shown strong interest in Freddy's girlfriend. The film bears striking resemblances to other films considered. Firstly, and perhaps most obviously, it is shot in real, deindustrialized locations and grounds itself in contemporary social issues such as racism and youth unemployment. Secondly, like the Dardennes, Dumont shows a marked liking for non-professional actors, although it should be said that, while the former clearly refuse to glamorize their performers, the latter seems to deliberately choose unattractive actors (Austin 2004). Thirdly, and more significantly, *La Vie de Jésus* seems to work on the same fragmented social terrain. Restricting itself to a purely local frame, the film tracks the actions and inaction of a tight cast of characters who, mainly seen on empty roads or in near empty streets and bars, seem to move in a space without any substantial network of social ties. The young, unemployed men have no language to describe and analyze a situation in which they have no work and seemingly no future. Freddy, the hero, is taciturn and inarticulate. His anger and frustration manifest themselves above all physically, notably in his series of falls from his moped, but also, of course, in the brutal killing of the young *Beur*. The film, like those of Zonca or the Dardennes, devotes itself to the close tracking of its characters' embodied interactions. However, whereas the body in those other film-makers was the surface upon which was produced the raw collision between subjective desires and socio-economic obstacles, the body of Dumont's characters seems to be the site of a struggle between spirituality and a primitive animality that depoliticizes what is shown despite the film's strong roots in the contemporary world. This is perhaps at its most evident in the treatment of violence.

The racism associated with the killing of the young *Beur* is connected with a sense of imploding national community. The unemployed young men do not seem meaningfully attached to anything beyond their own little circle and their own locality. Thus, their attitude when parading with their band behind the national flag seems one of mocking detachment rather than enthusiasm. They only engage more meaningfully with Frenchness when, in Freddy's mother's bar, they begin to ridicule the family of the *Beur*, underlining how the national now only retains meaning as a neo-tribalism that produces belonging through the exclusion of others rather than through any more positive integration of its citizens. In this *La Vie de Jésus* might seem close to other films discussed, such as *Marie-Line* or *La Ville est tranquille* where extreme nationalism seems the only form of collective belonging offered to the otherwise excluded. The specific trigger for the racist murder in *La Vie de Jésus* is the sexual jealousy provoked by the *Beur*'s pursuit of Freddy's girlfriend. If, in some ways, this might seem to depoliticize the racism, explaining it not by structural factors but by a purely personal vengeance, in other ways it points to the power of racism to connect to immediate, bodily experience, even as other forms of politics seem increasingly disembodied and distant.[6] However, the murder is not the only act of violence. There is also the sexual assault on the young girl that precedes it. While this latter act could be connected to the young men's bored frustration, it seems hard to see it as anything other than an act of senseless violence that confirms the young men's brute animality and retrospectively pushes us to see the murder in a similar light. Unlike in the other films discussed here, there are no obvious systemic violences that could rescue the violences of the margins for meaning by inserting them into a chain of equivalences.

However, there is a strong sense that the characters seek something else, some spiritual transcendence of their brute materiality. This is signalled at various moments, as for example at the time of the visit to the dying friend. One of the men finds an image of Lazarus raised from the dead and comments to Freddy that they need something similar. Freddy reacts with irritation to what seems a frivolous remark. While religion might make some sense of the death of their friend, it is not a path available to them. At the close of the film, another moment of spiritual transcendence is clearly indicated when, having been arrested for the murder and escaped on a moped, Freddy again falls off, but unlike on previous occasions, seems to find peace while lying looking at the sky. The film's title, *La Vie de Jésus*, of course cues us to see Freddy's life in quasi-religious terms. Divine and human, of the spirit and of the flesh, the biblical Jesus was sent to redeem a sinning, suffering humanity. Freddy and his companions are from a later, fallen age. Religion is no longer there to make sense of their lives and to give them a moral structure, as the often seen but never visited church reminds us. The nation, the God of a post-religious humanity, seems, as we saw, to have regressed to the tribal. Contemporary man is condemned to find his own spiritual transcendence and to bear his own cross, as Freddy's epilepsy perhaps indicates by always pulling him back to his bodily fragility.

A similar vision underlies the more ambitious and remarkable *L'Humanité*, a film that once more centres on a struggle between spirituality and brute animality as it plays itself out in the embodied actions of popular characters called upon to figure the human in all its frailty. Whereas in *La Vie de Jésus* the competing tendencies were both found in the central character, here the hero Pharaon, a painfully inarticulate detective, takes on a more clearly religious dimension, while his friend Joseph, a school-bus driver, is more associated with the bodily and the brutal. Between the two comes Domino, a woman factory worker, whom Pharaon desires but who is Joseph's girlfriend. Before the action begins, Pharaon's wife and child have been killed in a car accident, an event that perhaps casts light on the hero's sensitivity to human suffering and the willed and unwilled harm that people do. The action proper begins when Pharaon discovers the naked body of a young girl, an event that causes him to run in anguish across a ploughed field. There follows one of the most shocking shots of the film, an unwavering close-up of the child's muddied and bloodied vagina, a shot echoed later in the film by a shot of Domino's sexually aroused vagina which makes a clear reference to Courbet's famously scandalous painting *The Origin of Life*. The film would seem to suggest that if it is through the vagina that all human life issues, life is brutal and rooted in the physical. It reserves its most graphic moments for clinically shot, profoundly unerotic scenes of sexual coupling or masturbation. Violence remains at the level of the unseen, for the car accident, murder and sexual assault precede the action, but its lurking presence is suggested by Joseph's anger. It is also present at a more diffuse, impersonal level in certain modern behaviours such as fast or careless driving or the violent dissection of the rural terrain by the high-speed Eurostar train.

Pharaon, an almost inarticulate seer, is hyperaware of the violence and suffering of the world. He reproaches Joseph with the ugliness of his anger. When an Arab drug dealer is arrested, his unlikely response is to embrace the man, feeling the pain behind the act. His compassion is expressed in similar, physical manner towards a carer at a local asylum that he visits in search of a potential suspect. Finally, he gives Joseph a long kiss on the mouth after the latter is arrested for the murder of the child. The last shot of the film seems to show him in handcuffs, apparently having taken Joseph's place. If Freddy encapsulated the tension between the animal and the spiritual in the human, Pharaon is a more purely Christic figure. His ability to kiss the contemporary 'lepers', the drug dealer and the child murderer, and to take the sins of the world on his shoulders, have obvious biblical echoes. But one must remember that in Dumont's world the transcendental and the corporeal are irremediably enmeshed, that the embrace of the murderer has inevitably to be sexual as well as spiritual.[7]

The brute corporeality of Dumont's characters is constantly signalled by the *mise-en-scène*, both through the frequent close proximity to skin and bodies and through the crude frankness of the sex scenes. In case the point is missed, one sequence of shots when Pharaon first pats the hide of a large sow and then scrutinises the skin of his fat and sweaty chief would seem to go out of its way to underline it. A sequence that tracks Pharaon tightly as he cycles up a local hill, recording his effort, heavy breathing and sweating underlines how the film's most spiritual character is also tied to the body. But Dumont's camera also pulls back at certain moments to extreme long shot to show the smallness of the characters in the natural world. An obvious contrast to make here is the Dardennes' refusal, from *Rosetta* on, to draw back from characters always accompanied as subjects in the world and never objectified either by still, close scrutiny or by distancing long shots. But even in the earlier *La Promesse*, the long shots typically provided a view of deserted factories, providing an epic prehistory to the characters' shrunken present rather than pushing them back into nature. The smallness and animality of Dumont's characters might seem to be redeemed by the spirituality that the film also finds in them. Yet here also there is a sense of distance and, by implication, superiority. Pharaon has an artist forbear who, amongst other things, created religious paintings. When asked to comment on one work at a local exhibition he can only remark on the beauty of the blue with his usual painfully slow delivery. While the film gives itself access to a range of cultural and religious references, it condemns its hero to halting and limited language. Physically and culturally, it seems too ready to grant itself superiority and distance from its characters, despite its apparent commitment to the close tracking of their embodied experience and their refusal of the circumstances of their lives.

It is this broader context that one can begin to make sense of *L'Humanité*'s depiction of a brief, abortive strike. Discovering that their company plans to relocate production elsewhere in France, the workers go on strike taking the slogan of the 1995 national action, *tous ensemble*, as their own. But faced with the local mayor's refusal to meet them, they tamely subside. Domino comments that they are not very brave. The relocation, a gesture that shows no respect for the embeddedness of locally lived lives (chapter 8), might seem to be the socio-economic act of violence that rescues the other violences for political meaning. But the film does not work this way. Rather, as in *La Vie de Jésus*, where the senseless sexual assault on the young girl seems to at least partially defuse the political charge of the subsequent racist murder, the opening child murder tends to root all subsequent violences in the brutality of a fallen mankind. As in that earlier film too, the empty streets and the frequently seen but unvisited church suggests a humanity no longer taken in hand either socially or spiritually. This would seem to point towards the key thrust of Dumont's implied critique of the modern: a fallen, small humanity is out of its place in a post-sacred world of increasingly inhuman dimensions and speed.

We can now perhaps better appreciate why Dumont's films demand consideration alongside the other works considered in this chapter, but how, in the end, they stand out from them. They work essentially on the same ground. They figure small groups of characters who have no language to express their frustrations and desires and live in a hollowed out social space with neither collective values nor institutional frameworks to frame and make sense of their experience. Faced with this withdrawal of meaning, deprived of a past or a future, their struggles and suffering risk becoming senseless. The films commit themselves to these characters, tracking their actions and inaction with slow, careful attention, seeking to find meaning where none seems to reside. The characters, like those found elsewhere, are recalcitrant subjects who, although they have no language to frame their resistance, struggle against their reality, self-destructively in the case of Freddy, refusing its brutality in the case of Pharaon. However, Dumont's work diverges in essential ways. Firstly, through the superiority that, like Tavernier's *Ça commence aujourd'hui*, it gives itself compared to popular characters who are associated with brute animality and inarticulacy. One might object here that the other films similarly show characters who, deprived of a collective voice, express themselves above all through gesture and action. But the essential difference is that whereas those films tie their corporeality to the collapse of social mediations and the raw violences of the economy, Dumont tends to naturalize it in a way that is necessarily depoliticizing. This then opens onto a second key difference. While characters in other films can signal a radical break with a brutal reality by opting, albeit only through their gestures, for alternative values, Dumont's characters can only ever operate a partial break with a brute physicality to which they are intrinsically tied. Thirdly, because they belong to a fallen humanity and are at least partially objectified, the films tend to see them with compassion. If there is a division of labour in the contemporary world between a penal and a humanitarian treatment of social struggle and suffering, Dumont's films perhaps only avoid the former to fall more fully prey to the latter. This is perhaps the ultimate significance of Pharaon's embrace of the criminals, a gesture whose apparent radicalism masks its underlying conservatism.

As if reversing what is seen in Dumont, Alnoy's recent *Elle est des nôtres* begins from the premise of the divinity of humanity. Rather than tying Christine, its heroine, to the earth and to the body as Dumont might have done, Alnoy opens her film by showing her descending from a mountain. What she finds after her descent is a world whose relationships are brutal and cold but in which there is no shared public language or values that might name that brutality and coldness. In her social role as someone who temps in different companies, Christine is effectively treated as a non-person. Thus, for example, in a company cafeteria, someone pushes a chair back across her path as if she were invisible or did not exist. Later, in a swimming pool, something similar happens when a group of young men knock her into the pool, again as if she were not there. This latter incident enrages her, and in her fury she knocks her friend to the ground, causing a fatal blow to the head. Having murdered in a society that routinely eliminates people by treating those who do not meet its entry criteria as non-persons, she becomes 'normal,' is given an important full-time position and becomes a valued colleague and a desirable person. A male temporary worker, initially treated by her as a non-person, seems to pursue her, as if sensing her fallen divinity. After a trip to the mountains with him, back to the heights, she denounces herself to the police, reasserting the implicit sacredness of life by confessing to her crime. Like Dumont, Alnoy takes what is highly promising material for socio-political critique and then does something different with it by using a particular set of social relations – in this case the brutality of the world of work –to make a more general point about the inhumanity of people. The pool incident would seem to play a key role here. Unconnected to the world of work or to capitalist social relations more generally, it would seem to work like the chains of violence in Dumont to at least partially depoliticize systemic violence by absorbing it into a wider chain of inhumanity. What makes Alnoy's work far less politically regressive than Dumont's is her opposite starting point in the essential sacredness of the human. This radically different premise means that, rather than naturalizing socio-economic brutality, her film is able to retain an overpowering sense of its inhumanity.

Emergent Fragments

The contrast between the discussion in this chapter and that in the last might suggest that we were dealing with two radically different groups of films, one in which there was an elaborated leftist discourse of class that connected characters, however tenuously, to a tradition and one in which individuals and small groups were left face to face, body to body, with the violences of the economy and with few or any symbolic resources on which to call or with which to make sense of their experience. However, the real differences between the two groups should not blind us to underlying similarities. Because the first group show the decline of collective action and the crisis of a leftist discourse that once served to make sense of the world, raw, fragmented and mute struggle is already present within it in emergent form. This was the lesson drawn from discussion of *Reprise* and *Je pense à vous* in chapter 2: even as an epic dramaturgy of class comes apart, revolt is condemned to be local and immediate and to find new tools to make itself heard. The films already discussed in class terms in chapters 4 and 5 confirm this analysis, showing the emergence of the core traits of what we have termed an aesthetic of the fragment even as they bear witness to the undoing of the totalizing dramaturgy of class. Some (*Retiens la nuit, Ressources humaines*) are of particular interest here in that rather than moving from the totalizing narrative to the fragment, they seek to reverse the trajectory, taking a struggle that has become individual, corporeal and immediate and reconnecting it to a politically articulated story of collective action. We will come to them a little later.

Guédiguian, who might seem a paradigmatic case of a director determined to hold on to the old political language, is a good place to start for evidence of the movement from one dramaturgy to another. When we looked at his work we noted that, despite his strong sense of working-class traditions, the predominant focus was on small groups threatened in their intergenerational continuity. Thus broad class struggle with its aspirations for political transformation seemed to be mutating into a local struggle for bare life as one film title, *A la vie, à la mort!*, so eloquently suggested. The later *Marius et Jeannette* was able to evoke a tradition of resistance, but the particular story told was one of love-making in the concentration camp, that is, of a struggle that, deprived of all other resources, passed directly through the body and its most elemental desires as an affirmation of life in the face of death.[8] Along similar lines, the struggle of Michèle, the heroine of *La Ville est tranquille*, has become elemental, as Guédiguian himself notes.[9] No longer part of a group, she fights to feed her daughter's need for drugs and her granddaughter's need for food, contrasting bodily demands that place increasing strains on her own body. Finally, she kills her daughter to save her grandchild's future. However, rather than a politically elaborated aspiration, this is a future grounded only in being alive. Thus, even as Guédiguian seeks to make the fragments of the old politics productive, his films also bear witness to the rise of a new dramaturgy of social struggle.

A similar pattern underlies other films discussed in the same chapter where, although an articulated sense of working-class collective identity and tradition of struggle is retained, the class itself can no longer be found. Spoken by residual individuals or small groups, its language ceases to be a publicly shared idiom so that, although still having a voice and being able to name causes, struggle is tending to become mute and local. *Etat des lieux* follows a pattern along these lines. With its clear reference to the Marxist tradition, the film connects back, as much as any other in this volume, to an elaborated politics of class, yet in the end the hero struggles alone, using his body more than language as a tool. When harassed by his supervisor at work, he hits him and is fired. Later, when being interviewed to test his suitability for employment, he loses patience at the insulting nature of the questions and farts in his questioner's face. Finally, in a way that expresses all his pent up frustration and class resentment, he makes violent love to the wife of a bourgeois friend. It would seem that deprived of collective solidarities and institutional support, class struggle loses its voice and becomes brutal and physical. *Selon Matthieu*, another film with a strong sense of tradition, follows the same pattern. When the hero is let down by the unions and by his workmates, he is forced to seek revenge on his boss alone and drawing above all on his body. Firstly, he seduces his boss's wife, seeking to wound him through the flesh because conventional worker action has failed. Later, losing his temper, he headbutts him. His brother's ensuing fury with him for getting them both sacked is expressed not through words but through the repeated ramming of his car.[10] If one sought two key examples of works that showed that collective struggle was still both possible and necessary, one would choose Cantet's *Ressources humaines* and Cabrera's *Retiens la nuit*, both films about politically informed strike action. Yet, significantly, as if to underline the points made above, both have to start from struggles that have become mute, local and 'senseless' in order to reattach them to a politics and to restore collective meaning to them. One, *Ressources humaines*, does so essentially by bringing class conflict back into public visibility, the other, *Retiens la nuit*, by finding a terrain upon which to reconnect mute struggle with an articulated language.[11]

When *Ressources humaines* begins, as we saw, there seems to be no place for struggle within a consensual social order. However, once the film takes us onto the shop floor, we see that oppressive conditions and class resentment still exist although there is no longer a shared, public language with which to name them. This is made beautifully clear in the early sequence when the hero tours the factory on his own. As his father shows him how his machine works, a supervisor humiliates him, shouting at him and telling him that his slowness is hampering production. The workmate on the neighbouring machine intervenes, not by shouting at the foreman, but by barking at him. If, on the surface, this merely points to the supervisor's role as management 'guard dog', it indicates, at a deeper level, the workers' loss of a collective voice or, in Rancière's terms, their expulsion from the *logos* and their relegation to the domain of mere animal pain and noise. Something similar happens when the son again tours the factory, this time accompanying the manager. The latter approaches the same worker to shake his hand. The man holds up his oily gloves to keep him at a distance, providing silent testimony to his refusal to connive in the fiction of consensus but again underlining his lack of a political voice and the purely individual nature of his defiance. Another lone worker makes the same point in a more vulgar manner by raising his middle finger in the direction of the boss's back. What makes *Ressources humaines* profoundly significant is that, having underlined how corporeal struggle had become effectively detached from a voice of collective resistance, it then works to bring the two back together. Tellingly it does this through a physical rather than a discursive intervention in the fabric of the real. When the hero discovers that his father is to be sacked, he and a workmate climb over the factory rooftop at night, break in through a skylight, print out the telltale document and tape it to the factory door in order to force oppression back to the surface. From this stage on, although the struggle still has an embodied, individual dimension (the hero for example is physically ejected from the factory by his boss), it once again takes on a collective, public and discursively mediated form.

Another, somewhat different reconnection of raw corporeal revolt with the political occurs in Cabrera's *Retiens la nuit*. The film stages, as we noted, the encounter between Nadia, an impoverished single mother, and the striking railway workers of December 1995. It begins as, having seen her child's railwayman father on the television news, Nadia comes looking for him, considering, as she later reveals, the possibility of giving him an infant for whom she feels that she cannot care properly. Nadia is a decidedly physical presence in the film: she vomits and needs to be cleaned up; she gets burned by the strikers' brazier and needs bandaging; her child needs food and a clean nappy. Her urgent bodily needs help stress how, like characters in films by Tavernier, the Dardennes, Zonca or Guédiguian, she is locked into a fight for continued existence in the present. Her despairing willingness to give up a child underlines, as in other films considered, how the socially marginalized are threatened not just in their living conditions but in their very continuation as a group. She thus inhabits a different world to the strikers who, due to their relative prosperity and secure employment, are insulated from physical need. The latter engage in collective debate about their action. Building on a tradition of solidarity and protecting historical gains, they are at the same time fighting to protect a future for themselves and for the next generation. Through their encounter with Nadia, the two very different modes of appearance of struggle that we have described in this volume collide.

Unsurprisingly, the first result of this collision is mutual incomprehension. Long term, collective and mediated struggle seems unable to connect to immediate, individual revolt. Faced with her own immediate, physical need and that of her child, Nadia is intolerant of the strikers' discussions. Compared to her they seem privileged. For them, on the other hand, she is a burden, someone that they are willing to help but who causes them inconvenience and, when she criticizes their stance, irritation. The film would thus initially seem to concur with those who condemned the public sectors workers' fight by endorsing the politically disabling playing-off of workers who retained some rights and some power against the excluded. It would also seem to echo the early part of *Ressources humaines* where worker militancy seemed an outdated hangover from the past. But, like that film, *Retiens la nuit* does not leave things there. Instead, it works to find a common ground upon which to reconnect immediate, corporeal struggle with discursively mediated collective action. It does this through another contrived plot mechanism. The van in which representatives of the two main unions, the CGT and the CFDT, are driving Nadia round the edge of Paris runs out of fuel and the three are left, with Nadia's baby, in the cold of a December night. When they fail to bring any inhabitants of a comfortable suburban village to their doors to help, despair looms. However, picking up the strikers' slogan of *tous ensemble* ('everyone together'), Nadia leads the threesome in a warming jog back to the van where they huddle together to keep themselves and the child warm. Set against the wintry cold, a solidarity that had seemed purely abstract takes on flesh and re-roots itself in the world allowing Nadia's immediate embodied needs to reconnect to the values that the strikers defend. The next day, when the CGT representative speaks, Nadia has significantly become an attentive listener to a speech that now also addresses her by proposing an alliance between the workers and the 'excluded' against the neo-liberal drive that threatens both groups.

By bringing together Nadia and the strikers, Cabrera's film makes it own intervention in the debates that accompanied 1995 while reproducing the potentially counter-hegemonic convergence that the event had itself begun to operate. It might thus seem to only mirror political processes that had preceded it. Its originality lies rather in the way it intervenes in French cinema by establishing grounds on which, refusing its alleged fossilization, a leftist discourse can again take root in the world. In its mobilization of an elemental dramaturgy, it echoes other films we have considered in this chapter. But it uses the sharp contrasts that this dramaturgy permits (between the darkness of the night and the warm glow of street lights, the cold and the strikers' braziers, hunger and shared food and drink) to allow certain fundamental political choices to again make sense while laying the ground for immediate, embodied need to reconnect to the language and traditions of resistance.

Despite their effective reconnection of a leftist language with embodied struggle, *Retiens la nuit* and *Ressources humaines* help confirm to what extent an emergent aesthetic of the fragment is present in those films that still seem to have access to a totalizing leftist language of opposition. If films that work where fragmentation is more advanced have to find particular strategies to restore meaning, a voice and potentially political subjectivity to struggles and suffering condemned to the realm of animal pain and pleasure, those that retain or re-establish some access to a more fully developed politics put two very different dramaturgies of the social to work. While, on the one hand, they can still call on the pieces of the old left-wing dramaturgy of class (chapters 4 and 5), on the other they are obliged to find ways to give eloquence to emergent or existent fragmentation. The films where fragmentation is fully fledged draw their power from the proximity of raw struggle and the violent collision between resistant subjectivities and socio-economic obstacles. Films that retain some access to a language of class and to a tradition of struggle cannot draw on the same claustrophobic intensity, part of whose power is to make us wish for some release, some opening of political possibility, some restoration of meaning. What they can do is to remind us, by showing the trauma of its fading, why it was so vitally necessary to begin with.

Conclusion

Building on ideas introduced in chapter 2 and developed in chapter 3, this chapter has developed the notion of a paradigm shift in the mode of appearance of social struggle. At the core of its argument has been the transition from the totalizing, epic dramaturgy permitted by an explicit leftist politics to an aesthetic of the fragment. The fragment is not self-contained nor self-sustaining. It emerges from the shattering of something larger, from the loss of social connectivity, shared values and intergenerational continuity. Characters within it have no access to an overarching explanatory vision or to an elaborated politics. Their struggles and suffering pass above all through the body and are constantly threatened with meaninglessness. In Rancière's terms they have lost access to the *logos*, the language of public, political deliberation and are condemned to the realm of animal pain or pleasure. The films concerned are only politically productive to the extent that they resist this process. We have seen two essential ways in which they can achieve this. One is to make sense of the violences and sufferings of the margins by connecting them to processes at the centre, thus resisting the rise of meaninglessness. The other is to constitute the characters as desiring, creative subjects who, rather than being defined and immobilized by their reality, exist primarily through their struggle against it and their ability to reinvent values that refuse the ambient brutality. The next chapter will provide a more broad ranging evaluation of the films' mobilization of the resources of melodrama to restore political eloquence to struggle. We will then turn in the final chapter to the essential issue of spatiality. If almost all the films discussed here focus on the purely local struggles of residual groups or individuals who no longer have access to an overarching vision or language, they would seem ill-placed to provide any productive purchase on the processes of globalizing capital. In the same way that they must find ways to oppose a loss of voice and meaning, they must also find ways to reach outside their own narrow spatial frame in order to be politically productive.

Notes

1. In his journal entry for March 5th 1994, Luc Dardenne writes, 'The ethical consensus of pity that reins nowadys feeds off an aesthetics of the suffering, damaged, disfigured biological body that the media, principally through television images, endlessly propagate' (*'Le consensus de l'éthique de la pitié qui règne aujourd'hui se nourrit d'une esthétique du corps biologique souffrant, meurtri, défiguré, que ne cessent de propager les médias, principalement les images télévisées'*) (2005: 36).

2. The parallel rise of humanitarian and securitarian discourses bears clear echoes of the old divide between the deserving and the undeserving poor, the former deserving of assistance, the latter of reprobation and repression, with both groups cast as social objects with no right to challenge their position. *La Cérémonie* (chapter 5) points to the contemporary return of this kind of depoliticizing and objectifying configuration of the social. It also reminds us how quickly the deserving poor can mutate into their undeserving cousins if they become too vociferous or unruly.

3. '*Sale con de bourge*'.

4. A veteran oppositional film-maker, active since the 1970s, Tavernier has become increasingly prominent since the 1990s because of his leading role in professional organizations and engagement in contemporary struggles, as shown, for example, by the two documentaries, *De l'autre côté du périph'* (1997) and *Histoires de vies brisées* (2001), that he made with his son. The former came out of extended filming in the *banlieue*, the latter out of high-profile commitment to the struggle of the *sans-papiers*.

5. A central pillar of French national mythology is the notion of republican integration, the ability of France, as the classic universalist nation, to take little Bretons, Basques, Normans or indeed Italians, Portuguese or Algerians and turn them into French citizens. The school has usually been seen as the privileged vector in this integration, although work and political participation are also accorded a central place. The drama in *Ça commence aujourd'hui* is driven by the failure of two of the three pillars of integration – stable labour is no longer available to all, while politics no longer engages with local miseries. Consequently, the whole weight of the collapsing social edifice falls on the remaining pillar, the school.

6. This is similarly the case in Devers's *La Voleuse de Saint-Lubin* where, even as other political parties withdraw from popular areas, the Front National remains present and shows a strong capacity to make sense of the embodied struggles of the heroine, precisely because it so strongly politicizes white and non-white bodies.

7. When asked in a newspaper interview whether the final kiss expressed compassion, Dumont replied that it was sexual, an expression of the violence of desire passing through the body. But for him, as he immediately added, the body is the beginning of the soul, so that the embodied necessarily has a spiritual dimension (Royer 1999).

8. Similarly, in Siri's *Une Minute de silence* solidarity and resistance are above all embodied rather than discursive. The former is most evident in the shower scene where groups of men scrub each other's backs and the latter in the pitched battle with the police. There is little if any elaborated political discussion.

9. In the interview where Guédiguian commented that Michèle was an 'animal' character without a politics, he went on to underline how, in the absence of any elaborated discourse, each character was defined by their appearance and body (D., I. 2001).

10. Likewise in Jolivet's *Fred* a resistance that had been collective and discursive becomes raw and corporeal. This is most clearly visible in a scene where Fred's lover responds to her boss's denunciation of him to the police by throwing a blood sample in his

face, telling him that it is from someone with HIV. The sample is in fact harmless, but its use again signals the shift to a visceral politics of direct interpersonal collisions.

11. We will not return here to Liénard's *Une Part du ciel* or Charef's *Marie-Line*. They would nonetheless lend themselves to similar discussion in that both also work to reconnect a revolt condemned to be voiceless and individual to some form of embryonic, collective resistance, a resistance without words in *Marie-Line* but with a more conventional political language in *Une Part du ciel*.

7

MELODRAMATIC POLITICS

There is a common sense understanding that realism is deeply opposed to both melodrama and theatricality. Associated to a high degree with a flat, dedramatized and documentary-like recording of the world, realism would seem irreconcilable, on the surface at least, with the heightened and contrived effects of melodrama as well as with the declamatory and apparently artificial nature of the theatrical. Working in direct opposition to this particular strand of common sense, this chapter will argue that melodrama plays a consistently vital role in the politics of the films under consideration, intervening both at the level of form, as a way of restoring eloquence to a real that no longer speaks to us adequately, and thematically, by drawing on highly charged stories of individuals and families as a way to dramatize contemporary systemic violences. The chapter will also suggest that, although much less in evidence, an overt theatricality makes its presence felt at certain key moments of some films as a way of asserting the capacity of a radical politics to rupture the surface of the real and to challenge apparently fixed identities and roles. The discussion of melodrama will draw primarily on the seminal work of Peter Brooks on the subject, while the work of Jacques Rancière will provide a theoretical framework for the analysis of theatricality.

Brooks's work, *The Melodramatic Imagination* (1976), is mainly concerned with nineteenth-century fiction, notably the work of canonical figures such as Honoré de Balzac and Henry James. Perhaps the initial useful lesson that can be drawn from it is how writers whose names are indelibly associated with realism can also be shown to have systematic recourse to the resources of melodrama. Any assumption that realism and melodrama cannot be features of the same text is thus highly dubious. On the contrary, as Brooks shows, realist and melodramatic drives can exist in complex and productive tension both to engage with and to give eloquence to the real. Brooks's historical starting point is the French Revolution. For him, the Revolution represents the final nail in the coffin of a sacred order regimented by the representative institutions of monarchy and church. This old order was characterized by a moral transparency that allowed the value of people and things to be directly read off from the surface of the real. Deprived of any overarching moral framework, and lacking any shared sense of the place and worth of people, the post-revolutionary world is, in contrast, opaque. Things no longer signify their social and moral worth. Significance is something that artists must work to restore. Whereas a realism that sought to record the surface of the real would simply reproduce the moral opacity of the world, the resources of melodrama can be mobilized to penetrate beneath the surface and to produce a heightened real, one that again speaks to us in moral terms of the worth that we should attach to people (Brooks 1976: 14–23).

Melodrama, as Brooks delineates it, has certain key features. Firstly, in its push to move beyond surface appearances, it is driven to produce climactic moments when characters confront one another with full expressivity to fix the meaning of relationships. This expressivity is characteristically rooted in accentuated gestures and statements. Secondly, in its drive to restore moral legibility, melodrama develops an essentially Manichaean worldview. Figuring neither indecipherable complexity nor infinite shades of grey, it draws its power and excitement from the conflict between black and white, good and evil. Whereas realism in its more objectivist variants might be associated with a cold, analytical eye, melodrama calls for strong emotional engagement through the staging of heightened conflicts and through a characteristic recourse to suspense and brinkmanship. This amplified register is tied intrinsically to a focus on individuals: good and evil are not abstract forces, but are attached to characters. Because, in a post-sacred world, there are no ultimate moral guarantees, morality has to be brought within the world as a hidden truth to be found in people and things and to be restored to visibility (Brooks 1976: 1–17).

This need to bring out what would otherwise be condemned to remain hidden helps explain the complex interplay within melodrama between the gestural, the prelinguistic and the linguistic. While there is a drive towards a heightened, emphatic use of language, there is also a sense that language has become inadequate, that there is an occult moral level of meaning that a fallen language is inadequate to express. Melodrama thus tends towards a paradoxically eloquent silence within which what Brooks calls the 'text of muteness' serves as a supplement to the words (Brooks 1976: 62). Gestures, attitudes and prelinguistic cries and sounds point towards a gap in the linguistic code, underlining its inability to convey a true fullness of meaning while at the same time helping to compensate for that same inability. If there is always a sense that words may have broken free from underlying truths, gesture and inarticulate cry would seem to look back towards some mythical, primal language within which there was no gap between code and meaning and words were intrinsically tied to what they signified. Melodramatic gesturality thus both underlines and compensates for a lost fullness of meaning, helping once again to make the world eloquent (Brooks 1976: 56–80).

Brooks provides a compelling account of why melodrama was so important in the nineteenth century and how its devices were of such importance in classic realist novels whose central mission was to again make the real meaningful, underlining in the process that realism and melodrama, despite the clear tensions between them, could be interdependent rather than antithetical modes. We will explore here how, in somewhat similar fashion, contemporary French social-realist cinema has systematically drawn upon melodramatic devices to restore a lost eloquence to the socio-political world. But before we do so we should remind ourselves why the current turn to melodrama was necessary in the first place. Within Brooks' original argument, the French Revolution is the cataclysmic event that explains the collapse of the sacred order and the need for melodrama's compensatory restoration of transparency. In the contemporary period, and within the argument that this book develops, the parallel cataclysm is the collapse of the twentieth century left, an event whose consequences were explored, drawing on emblematic films, in the third chapter. While a leftist dramaturgy once served to render the socio-political world transparent, giving sense and direction to actions, naming oppressions and dividing the world between class allies and enemies, the world has now become opaque. Oppressions of course remain and, due to the major shift in the balance of forces, have indeed deepened but are now deprived of the sense that might once have attached to them. It is in these circumstances of a loss of transparency and meaning that we can make sense of the cinematic turn to melodrama.

The melodramatic turn is implicitly theorized in one of the films considered in chapter 3, Le Roux's *Reprise*. I suggested that it could be seen as showing the moment when raw, individual revolt of the kind routinely found in current cinema was detached from an overarching leftist language and dramaturgy. Revolt was embodied in *Reprise* by one young woman worker. Significantly, as she found herself abandoned by those supposed to represent her and had to take her own representation in hand, the strategies to which she turned were profoundly melodramatic. While those around her sought to dedramatize the moment by presenting it as just one phase of an ongoing process and by speaking in measured, controlled and even subdued tones, she was forced to amplify and project her feelings. Refusing the 'reasonable' positions of those around her, she adopted a profoundly emotive register. Not only did she turn to a heightened language to denounce the disgusting and oppressive working conditions to which they were returning, she also mobilized the expressive capacity of her face and her body to dramatize the situation, waving her arms as she reminded her listeners of the embodied oppression faced by those who worked directly with the filthy raw materials of battery production. Thus, as her revolt became raw, as it lost its stage, she was forced to turn to essentially melodramatic strategies to try to compensate for the broader silencing of a collective voice. Something similar, we would argue, can explain the contemporary turn to melodrama.

It was also in our discussion of *Reprise* that we first turned to Rancière's perhaps counter-intuitive comment on the profoundly theatrical nature of an authentic politics. In direct opposition to any position that might define a radical politics as one that cuts through the false consciousness of ideology to reveal the fixed 'truth' of the social and of the real, Rancière equates the political with the splitting of the real. A radical politics can only emerge when, refusing its silencing and subaltern role, an oppressed group takes voice to refuse the existing distribution of the commons and the right to public speech, thus proposing a reordering of the real. This refusal is necessarily theatrical. What it does essentially is to propose a new dramaturgy, that is, a rewriting of roles and voices (Rancière 1995: 49, 80: Hallward 2006). Within such an analysis, the radicalism of 1968 lay precisely in the way that students and workers moved out of their existing identities and roles and took voice in public space, turning the street and the factory forecourt into improvised stages for their radical theatre.

Rancière's notion of the necessary theatricality of an authentic politics can be usefully held in productive tension with Brooks's account of the melodramatic. If we take the core of Brooks's discussion to be that melodrama works to bring the unseen to the surface, there is a danger that this could be taken to mean that films are somehow politically productive when they bring fixed but hidden qualities or identities back to visibility, rescuing, for example, the working class from its current obscurity and reasserting its positive worth. What Rancière usefully reminds us is that what needs to be returned to the surface is not a fixed identity, however positive, but a construction of the social based on subaltern struggle. This is something to which we shall come in the middle part of the chapter when we consider those films within which, at key moments, characters step out of their existing role to reclaim a right to public speech and to polemically challenge the social order. Such moments serve to remind us that it is not sufficient to foreground contemporary social misery. This in itself has little political use-value and is at best humanitarian and patronizing in its thrust, at worst voyeuristic, offering the suffering of the margins up for our horror and our pity. Politics re-emerges, the films help remind us, when, refusing their marginal and silenced social role, the oppressed take voice and become speaking subjects not objects to be looked upon. The chapter will conclude by returning full square to melodrama to consider the films' focus on affectively charged stories of individuals and families. Staples of melodrama, such features have traditionally been considered anathema within a properly political cinema. If we are to suggest that recourse to them can play a positive political role in contemporary committed films, we will have to show that they can offer a privileged way into current social struggles.

Melodramatic Realism

We noted how a range of critics have converged in associating the current wave of socio-politically engaged films with the term realism (chapter 2). Whereas some saw this new realism positively, pointing towards its ability to re-engage with social oppressions and struggles, others – notably the *Cahiers* critics – were highly critical, suggesting that it repeats the sins of earlier variants by immobilizing the social and allowing the political to be absorbed by the conventions of fiction. There would seem, however, to be a minimal consensus that, in one way or another, the strand of cinema concerned can usefully be labelled realist, even if the precise content and valency of this term are clearly matters of considerable contention. By the end of this chapter, we should be better placed to offer our own evaluation of this realism. But we should perhaps begin here by briefly reminding ourselves how the body of films concerned might be judged realist.

The films' realism could be considered to operate at a range of levels. Firstly, the films examined can be considered as realist at the thematic level, that is, they deliberately engage with contemporary socio-political issues and debates, such as unemployment, the *banlieue* or the world of work. Secondly, the films have stylistic features commonly associated with realism: thus, with the partial exception of *La Haine*, they choose to present us with an unpolished, naturalistic image. One might say that this image was quasi-documentary in its look, except for the fact that, refusing the pseudo-objectivity of documentary, it chooses to track characters, recording the collision between their subjective desires and the obstacles that they encounter in the world around them. The close tracking of individuals is often carried out using a breathless and unsteady handheld camera – a characteristic that has become almost a stylistic tic due to its widespread use. It is also a characteristic that adds to the films' stylistic roughness. In this it is abetted by the general avoidance of star actors and the widespread use of non-professional performers (Austin 2004; Beugnet 2000: 62). Thirdly, a sense of realism is reinforced at the narrative level by a predominance of what *seem* to be loose, episodic plots. Whereas tightly constructed plots might leave little space for engagement with the complexity of the real, episodic plots, as Bazin notes in his discussion of Italian neo-realism, seem much more open to it and can thus enhance a sense of realism. There is thus a range of reasons to do with theme, casting, style and plot which mean that the films under study might be grouped under the label of realism. Their melodramatic qualities are perhaps less obvious and will need explaining here before we move on to discuss the political effectiveness of their combination of realism and melodrama. Certain features that might be described as melodramatic will attract our particular attention. These are: the production of moments of confrontation and collision; the corporeal and the gestural; the restoration of ethical transparency to a world that has become opaque; the emotive focus on individuals and families rather than abstract forces.

Manufactured Collisions

The language of class and of class struggle used to serve to name social domination, exploitation and alienation. With the triumph of globalizing capital and the effective defeat of the organized working class (chapter 1), oppressions have become much more difficult to name. The language of class has been replaced to a considerable extent by the language of exclusion. Drawing the dividing line between those in work (deemed to be privileged) and those out of work (deemed to need help), this latter discourse further renders a conflictual account of the social hard to sustain. If those in work are privileged, it becomes impossible to denounce their domination, exploitation or alienation. If those out of work are opposed to the employed, it ceases to be possible to connect their situation to systemic violences. Both those in work and those unemployed are condemned to silence, the former because they can have nothing to complain about, the latter because, needing assistance, they are above all social objects rather than subjects with a legitimate grievance. This delegitimization and silencing of a polemical framing of social relations is further aggravated by two other factors. Firstly, there has been what one might call a spatialization and pathologization of the social, a phenomenon whose chief symptom has been the obsessive focus on the *banlieue* as an epicentre of social ills. Whereas class opened onto the possibility and need for systemic change, the *banlieue* would seem to call above all for a localized and purely spatial fix. Discussion of it can help keep the problems of the margins at the margin rather than readdressing them to the centre. Its problems and those of the underclass more generally are cast as pathologies, at best worthy of our compassion, at worse purely destructive tendencies requiring policing and repression. Secondly, there has been a substantial decline in the social visibility of production and a concomitant rise in the prominence of consumption. If hierarchies were immediately evident within production, consumption, with its utopian promises and apparent democracy, can only serve to obscure them. These broader shifts help explain contemporary French cinema's recourse to the production of melodramatic collisions to make oppressions again visible and to ensure that the problems of the margins are readdressed to the centre. Let us now move to consider some examples.

We might begin by noting how many of the films under analysis take us into the world of work thus bringing social barriers and hierarchies back to the surface. This in itself could not necessarily be constructed as a melodramatic strategy did the films themselves not first suggest that the violences and inequalities of production were hidden. It is because they work to bring something hidden back to the surface that they can be seen as intrinsically melodramatic. Thus, for example, and as we noted in chapter 5, Cantet's *Ressources humaines* initially seems to present us with a world ruled by consensual co-existence and class fluidity before gradually revealing hidden class barriers and hierarchies. Rather than simply documenting the surface of the real, it suggests that its violences first need to be restored to visibility. Thus, when the hero wishes to tour the factory, the door is initially closed in his face. Later, we will begin to suspect something unpleasant is being prepared as he finds other doors closed and blinds shut in a way that makes issues of visibility and opacity a central part of the film's visual economy. Given this, it is no accident that the turning point in the film is when the hero breaks into the head of personnel's office to print out the confidential letter with details of forthcoming redundancies. When he sticks the letter to the front door he restores transparency to the world allowing, in true melodramatic style, for hidden wrongs to be brought to the surface and named. Interpersonal relations in the film have a similarly melodramatic economy. Although the film is far too sophisticated to have characters that are simply good or evil, it does nonetheless work towards climactic moments when wrongs are named and their perpetrators denounced. Thus, for example, once the hero has learned of the redundancies, he pulls his boss out of his meeting and denounces him as a coward. Later, he will publicly accuse his father of making him ashamed of his origins, thus bringing what had been a hidden humiliation to the surface. Films such as *La Cérémonie* and *Marion* likewise work to restore the visibility of class domination, bringing working-class and bourgeois characters into collision in situations that initially seem pacific and within which, as we saw, there was no longer a language to name class inequality.

The few *banlieue* films to which we make specific reference also work to make class differences reappear. *La Haine* primarily achieves this by sending its characters into the centre of Paris and bringing them into contrived collision with class others while using their movements to render visible social, cultural and economic barriers to true freedom of movement. *Wesh wesh* sends its illegal migrant hero to seek a job from a *Beur* employer as a way of underlining that his social exclusion is not simply a question of ethnicity but also has a class component. Finally, Richet's *Etat des lieux* consists almost entirely of a series of collisions that are designed to bring social and political fault lines into visibility. Thus it could be argued that, despite their usually semi-documentary look, *banlieue* films tend to be driven by essentially melodramatic narrative schemata.

Another group of films work to oppose the utopian promise of consumption by looking behind its glossy surface to reveal inequalities, exclusions and oppressions. This is done through a range of mechanisms. In some cases characters are deliberately moved between the constraints and inequalities of production and the apparent freedom and democratic openness of consumption as a way of giving the lie to the latter. In others, characters from different social groups are brought together in the face of consumption as a way of pointing towards their unequal economic capacities and their contrasting class-related attitudes to what they buy. Finally, a not insignificant number of films show us characters who work in places of consumption, thus pointing towards its messy and oppressive underside rather than stopping at its utopian surface. Thus, for example, Zonca's *La Vie rêvée des anges* moves its characters between sweatshop labour, shopping centre and nightclub doors, drawing attention to the oppressions, exclusions and inequalities that undermine the apparent promises of leisure and consumption. Having shown its heroine's initially failed attempt to obtain free paint from a disused cement works, Guédiguian's *Marius et Jeannette* then pointedly shows her at a supermarket checkout as she takes money for someone else's purchase of paint. Cabrera's *Retiens la nuit* takes its striking railway workers and its single-mother heroine to a supermarket as a way of underlining economic differences between them. Along similar lines, Marion Vernoux's *Rien à faire* (1999) takes a supermarket as the central locale of an extramarital romance between two unemployed characters, a bourgeois high-flyer and a working-class woman, thus drawing attention to radically different relationships to consumption. A good number of other examples could be mentioned but it is perhaps more useful to mention two films which reflexively engage with their unmasking of consumerism. These are Charef's *Marie-Line* and Devers's *La Voleuse de Saint-Lubin*.

Marie-Line focuses as we saw on a group of cleaners in a shopping centre. The workers are low-paid indigenous workers, immigrants and illegal migrants. They work at night unseen by consumers. When labour inspectors come, the migrants are forced to hide. Their children, when they are obliged to bring them with them, are left at the back of the shop. By choosing to show what happens at night, at the back and in the illegal economy, the film works to disrupt and go behind the smooth surface of consumption. By foregrounding the labour of cleaners, whose task is well done only if it is unseen, it further works to highlight the active 'invisibilization' that is required for consumption's sanitized image. Something similar happens in *La Voleuse de Saint-Lubin*. Its central character works as a cleaner in a meat preparation plant, washing away blood and cleaning waste even as the other women pack the meat into the pristine, cling film wrapped packages that will appear on the supermarket shelves. The film thus again actively works to highlight the active sanitization required to produce consumption's clean image and to render messy violences invisible.

Taken together, the films considered can be seen to refuse the current pacified and sanitized face of the social. Bringing their characters up against class others and against socio-cultural and economic barriers, they collectively work to bring underlying social fault lines back into visibility. The collisions that they force, as we noted in chapter 6, are often raw and corporeal. What we will now consider is how light might be cast upon this corporeality by Brooks' understanding of melodrama.

Corporeality or the Text of Muteness

Brooks suggests that melodrama's focus on the gestural and the embodied has a double thrust. While it indicates a loss of language and of transparency that makes moral worth hard to know and to name, it also helps compensate for that loss by restoring a mute eloquence to the world (Brooks 1976: 56–80). This double thrust helps explain the recourse to the corporeal in films that have to engage with a situation in which social struggles that were once made public and meaningful by a polemical discourse of class are now condemned, in Rancière's terms, to the realm of animal noise and suffering. The raw, corporeal nature of the conflicts that run through the films considered serves to underscore yet compensate for the falling silent of the leftist language that was once available to name and give meaning to social struggle.

While one would generally tend to place Guédiguian's *Marius et Jeannette* at the verbose end of the melodramatic spectrum alongside, for example, the work of Tavernier, there is one particular scene in the film that perfectly illustrates the argument here. It comes when Jeannette is ordered into the supermarket manager's office to be fired. Her fellow checkout women can see what is happening through the office window but are prevented by it from hearing anything. What is seen is thus effectively a pantomime that, despite the absence of sound, is doubly eloquent.[1] If it points to the silencing of struggle, it also resists it, as the combative body language and ample hand and arm movements of the two protagonists offer clear testimony to the disagreement that the manager had attempted to keep private. The scene continues. When the manager steps out of the office, Jeannette grabs the public address microphone and uses it to harangue the assembled shoppers with an ironic exhortation to consume and run up debts. The manager returns and another struggle ensues as Jeannette is silenced for the second time. This alternation between amplified language and mute gesture suggests the underlying similarity of function of two forms of communication that might on the surface seem to be polar opposites. In a situation where there is no collective voice and struggle is denied a stage, both pantomime and heightened verbal expression serve to point to yet refuse its silencing and privatization. They can be seen at work across the range of films studied here. If some (those of the Dardennes and Zonca for example) choose to privilege the corporeal, others (those of Guédiguian, Tavernier's *Ça commence aujourd'hui*) lean towards verbal inflation. Despite these marked differences, and because all the films tend to focus on small groups and individuals detached from broader solidarities and institutional mediations, the corporeal retains a centrality rooted in its ability to track the uncushioned impact of systemic violences and the raw, often physical nature of unstructured resistances.

The 'text of muteness' is at its most developed in the films of the Dardenne brothers where the physical becomes the prime vehicle for expressing characters' collisions with social obstacles and embodied others. Thus, to take just one example, when the eponymous heroine of *Rosetta* loses her job in a bakery, a tussle ensues between her and the owner, as she tried to hold onto a bag of flour and continue work and he tries to take it away from her. Rosetta's distress and resistance are expressed not through facial close-ups nor, primarily, through dialogue, but above all through physical gestures and struggles whose expressiviness is magnified by the proximity of the camera to the protagonists' bodies and the mobility it has to assume to track them. If we inevitably infer some sense of psychological interiority from the heroine's gestures, her body's surface retains a certain opacity. What the film tracks in the end is not an individual psyche but the interaction between the embodied desire to belong and the obstacles to that belonging. Because of this, what is brought to the surface is a social rather than a psychological occult. Enforced social marginalization, peremptory sackings and primal resistances to them are brutal processes that normally remain hidden. Rosetta's body acts as a screen on which they can be played out and melodramatically brought to the surface. Despite the preachy wordiness of Tavernier's *Ça commence aujourd'hui*, the body also plays a constant role within it as a way to figure forth underlying violences. As the film progresses, we are confronted with a series of mute signals of distress: a child who has come to school with his pyjamas under his clothes, a boy who will not speak, a mother who falls drunk to the ground, a baby left in the school yard, a child with bruises. These mute signs are taken up by the film's hero who interprets them, verbalizes them and brings them forcibly to the notice of public institutions. But this subsequent reworking in a heightened, melodramatic language should not distract us from the initial stimulus, the body's mute text, that brought social suffering to the surface.

Ethical Choices

If we can broadly explain the rise in prominence of the body as a privileged locus of expressivity by the loss of a language of political opposition, the same traumatic shift also helps to explain the recurrent presence of ethical questioning in the cinema we are considering here. As we showed when discussing the Dardenne brothers' *Je pense à vous*, the forced production of moments of ethical transparency is intrinsically tied to the need to compensate for the loss of a collective value system and an elaborated political language that might once have served to make sense of social interaction (chapter 3). We developed this insight in chapter 6 when we showed that the Dardenne brothers repeatedly drove their central characters into collisions with others in extreme situations in ways that obliged them to make fundamental choices that in turn restored some ethico-political meaning to a savage universe deprived of inherited values. This discussion of the Dardennes' work helps us to understand why, faced with the same devastated socio-political terrain, other contemporary films also have considerable recourse to the production of moments of transparency as a way of restoring ethical sense to the world.

We noted, however, that there had been an important evolution in the brothers' recent films that could also cast light on the works of other film-makers. While *La Promesse*, *Rosetta* and *Le Fils* all place their characters before a fundamental choice relating to the nature of their interaction with the other, this choice evolves. In *La Promesse*, the son keeps faith with the dead migrant and his widow by breaking with the man, his own father, who oppresses him and exploits migrant labourers. There is thus a third person in the equation. The 'I' and the other, the son and the migrant's widow, can still come together in opposition to the oppressor, thus restoring, *in extremis*, an oppositional politics reduced to its most minimal level. *Rosetta* still figures the oppressor, in the shape of the employer who holds tyrannical power over the worker. Although the heroine never manages to forge even a temporary alliance with Riquet, her fellow worker, her interaction with him is conditioned by the presence of a third party whose arbitrary power explains and inflects interactions in a way that still point towards a political explanation. But, in *Le Fils*, the context is refined still further. The third, exploitative party disappears. All that is effectively left is the collision between two main characters. One can of course argue that the theft of the car radio that sets all in process still connects to a politics by showing the socially destructive nature of a world where commodities take preference over human life, but this is a diminished politics, one that while still constituting a radical refusal of systemic logics no longer points the way to an alliance of the oppressed against an oppressor. The Dardennes' work thus helps us account for the repeated presence of moments of ethical transparency across the body of films discussed while reminding us of the need to question their political value. It is with lessons learned from their work in mind that we can approach the ethical dimension of the other films considered.

We should perhaps begin with a cluster of films that emulate *La Promesse* by staging the encounter between members of the indigenous population and migrant workers, the latter being, as we shall see, emblematic figures of the contemporary period. We have already discussed most of the films concerned, but one of the most interesting, François Dupeyron's recent *Inguélézi* (2003) is one we have yet to consider. *Inguélézi* shows us a woman who, like Igor in *La Promesse*, is pushed to make a commitment to an illegal migrant by an entirely improbable, melodramatic plot turn. The film picks the woman up as she attempts to come to terms with the death of her husband. While driving at night, she stops by a burnt out lorry allowing an illegal Turkish immigrant to climb into the boot of her car without her realizing it. When she discovers his presence, she initially treats him with kindness but wants him to move on. Slowly, she finds herself sucked into an ever greater commitment, until she finally agrees to smuggle him to England, the destination that he has indicated to her through the one word, *Inguélézi*, that seems to bridge the language barrier between them. The film has confronted her with her responsibility towards the other, not as an abstract or theoretical question, but as a presence improbably thrust upon her that forces her to make a clear ethical choice between radical commitment or abandonment. If the underlying logic of the humanitarian is to express an apparent commitment to an other who is in fact held at a distance and safely objectified as a suffering object, *Inguélézi* suggests what a truly ethical humanitarian commitment might mean by abolishing the insulating distance between self and other and by constituting the other as an actively desiring subject. In this it might seem to come close to reproducing what had already been seen in *La Promesse* where Igor also found that he was confronted with his responsibility to the other not in general or abstract terms but in the shape of the demanding, physical presence of the widow and her child. But the crucial political difference lies in the way that *La Promesse* framed the encounter in the presence of a third, exploitative character, a situation that opened the way towards an alliance, no matter how fragile, local or temporary, of the oppressed.

Une Minute de silence, *Sauve-moi* and *Marie-Line* all give a prominent place to migrants in narratives where ethical decisions play a central role. Interwoven with the former's pit closure drama is another narrative strand that centres on a people trafficker and the willing and unwilling East European women he brings in for the Western sex trade. If the mine, its workers and their tradition of collective solidarity represents the old order, the trafficker would seem to represent the temptation, moral confusion and barbarity of the new. One of the two heroes, Mimmo, is initially seduced by this lifestyle and seems ready to work with the trafficker as he feeds off the wreckage of East European state socialism. However, the film's climax pushes him to an ethical decision by making the trafficker's departure coincide with the miners' last stand against the riot police. He can either remain defiantly faithful to his comrades or profit from the human misery of the new order. He chooses the former, aligning himself with values that seem historically condemned but saving himself as an ethical being. If his story is in some ways parallel to that of Igor in *La Promesse*, there is also a key difference that has its roots in the presence of an explicit dramaturgy of class struggle in *Une Minute de silence* and the absence of such a thing in *La Promesse*. While, like other Dardenne characters, Igor has to create values where none seem to exist, Siri's hero can call upon the values of the past to resist a fallen present.

Vincent's *Sauve-moi* develops its ethical dimension in a less concentrated manner. It first shows its main character's sustained support of the Romanian migrant woman he found at the railway station, an attitude that contrasts with the embarrassed indifference of the middle-class doctor that the woman had come to find. Although this initial commitment places material demands upon the hero, it does not cause him major inconvenience. However, the film pushes things further, clarifying its politics, when it has him work for the local debt collector, a position where he is increasingly asked to choose between helping or exploiting those who live in misery. The dilemma is positively resolved when he and the debt collector go to the house of the mother who is asked to pay for the medical tests of her dead son and he sides with the mother against his boss. Like Mimmo in *Une Minute de silence* and Igor in *La Promesse*, he finally refuses to exploit the social ruins of the new world. The film is interesting for how it combines the kind of radicalized humanitarian commitment to the other found in *Inguélézi* with a more overtly political decision to side with the oppressed against the oppressor. This combination is more fully developed in *Marie-Line* whose heroine is pushed to choose between establishing solidarity with her team of legal and clandestine immigrants and siding with the bosses who exploit them and her. By developing its central dilemma in a situation clearly structured by class relations, *Marie-Line* ensures that it pushes its heroine to an ethico-political and not simply an ethical decision. Although its heroine has, as we saw, no words to express the politics behind her choice, the film nonetheless works to develop the figure of the migrant in a class-centred narrative.

The migrant is a key figure of our times. Coming from outside our frame of reference, for reasons that are felt to be obscure, he or she is an incarnation of the opacity of the new world and of our uncertainty about how we should deal with it.[2] But, embodying the unknown consequences of threatening global processes, he or she also seems to offer an easy solution to them. If globalization signifies a more general weakening of boundaries and territorial sovereignty and an increase in cultural and economic flows, policing and exclusion of migrants seems to offer a compensatory restoration of frontiers and comforting reassurance of the rooted belonging of the settled population. Rejection of the migrant is a key component of the contemporary rise of xenophobic nationalism across Europe. By placing an ethical commitment to the migrant at their centre, films first force an engagement with the uncertainty and opacity of the new world and then take clear anti-fascist stances. But these stances, moving to our second point, are not uniform. Where the encounter with the migrant is framed simply as an encounter between self and other, it can only open onto a defensive anti-fascism or a radicalised humanitarianism, that is, a commitment to the other not as mediated, safely distanced figure but as a distinctly inconvenient bodily encumbrance. But where the encounter connects to local struggles against an oppressor or exploiter, where there is a central cast of three and not simply two, it points towards the possibility of moving beyond anti-fascism and humanitarianism towards a renewed political configuration of the social terrain.[3] Thus, if the filmic encounter between the uprooted migrant and the once but no longer integrated working-class remnant might seem to underline above all the devastated nature of the contemporary order, it might be seen, in another way, as opening up a fragile utopian possibility not without echoes of that generated within the *film de banlieue* by the coming together of different ethnic groups within still essentially class-driven narratives (chapter 4). To the extent that the migrant and the disinherited worker can reinvent values such as equality and solidarity outside of the fading boundaries of the nation-state, they might be seen to be looking towards an emergent post-national politics of the sort that must be found to confront neo-liberal globalization.

A similar tripartite dramaturgy of 'hero', other and oppressor can be found, but without the presence of the migrant, in films such as Ameur-Zaïmeche's *Wesh wesh* and Moutout's *Violence des échanges* where characters are faced with violences done to others and have to choose whether to walk away, collaborate actively in oppression or side with the oppressed. Although the main drama of *Wesh wesh* involves the inhabitants of the *banlieue*, the story is broadened by the development of a relationship between the hero and a white woman schoolteacher. The latter is clearly broadly sympathetic towards the *banlieue's* inhabitants, yet the film deliberately pushes her into more decisive ethical stances. Initially this occurs when she is brought face to face with an incident involving racist police officers who are harassing some young *Beurs*. She intervenes courageously. She later discovers that the hero, a victim of the *double peine*, is back in France illegally and has to decide whether she will continue their relationship or break with him. Again she makes a positive commitment. While her involvement might seem to serve above all to broaden the potential appeal of the drama, it serves more specifically to develop the political dimension of the film by underlining the ethical responsibility of individual French people when faced with discriminatory statutes, racism and social exclusion. In its underlying dramaturgy, Moutout's film's opening sequence echoes the staged collision with the racist police in *Wesh wesh*. As its young hero travels to work in a packed metro carriage, he sees a young woman who is being sexually harassed by a smartly dressed man. He could turn away like the rest of the people in the carriage. Instead, he intervenes, telling the man to stop, and finds himself exposed to public embarrassment when the latter seeks to turn the tables and present himself as an innocent victim. Later, when his company put him in a position where he must select people to be sacked, his courage fails him and he goes along with a process with which he is initially deeply unhappy. The film deliberately plays off the initial brave reaction with the later cowardly one as a way of raising the whole issue of the responsibility of the individual in the face of acts of individual or collective violence. The first intervention, while courageous, may not in itself seem a radical political act. But it does nonetheless have the essential cast of three (self, other and oppressor) that we have suggested is necessary for a political framing of social interaction and it does place the hero in an uncomfortable situation, so that it is not a mere gesture without cost. The failure to intervene in the second case builds on this initial dramaturgy, suggesting that the truly courageous act is the one that, opposing oneself to systemic needs, places ones own future at risk while opening up potential alliances with other exposed to systemic violences. What the two moments have in common is that they confront an individual with a choice. The limit that they both share is their failure to develop the potential alliance between hero and oppressed. Both the workforce and the woman on the train are relatively passive figures.

Political Theatre

Closely related to the moment of ethical decision are those instances in the films where, choosing to publicly confront their oppressors, characters courageously step out of their subaltern role, cast off their imposed silencing and denounce existing socio-political arrangements. While the moments of ethical transparency considered above restored a sense of choice and of value to a fallen world, the eminently theatrical moments considered here can be seen as connecting back to a more conventionally framed politics by reminding us that an oppositional movement needs, as Rancière notes, to generate a public disagreement about the existing distribution of social roles and the right to public speech. The problem, as we have noted, is that the stage built by leftist mobilization has been dismantled. When characters in films wish to propose an alternative dramaturgy to that laid down by the existing social order, they must simultaneously create a public stage for it, either by opportunistically appropriating an existing one or by improvising one where none seems to exist.

The strategy of appropriation can be found in several important cases. Liénard's *Une Part du ciel* is an excellent example to begin with. Its leading characters twice lay claim to a stage that has been set up for more conventional purposes and use it to enact their radical theatre. The first case is when one of the two heroines uses a union meeting to mount a public challenge to the union representative, denouncing the union's acceptance of insecure jobs and poor conditions while simultaneously reaffirming the women workers' right to a say in negotiations with management that effectively exclude them. The second example occurs when the other heroine, the imprisoned one, uses a concert party as a way to mount a public challenge to the women prisoners' situation and lack of a voice. Those who perform before her tamely deliver an Edith Piaf love song. Reworking the lyrics of the same song, she launches a call for defiant independence and resistance while asking the women prisoners to face up to their real situation. If the film's prison stands in metaphorically, as we noted, for a society where dissent seems impossible and where people seem trapped within the *status quo*, the woman's taking of political voice allows for a polemical renaming of the social order and the re-inscription of a recalcitrant political subjectivity in a place where it might seem that none could emerge. Along somewhat similar lines, the heroine of Devers's *La Voleuse de Saint-Lubin* uses the trial that follows her theft of food as a forum for launching a public attack on a society where people cannot feed their children adequately and where politicians fail to intervene. The trial is set up to reaffirm property rights and to treat the heroine as an object to be judged but she re-orientates it to refuse the existing social order and to assert her right to public speech (O'Shaughnessy 2005). Something similar occurs in Tavernier's *Ça commence aujourd'hui* when the politician's public meeting is interrupted by the social worker who, refusing his complacent endorsement of the neo-liberal order, reminds him of the lack of resources available to deal with rising social problems. A final example can be found in Charef's *Marie-Line* when the heroine subverts the company prize-giving session by playing the tape of Algerian music that had belonged to the expelled woman migrant worker. In each case, a stage set up to legitimize the *status quo* is heroically commandeered by an isolated figure who casts off his or her allotted passivity and silence to make a defiant claim to a voice. The ingenuity that the characters have to show to create a stage underlines the scarcity of politics in a contemporary order that, in thrall to neo-liberalism, seeks to foreclose the space of dissent.

In other cases, there is no effective public stage that the characters can commandeer. Their performances have to turn neutral public spaces into political stages. One might suggest that this happens in a diffuse way in those *banlieue* films that, drawing on the repertoire of hip-hop, seek to inscribe a collective oppositional subjectivity on the urban landscape through the use of dance, graffiti and scratch music. There is also an element of diffuse theatricality whenever challenges are made to the existing control of public spaces. Thus, for example, in *La Vie rêvée des anges*, when the two heroines seek entry to a nightclub, the bouncers tell them that they could enter if they were dressed attractively. Their reaction is to cast scorn on the club, calling it a 'bourgeois haunt' where they would not wish to set foot, thus throwing back the negative judgement cast upon them while again asserting their right to the exercise of a public voice. This is vestigial political theatre acted out upon a short-lived and fragile stage with disconnected fragments of the old script of class struggle.

The theatrical moments when characters mount or create a public stage to challenge the existing order could be seen as one melodramatic strategy amongst others. But it is important to remember the specific role played by these moments in reasserting an oppositional political subjectivity within a framework of struggle. By underlining the importance of recalcitrant subjectivities, they also help us make sense of films such as *Rosetta* where characters have no public stage or voice and no political script but nonetheless resist. Their refusal of their allotted role and silencing forces, in its own way, the kind of theatrical splitting of the real that Rancière associates with an authentic politics.

Individuals and Families: Melodrama's Stock Cast

The Dardennes' *Rosetta* finds herself at the intersection of individualism and the family but is able neither to become an autonomous individual nor to find security in a residual, dysfunctional family unit. Played out in the interpersonal arena, melodrama's core terrain, her story nonetheless constitutes a fierce critique of the current order, thus seeming, at least partially, to give the lie to politically progressive accounts that have traditionally equated individual and family-centred stories with conservative positions. Condemnation of such stories has occurred on both cinematic, and generic grounds, with inevitable overlaps due to shared ideological roots. The specifically cinematic rejection of individual or interpersonal narratives has essentially two dimensions. On the one hand, narratives built around individuals and their relationships are felt inevitably to allow systemic and collective dynamics and truly political questions to be absorbed or obscured by the interpersonal and the affective. On the other hand, the kind of empathetic engagement that interpersonal dramas engage is considered anathema to the sort of distantiated, questioning and analytical response required by genuinely progressive fictions. Arguments along these lines are exemplified in the sort of response to the films that we earlier identified in the pages of *Cahiers du Cinéma* (chapter 2). But beyond these specifically cinematic objections, there is a broader ideological critique of individualism and the family that can clearly be made. Individualism, put simply, is a key value of the right, with its traditional political hostility to both public or state intervention and to core leftist values of collectivism and solidarity. Along similar lines, the family has conventionally been castigated by progressives as one of the primary loci of moral conservatism and social immobilism. Associated with the reproduction and normalization of existing gender hierarchies and of heteronormative sexualities, the family is something that progressive politics has often felt moved to condemn.

A reminder of a now perhaps unfashionable dislike of the family institution can be found in Badiou's *Le Siècle* (2005), a work which, rather than condemning the twentieth century, as is now prevalent, for its attempts to invent a new humanity, seeks to understand and restore validity to that ambition. Badiou notes the essential dissimilarity between fascist and leftist understandings of the nature of the new humanity to which they both aspired. While fascist aspirations always involved restoration of some lost, authentic identity, the left's vision implied the refusal of all existing ties whether of family, property or nation. The family, more specifically, was viewed as the primordial bastion of egotism, particularism, tradition and narratives of origins. The contemporary retreat from a radical critique of the family is thus symptomatic of a more general evacuation of the political aspiration to invent a better humanity (Badiou 2005: 100). Badiou's comments usefully remind us of the enormous ideological baggage of the family and the difficulty of mobilizing it within a progressive politics. If it ties individuals to their origins, it is clearly an obstacle to any progressive social redefinition. Moreover, to the extent that it legitimizes a selfish preference for those with whom one has blood ties rather than for strangers, it has clearly been and remains open to appropriation by the racist right.

On the more positive side, and returning to the narrower domain of film studies, there has been a considerable re-evaluation of the progressive credentials of melodrama in general and family melodrama in particular. This re-evaluation has been inspired in part by the feminist drive to politicize the personal. It is usefully encapsulated in the following statement by Bratton, Cook and Gledhill: 'rather than displacing the political by the personal, melodrama produces the body and the interpersonal domain as the sites in which the socio-political stakes its struggles' (Bratton, Cook and Gledhill 1994: 1). Chiming with my own work on the political usefulness of contemporary melodrama (O'Shaughnessy 2005) and with an analysis of Cantet's films by Higbee (2004), Bratton, Cook and Gledhill's comments usefully underscore the potential productiveness of the form. But one would also do well to remember the negative baggage it may bear and pay close attention to the precise political uses to which it is put.

Uses of the Family

The family is used in three main ways across the films considered. It is used to show how the working class as a group is deprived of a future, not simply in its values but, more dramatically, in the continuity of its physical being. It is mobilised more generally to figure the consequences of economic violences and class divisions. Finally, it is used to bring out the tension between a preference for consanguinity and an openness to alterity. The family is associated with close bodily proximity and strong affective ties. When it becomes a stage for such broader systemic shifts and questions, it serves to put melodramatic flesh upon them and to give them a strong affective resonance.

A considerable number of films use the family to condense and dramatize the loss of a future. The issue is one that runs through the works of Guédiguian and the Dardenne brothers, but which also comes to the fore, for example, in Devers's *La Voleuse de Saint-Lubin*, Tavernier's *Ça commence aujourd'hui*, Cantet's *Ressources humaines*, Poirier's *Marion* and Beauvois's *Selon Matthieu*. In Guédiguian's films, although the families embody residual resistance and the continued transmission of traditional working-class values, they are nonetheless deeply threatened in their intergenerational continuity. Parents struggle, as we saw, to provide not simply for their children's future but also for their continued physical well-being. Similarly, in *Ça commence aujourd'hui*, some parents find themselves unable to feed their children, to keep them warm, or to get them to school, thus placing their present well-being and their future at risk. *La Voleuse de Saint-Lubin* shows a mother who cannot afford the meat that her daughters need for healthy growth. *Ressources humaines* and *Selon Matthieu* show sons who are forced to deal with their fathers' loss of a job, a redundancy which is a symbolic death in the former case but leads to a real death in the latter. In contrast to Guédiguian's films, the Dardenne brothers show a world from which traditional solidarities have been erased and with which dysfunctional and incomplete families can no longer deal. Neither the unscrupulous single father of *La Promesse* nor the alcoholic single mother of *Rosetta* can help their children make productive sense of their worlds or their encounters with others. Moving things a generation further on, the innocently irresponsible child-father of *L'Enfant* explores what happens when an abandoned generation of children themselves become parents and are forced to reinvent an ethic of care *ex nihilo*. Taken together, the films use the family unit as a way to put flesh upon socio-economic shifts and struggles and give them a powerful affective resonance instead of evoking them in disembodied or abstract terms.

Social representations of the family are traditionally highly normative. The good family is one where parents work selflessly to ensure the current and future security and well-being of their children. Because of this the family is also a powerful site for the generation of a sense of the unnatural. Parents deemed not to care for their children are routinely portrayed as monsters. Indeed, traditional folk tales provide an ample repository of monstrous parents, mother or father figures who abandon or kill children in their hands. The current wave of social cinema is not without its own monstrous families. *Rosetta* shows a mother who walks away from a daughter who may drown and, later, a daughter who attempts to kill not just herself but also her mother. *La Promesse* shows a monstrous father who makes his son an effective accomplice to a killing. *La Ville est tranquille* shows a mother who feels forced to kill her own daughter. *Retiens la nuit* and *Marion* show parents who come close to giving away their children. *Ça commence aujourd'hui* shows a mother who kills herself and her children and a stepfather who beats his stepson. *Le Fils* shows a father who draws back *in extremis* from monstrosity by refraining from killing his son's young murderer, instead working with him to restore the broken paternal link. Rather than suggesting that this monstrosity is somehow intrinsically rooted in the family, the films use it to bring the monstrous face of socio-economic forces and class inequality to the surface. It is precisely because the family is so strongly associated with care and nurturing that destructive behaviours can resonate so strongly in its frame.

However, when the duty to nurture becomes tightly tied to the question of biological relatedness and especially when it is connected to a sense of the national, apparently positive family traits can themselves mutate into something profoundly monstrous and serve to ground and legitimize racism and fascism. Thus, for example, the eponymous heroine of Charef's *Marie-Line* finds that the only way that she can find jobs for her family members is by declaring loyalty to the local Front National. It is only when she widens her maternal role and starts to care for migrant workers and, more particularly, their children that she can save herself. Similarly, in the Dardennes' *La Promesse*, and in the absence of other collective norms of behaviour that would allow positive connection to others, the father/son tie serves as a justification for an abject denial of the rights of migrants. It is only when, forsaking the bonds of blood and realigning himself with an African widow and her child, that the hero can form a new, unconventional and temporary 'family' and, in the process, save himself from monstrosity. More broadly, Guédiguian's films have systematic recourse to unconventional, multi-ethnic and opened-out families as a way of figuring their resolute opposition to racism and of avoiding the pitfalls which might otherwise accompany their family-centred narratives.

In this anti-fascist mobilization of the family the films show some convergence with what has been another notable strand in recent French cinema, a strand that, beginning with the conventional two-parent family, opens it up to gay sexualities. Exemplified by work such as François Ozon's *Sitcom* (1997), Alain Berliner's Franco-Belgian *Ma Vie en rose* (1996) and Josiane Balasko's *Gazon maudit* (1994), this line of film-making has used family settings and the comic genre to help take gay and non-heteronormative cinema firmly into the mainstream while at the same time underlining how the traditional family needs to be profoundly reworked if it is to become useful for sexually progressive works.[4] Situated somewhere between the two strands described, Jacques Martineau's and Olivier Ducastel's remarkable *Drôle de Félix* (1999) tells the story of a gay, unemployed, HIV-positive *Beur* who, after leaving a northern port to find his father and his origins, manages instead to establish a series of temporary and non-biological 'family' links to an adopted 'brother', 'grandmother', 'cousin' and so on. His journey also sees him stumble into a racist murder and refuse to pass through the National Front controlled town of Orange. By connecting its radical reinvention of the family and its refusal of a narrative of origins to an overt anti-fascism, *Drôle de Félix* serves to underline the dangers associated with non-critical appropriations of the family. Although its anti-fascist mobilization of a non-biological, ethnically mixed family converges with that found in films discussed above by directors such as Charef or Guédiguian, its refusal of the traditional, patriarchal family goes a deal further than what is found in the broadly social-realist films discussed above that broadly refrain from any problematization of gender roles and sexual identities within the family.

Patricia Caillé has laid charges of gender conservatism at the door of Cantet's *Ressources humaines* suggesting that, even as the film works to reground a critique of capital, it reverts to a highly conservative representation of the family, showing the crisis of labour as a predominantly male drama while condemning the mother to domesticity and self-effacement. Although the family has a daughter who works in the same factory as the father and son, the drama is essentially played out between the males (Caillé 2004). Caillé's reading is usefully complemented by an article by Will Higbee. Higbee initially notes how recent French social-realist films have focused on incomplete or dysfunctional families, locating their dramas 'in an environment where traditional support networks of community and family have broken down'. He suggests that these representational traits are 'consistent with the critique of the traditional family unit found more generally in contemporary French cinema' (Higbee 2004: 240). Contrasting Cantet's two films with these more general trends, he notes how they attach their dramas to male working-class and middle-class 'professionals'. Because the 'crisis of masculinity' that they figure affects socially integrated groups, the films point to the extent of alienation and social division in today's France (Higbee 2004: 247–8). There are problems with any suggestion that the white, male worker is socially integrated given the prolonged assault on the working class that has taken place over the last thirty years. It may also be dangerous to read Cantet's films through the lens of a 'crisis of masculinity', as analyses framed in such a way risk pushing socio-economic and class questions into the background. Nonetheless, Caillé and Higbee's analyses remind us of the need to consider the gender politics of those films that choose to return to the family to stage their dramas of social disintegration. Broadly speaking, the films considered in this work privilege class and the socio-economic over questions of gender. Although they repeatedly show disrupted, dysfunctional and reworked family structures, their mobilization of the family is driven by a desire to dramatize socio-economic violences and to oppose fascism rather than by an attempt to question the gender and sexual dynamics of the family. But, having made this broad comment, one is immediately driven to qualify it in a range of ways.

One should begin by noting that the distribution of roles amongst the collective cast of the films discussed is clearly gendered. Thus, for example, the defeated, discarded or devalued skilled worker found in Guédiguian's films, Beauvois's *Selon Matthieu*, Jolivet's *Fred*, Richet's *Etat des lieux* and the Dardennes' *Je pense à vous* is an exclusively masculine figure. The drama of unemployment inevitably has a male face in these films, as it does in the *banlieue* films discussed in chapter 4. Such films could undoubtedly be read in terms of a crisis of masculinity, as long as one notes, firstly, its class dimensions, and secondly, that the films show this crisis as a humiliation rather than liberation from an oppressive social role. The exploited, relatively unskilled workers seen in *La Vie rêvée des anges*, *Rosetta*, *La Voleuse de Saint-Lubin*, *Marie-Line*, and in Masson's and Guédiguian's films are women. Women in several of these films move between unemployment and employment, but whereas the loss of skilled male labour is shown as a single, traumatic event, women's unemployment is shown more in terms of an ongoing survival struggle. Although less prominent, unskilled male labour is not absent from the films: the hero of Zonca's *Le Petit Voleur* is a bakery worker; the steelworker in *Je pense à vous* finds himself labouring in the latter part of the film; *Sauve-moi* has male supermarket shelf stackers in addition to its woman hotel cleaner. However, when men are seen performing unskilled work, their personal humiliation tends to come to the fore, whereas, in the case of the women, the exploitative and alienating nature of their labour is what is emphasized. The acquisition of a skilled craft is a route to social re-integration potentially open to the young men of the Dardennes' *La Promesse* and *Le Fils* but not to the heroine of their *Rosetta*. Moreover, in contrast to the unemployed skilled male workers, the women, with the exception of those of Guédiguian, have little or no access to an elaborated discourse of class.

We might be tempted to conclude that the social worlds of the films are thus gendered along traditional and indeed conservative lines. They seem to mount little explicit challenge to the established gender order. It would seem that, seeking to oppose neo-liberalism's hegemonic drive, they are primarily concerned to reassert a class-based construction of the social and to draw attention to economically grounded alienation, domination and exploitation in general and not to their specifically gendered dimensions.

This conclusion requires still further refinement. Although the films have no explicit feminist content, there are elements of what one might call 'latent' feminism running through them. Firstly, their women characters, whether it be the younger ones fighting marginalization or the different Mother Courage figures, actively resist their situation. Even in Cantet's apparently male-centred *Ressources humaines*, the most combative and clear-sighted character is the woman trade unionist. Secondly, as Austin has discussed with specific reference to *Rosetta* and *L'Humanité*, the portrayal of their leading female characters has little or anything to do with cinematic conventions regarding female stardom. Framed by a broadly naturalist *mise-en-scène* and cast as resistant, struggling subjects rather than attractive objects, they clearly avoid the visual fetishism traditionally associated with star performers (Austin 2004: 251–63). Thirdly, some films show groups of women coming together to resist a domination that may be institutional or economic in its roots, but which also wears a predominantly male face. This is clearest in Liénard's *Une Part du ciel*, where the two heroines are ultimately opposed to three males: a trade union representative, a factory manager and a prison governor. But it is also strongly felt in Charef's *Marie-Line*, a film whose heroine refuses to provide the sexual services that her manager requires, renounces her highly traditional dream of marriage with a farmer and instead commits herself to solidarity with the exploited women she supervises. Fourthly, and as we have noted, the films politicize the familial, the personal and the affective in a way which bears echoes of the feminist slogan 'the personal is political'. Fifth, a proportion of the films considered were made by women, namely Devers, Cabrera, Masson and Liénard. These directors all foreground the struggles of women in their films, with Devers and Cabrera paying specific attention to the difficulties faced by struggling single mothers.

Should we thus abandon our initial conclusion and suggest that there is a strong feminist component within the films considered? This would be a precipitate move. The struggle of the women in the films is not in general explicitly framed as a struggle against gendered oppression. Thus, for example, when Isa and Marie in *La Vie rêvée des anges* are told that they would get into a nightclub if they were dressed more suitably for young women, the words of abuse that spring to Marie's lips refer to class and not gender. More generally, the freeing of the women characters from the objectifying constraints of female stardom is part of a broader turn to a 'brute' realism while the taking of political and social struggle into the personal domain seems to draw as much on the melodramatic tradition as on feminist politics. Finally, although the women directors do pay specific attention to the predicaments of working and unemployed women, so do some of the men, such as Guédiguian, Charef and the Dardennes. It is in fact striking that Charef (in *Marie-Line*) and Guédiguian (in *A la vie, à la mort!*) pay specific attention to the sexual harassment or worse of women at work while Beauvois's *Selon Matthieu* shows a keen awareness of the regressive machismo involved in its hero's seduction of his boss's wife as a form of class revenge. In contrast, Cabrera seems to go out of her way to avoid making a specifically gendered claim in *Retiens la nuit* despite what seems a clear debt to a feminist politicization of the personal. Significantly, it is a *woman* trade-unionist rather than the men who tries to maintain precisely the firm dividing line between the political and the personal that feminism worked so hard to problematize. If one were to seek to build a case for a feminist cinema created by women, one would have to look to the celebration of the solidarity of the bakery women and the women prisoners in Liénard's film or to Masson's exploration of the social entrapment of working-class women in *En avoir (ou pas)* and *A vendre*.

Both of Masson's films show young women of working-class or peasant origins who try to liberate themselves from their backgrounds and social pressures placed upon them either by seeking a new life in another town (*En avoir (ou pas)*) or, more radically, by turning the self into a commodity to free it from all ties and obligations (*A vendre*). In both cases the attempts at self-liberation fail because the heroines cannot in the end deny human interconnectedness, because socio-economic circumstances inevitably rein them in and because commodification of the self leads to alienation not freedom. If the autonomous individual is one who has the liberty to chose his or her own social role, it would seem that women from the lower end of society lack the resources to become individuals. By the end of *A vendre*, the heroine has escaped from marriage only to face destitution on the streets of the U.S.A. At the conclusion of *En avoir (ou pas)*, the main protagonist has come back to low-paid work and a relationship with a working-class man.

Impossible Individualism

Although the family as a residual source of social connectivity plays a strong role in a good number of films, others, like those of Masson, show characters who seek to be autonomous individuals. In opposition to the type of argument mentioned above that suggests that individual-centred dramas are formally and ideologically regressive vehicles, I will argue that they can be effectively mobilized for political critique in a number of different ways. Firstly, they can show the impossibility of individualism for the economically disadvantaged. Secondly, they can highlight the ethico-moral self-destruction that follows from an espousal of individualism. Thirdly, they can show how the autonomous individual is a fiction.

Castel has suggested that one of the inevitable consequences of the contemporary weakening of collective solidarities and state support mechanisms is that people are forced to become individuals without the resources to do so successfully. Alongside the narcissistic, conquering individual, who wrongly attributes his or her socio-economic success to purely individual qualities, there arises the figure of the 'negative individual' or 'individual by default', the person who is obliged to take responsibility for him or herself but cannot possibly do so due to a lack of the necessary material and symbolic resources (Castel 1995: 747–69; Castel and Haroche 2001: 128–29). Such 'individuals by default' are key figures in current social cinema. While they do not necessarily offer any positive way forward beyond individualism, they work against its ideological hegemony by showing its destructiveness and ultimately its impossibility. Poirier's *Western* serves as a useful example. As the film begins, its hero seems a model of autonomy as he circulates in his car on the *autoroute*, able to pick up, with consumer-like choice, the hitch-hikers he deems attractive. However, once he loses his job and the money that went with it, his apparent freedom of movement and choice is quickly curtailed showing how his autonomy was entirely contingent on his place within a socio-economic order not of his making. Although his loss of his employment and eviction from the protective bubbles of his car and his wallet are initially experienced as an individual disaster they become liberatory when they permit a positive re-engagement with others.

Rosetta works rather more austerely to show the impossibility of individualism. Its heroine struggles to be independent and not to depend on others or charity but eventually finds that she cannot stand alone. For those at the bottom of the pile, individual autonomy requires a heroic effort that is ultimately unsustainable. Because of its working through of an individual-centred story, *Rosetta* has been rightly called conformist but wrongfully condemned as a result (Garnier 2001). The film shows the profound destructiveness that ensues when an individual internalizes systemic norms of competitive individualism. Under such conditions, each becomes the enemy of each in a way rendered eloquently visible when the heroine is tempted to let a young man drown so that she can take his job. Something similar happens in the case of Marie in *La Vie rêvée des anges*. Whereas Isa, the other heroine, is constantly drawn towards others, Marie is defiantly individualistic, seeking to escape from her precarious social situation through a relationship with a young bourgeois man. When her friend literally stands in her way, she takes a weapon in hand, apparently ready, like Rosetta, to destroy the other to get what she wants. Her relationship fails – the young man is just using her – and she commits suicide. For those at the bottom, espousal of individualism leaves them suspended between destruction of the other (cast as competitor) and destruction of self (when the sought for autonomy and mobility inevitably fail to materialize). At the ethical level, the two destructions merge. By destroying the other and denying interdependence, one effectively destroys the self as a moral being.

Something similar can be found in those very few films that engage with apparently triumphant individualism like Moutout's *Violence des échanges* where, forced to choose between his place as conquering individual and his responsibility to others, the hero makes the wrong choice and effectively destroys himself as an ethical being even as he seems to succeed. A broadly parallel situation arises in Alnoy's *Elle est des nôtres*. As long as the heroine has no permanent job she does not exist in the eyes of those around her. It is not until she has killed someone that she is accepted and, as if by miracle, given a job. We live in a world, the film suggests, where to achieve individual recognition we have to accept the destruction of others and our own moral self-abolition through the internalization of nihilistic systemic norms.

L'Emploi du temps mirrors and complements these two films by again showing that triumphant individualism is destructive of self and others, but by also demonstrating that it is an ontological impossibility. Initially, the hero seems a figure in total command, one who circulates freely and independently in his car. Because he visits decisions on others less well placed, he seems a powerful figure. However, as we have noted, it is soon revealed that he has been sacked by his company because of a tendency to keep on driving rather than turn off where he was required. Rather than springing from him as an individual, his apparent mastery was entirely dependent on his place in the system and was thus a contradiction in terms. He could only be a conquering individual when not his own person. His invention of a false job initially seemed to give him a genuine liberty. He could dispose of his time as he saw fit and go where he wished. Yet, as we saw, this autonomy is both materially unsustainable (self-determination is expensive) and a self-deception (he is connected to others and thus constrained in his actions). A trip to the mountains with his wife underlines the impasse he finds himself in. When the couple go for a walk in the snow they nearly lose each other in the mist. While the height they are at and the emptiness of the terrain seem to reflect the hero's aspiration for heroic freedom, the surrounding emptiness shows that he can only be free outside of society. Because he is a social being who exists through his connection to others, when he breaks free from them they literally fade in the mist. He must come back from the brink to accept connectedness to others and systemic constraints. Poised between alienation within the social order and self-abolition outside it, the hero shows that the autonomous individual has nowhere to go.

Taken as a group, the different films work to mount a sustained assault on the ideological individualism that is currently hegemonic by showing that those at the bottom do not have the resources to be individuals, that competitive individualism involves the destruction of self and others and that, based on a denial of human interdependence and systemic constraints, the autonomous individual is an ultimate impossibility. The turn to individual stories is not simply a repeat of the earlier 'error' of undermining progressive content through the adoption of a cinematically and ideo-logically regressive form. It is a productive response to a situation where collective instances have been substantially weakened and individualism seems unchallenged.

Conclusion

In the years following 1968, a revolutionary new cinema seemed called for that would be adequate to the radical socio-political break that was sought. Contemporary film works in the aftermath of a defeat. Its mobilization of individual and family-centred stories and melodramatic strategies in a broadly realist mode of film-making might seem to represent a return to discredited forms symptomatic of a broader abandonment of radical aspirations. Post-1968 theory rejected realism because of its tendency to immobilize the world, locking people and structures into their existing states in a way that could only be reactionary. Dramas that developed emotional involvement through empathetic engagement with characters were condemned for their escapism and their incapacity to generate the kind of distantiation necessary to produce actively reflective spectators. Films that focused on individuals were felt inevitably to subvert whatever progressive content they might have had through their failure to focus on the structural and the collective (chapter 2). While we should not simply reject these judgements, we should recognize that they were contingent on a specific set of historical circumstances and thus cannot simply be transposed to the very different circumstances of the present. We instead need to evaluate the effectiveness of a given set of choices of form and content in a specific context. What has been argued in this chapter is that, far from simply reproducing old errors, the contemporary films considered deploy a range of strategies with considerable political effectiveness. Thus, rather than merely generating emotional responses, melodrama has become an essential vehicle for restoring eloquence and ethical transparency to a real that, following the implosion of the old leftist imaginary, no longer seems to speak to us. Far from being simply regressive, family and individual-centred narratives have become useful vehicles for figuring the destructive impact of triumphant neo-liberalism. The individuals figured by the films are not simply immobilized by absorption into an existing reality, they are shown to struggle against it. Through their struggles and their movements, they show their refusal of that reality while simultaneously bringing social fault lines and barriers back into visibility. Finally, through their determination to exist as subjects and their capacity to mount theatrical challenges to the existing distribution of the right of meaningful public speech, they refuse both their silencing and their objectification while contesting the current evacuation and pacification of the political terrain.

We suggested in chapter 2, drawing on Bazin via Jeancolas, that the films considered might have key traits in common with Italian post-war neo-realist films, not simply in terms of their often loosely structured narratives, their deliberately unpolished look and their frequent recourse to amateur performers, but more importantly in the way they stage an encounter with an unpredigested real, a real that, no longer able to call upon an existing politics or framework of values, drives us to find meanings and a politics retrospectively. One aspect of neo-realist cinema that Bazin lamented was its melodrama, an unfortunate characteristic that he felt to be rooted in the film's Italian provenance rather than in any intrinsic necessity.[5] Yet, it could be that both the original neo-realist films and their contemporary descendants needed to be melodramatic, the former because they had to make meaning re-emerge from the ruins of the post-war world, the latter because they operate in the ruins of the old leftist imaginary and in the social wasteland built by neo-liberal globalization.

Notes

1. As Brooks notes, the pantomime was one of the main precursors of the melodrama. Its capacity for non-verbal communication was honed at a time when only certain Parisian theatres were allowed to perform scripted works and others had to resort to and perfect mute forms (Brooks 1976: 62–4).
2. This vision of the migrant draws on Zygmunt Bauman's rather broader notion of the stranger and his or her power to disrupt. Bauman writes, 'The stranger is, by definition, an agent moved by intentions that one can at best guess but would never know for sure. The stranger is the unknown variable in all equations calculated when decisions about what to do and how to behave are pondered' (Bauman 2003: 106).
3. Generally, the films studied tell us relatively little about why the migrant has come. Their place of origin and the places that they have been through remain firmly off-screen, and their reasons for coming, although hinted at, are not usually explored. Coming from outside story space, they remind us that what happens within that space connects to global processes. But whereas there was once a language of leftist internationalism and of anti-colonialism to make sense of processes elsewhere, the enigmatic presence of the migrant serves to remind us of the lack of a framework to connect what we see to a broader understanding.
4. For a discussion of the reworking of the heteronormative family in recent French cinema, see Ince (2001).
5. In his discussion of Italian neo-realism, Bazin approvingly notes how the films reject the well structured plots of conventional fictions as part of their opening onto the

real before adding, 'unfortunately the demon of melodrama, which Italian film-makers can never quite resist, wins out here and there, reintroducing a dramatic necessity with rigorously predictable effects' (*'malheureusement le démon du mélodrame, auquel ne savent jamais résister tout à fait les cinéastes italiens, gagne ça et là la partie, introduisant alors une nécessité dramatique aux effets rigoureusement prévisibles'*) (Bazin 1990: 275).

8

ELUSIVE CAPITAL

Completing an exploration of the new face of committed cinema in France, this chapter approaches the vital question of its treatment of space. Previous chapters have shown how the pieces of an old dramaturgy of class can still be put to work to oppose neo-liberal triumph and how essentially melodramatic strategies can be mobilized to restore a lost eloquence and transparency to social suffering and struggle. However, what they have not dealt with sufficiently is the spatial asymmetry between on-screen resistances and an increasingly globalized causality that has effectively moved out of story space. Chapter 3 provided a genealogy of this asymmetry by underlining the disabling consequences of a double spatial shift: firstly, globalizing capital has been able to abstract itself from local face-to-face confrontations: secondly, a totalizing leftist dramaturgy that had once raised local, particular struggles to a general level has come apart. It could be that those critics who accuse the current wave of films of simply repeating old errors ironically neglect their main Achilles' heel by omitting the crucial spatial dimension from consideration. Their real weakness is perhaps not their apparently hackneyed recycling of the resources of realism and melodrama but a crucial inability to figure the systemic dynamics of globalizing capital within the narrow spatial framework of realist fiction. This chapter explores this central question, suggesting how one might understand the novelty of the spatial dynamics of the films while paying particular attention to strategies that they mobilize in order to compensate for the limitations of spatially circumscribed fictions. These limitations will be underlined by a contrast with the current wave of anti- and counter-globalization documentaries.

A provisional way to understand the novel spatiality of current social realist film is through an examination of how it proposes a reworking of the symbolic geography of the nation by choosing to focus on the margins rather than the centre, by revisiting the world of work and by figuring a decidedly unpastoral rural and regions in the throes of deindustrialization. Thus, for example, *La Haine* and *Wesh wesh* take us to the rundown outer suburbs of Paris rather than exploiting the photogenic and cinematically hyper-exploited locations at the city's heart. Thus too, films by Dumont, Tavernier, Zonca, Beauvois and Masson locate part or all of their action in the socially deprived north of France, an area separated by a national boundary but only a small distance from the equally depressed Belgian town of Seraing where, since the beginning of their careers, the Dardenne brothers have stubbornly and faithfully chosen to work. At the opposite end of France, Guédiguian has, until his recent Paris-centred Mitterrand film, *Le Promeneur du Champ de Mars* (2004), obsessively returned to Marseille and its deindustrialized suburb of L'Estaque, thus largely avoiding the more familiar and picturesque locations in the city's historic port area as well as the Provençal countryside that, since Claude Berri's *Jean de Florette* (1985) has become a favourite location for heritage cinema. Living in the countryside, Poirier has nonetheless refused to feed off the tourist charms or folksy stereotypes of rural France, but has instead chosen to put social problems (poverty, unemployment, racism) back into a zone from which they are normally evacuated. The films thus propose, as Beugnet (2000: 55–58) accurately notes, a symbolic geographical reordering entirely consistent with a commitment to the representation of social suffering and struggle. If a larger budget and more purely commercial French cinema seems intent on either peddling a commodified version of the national on international image markets or on producing 'post-national' English language or international genre films (Danan 2000), the low to medium budget cinema figured in this volume might seem resolutely national in its address. Substantially dependent for survival on distribution within France's borders, it brings issues of national concern to the public's attention. To the extent that this same cinema is used to stimulate public debate both within and outside the commercial cinema circuit (chapter 1), it might seem to be defending a French republican civic culture in the face of a commodified, international image market while opening a gap between a cinema that merely seeks competitive advantage in global markets and one that actively seems to resist globalization. But the resistance generated by the latter would begin to ring decidedly hollow if, at the level of representation, the films were profoundly unable to figure the dynamics of neo-liberal globalization and were only able to bring its local consequences to public attention. Only some more detailed examination of the films will allow us to gauge how effectively they respond to this challenge. Cabrera's *Retiens la nuit* is a good place to start.

A Novel Spatiality

In *Retiens la nuit*, the situation of both the unemployed Nadia and the strikers is intrinsically connected to the ability of capital to relocate its production and to undermine the power of nation-states and the position of the working class. Neither the state-led attack on public sector workers to which the strike is a response nor Nadia's experience of economic vulnerability can be understood outside this broader dynamic. There is a moment in the middle of the film when, riding in the strikers' van round Paris, Nadia picks up a little plastic hippopotamus from the dashboard and reads the words 'Made in China' from the back of it, thus providing fleeting connection to a causality that has migrated outside of story space. As the film ends, the CGT representative's speech makes a more adequate connection to the systemic, describing the mechanisms by which workers are kept cowed and set against each other. Unlike Nadia, he has the inherited symbolic resources to name broader processes. Yet the strikers' actions are addressed initially to the state as their employer and guarantor of their social rights, rather than directly to global capitalism. Compared to an earlier generation of political films, there has been a radical shift in causal and spatial dynamics. As we noted when we considered Karmitz's *Coup pour coup* and Godard's and Gorin's *Tout va bien* (chapter 3), there used to be a broad spatio-symbolic symmetry between the two sides involved in social conflict. At a local level, this meant that an enemy could be identified and opposed, face to face. At a more general level, the universalizing frame of class and anti-imperial struggle meant that each local struggle had a general significance and, rather than being condemned to narrow particularity, was implicitly international in its reach. *Retiens la nuit* reminds us how this symmetry has been lost.

A recent work by Balibar can help us explain this shift and will provide the theoretical backbone for this chapter. Balibar suggests that it is useful to distinguish three types of universalism: the real, the fictional and the ideal. The real universal is made up of the concrete material interconnections and flows that bring together different spaces. The fictional universal is embodied by instances such as the great universal religions and, in more recent historical time, the nation-state form that serve to locate and identify people symbolically within global space. As Balibar notes, drawing on Hegel, the nation forcibly detached people from local allegiances but offered a compensatory reattachment of identity at a higher level by giving them a national belonging that simultaneously located them within an international order. In implicit opposition to this fictional universal is the third form, the ideal, as expressed classically in the French revolutionary declaration of the universal rights of man or in left-wing internationalism. While the fictional locates people, it does so in a way that is not of their choosing. The ideal, in contrast, is how those normally denied a voice may begin to lay claim to the spaces to which they have been assigned or to challenge their boundaries. Currently, Balibar notes, the real universal reaches ever more intensely into people's lives as they are connected to globalizing economic flows (Balibar 1997: 412–54). At the same time, there has been a weakening of the other two instances. The nation-state no longer provides the same level of protection either of its national economy or of its citizens: the real and symbolic homes it once offered now no longer offer the shelter they once did. More traumatically still, as we noted in chapter 1, left-wing internationalism has effectively collapsed. What this means is that, at a time when the need to make sense of material global processes (Balibar's real universal) is at its most urgent, the resources that one might call upon to make sense of them, to locate oneself within them or to challenge them have either weakened or collapsed.

The drama of *Retiens la nuit* suggests how this momentous shift might work its way through at the narrative level. The railway workers' action in the film can be seen as an interpellation of the failing mediating instance, the nation, again demanding of it the protections that it once afforded. Nadia's own drama seems trapped at the level of Balibar's real universal, that is, although her socio-economic vulnerability is intrinsically connected to global processes, she has no symbolic resources or ideal values with which to locate herself within those processes or to oppose them. She lives, one might say, at the level of a real profoundly conditioned by the global but experienced as immediate local need. Part of the political work that the film does lies in its refusal to leave her at this level. By having her read 'Made in China' on a material object, a fragment of the globalized real, the film enables her to connect at a minimal, sub-sentence level to causes that she can no longer describe or confront in a way that is perhaps derisory but which avoids the politically debilitating self-enclosure of the story. But the film goes further. Her trip to the edge of the capital and her improbable collision with the trade-unionists effectuate a forcible reconnection of her embodied local misery with the national, political level or, in Balibar's terms, with the fictional universal. Moreover, her final realignment with the strikers' fight begins to suggest how a broad front might be recreated to oppose neo-liberalism, rescuing the workers from defense of a particular interest and Nadia from mere embodied suffering in the name of a universal ideal of solidarity.

Retiens la nuit helps point towards the novelty of the causal and spatial dynamics of the films we are examining here. There has been, one might say, a double dislocation with which they must cope at a narrative level. On the one hand, a causality rooted in global economic processes has migrated out of story space and effectively become disembodied. On the other, connection to the nation-state, for so long the implicit or explicit frame of French cinematic narratives, can no longer be taken for granted. Almost all the films considered here focus on the struggles of groups or individuals who no longer seem able to oppose or even confront what oppresses them. Nor are they able to connect meaningfully to some larger body that could raise their struggle from the local to the national or international levels. In many of the films the characters no longer even have a language to name what has happened to them. The consequences of the global are all around them but they cannot insert them into a meaning-giving narrative. What we will therefore now do is track these shifts across the broader corpus of films. We will pay particular attention to how they resist politically debilitating entrapment within the local by figuring dislocation within their visual economy, by finding ways to 'short-circuit' from the fragment to the totality, by interpellating the national as failing mediating instance and, finally, through recourse to choral structures that, by allowing some assemblage of fragments, help restore a lost sense of totality.

Spatio-symbolic dislocation is not the only issue in *Retiens la nuit*. The film also underlines how mobility has become a key issue in contemporary realist cinema. At a macro-level, the strikers' inability to confront the forces that they oppose in any direct way points to the profoundly unequal mobilities of capital and labour at the current time. While the former seems limited to spatially circumscribed struggles, the latter is able to outflank local oppositions and distance itself from the resistances it provokes. The film at least partially compensates for this disabling asymmetry by productive use of the micro-spatial level. Thus, rather than fixing its heroine in the social context of exclusion, it allows her to move, to test out social barriers, to signal her refusal of fixity and to provoke the collision with the railway workers that will force a dialogue where none previously existed. While other films may differ in their occupation of the macro- and micro-spatial levels, mobility will repeatedly reveal itself as a key issue. We will return to it in the second half of the chapter.

Figuring Dislocation

There is a cluster of films that, following in the footsteps of the Dardennes' *Je pense à vous*, figure two different scales of narrative within the same story space and thus retain residual access to a totalizing explanatory frame. In that earlier film, the epic story of class defeat that preceded and explained the origins of the main, small story of individualized social struggle was still part of the film narrative. However, in most of the other films that we will consider here, the epic battle is lost before the film starts. This is the case, for example, in the Dardennes' own *La Promesse* where the empty factories provide mute testimony to the defeat of the organized working class. The small foreground drama of hyperexploitation, fragmentation and disarray finds its origins in this silent backcloth. The film holds background and foreground in tension to invite us to ponder the nature of their interconnection. There is, for example, an early sequence showing the father and son of the story drive a new contingent of illegal immigrants into the old industrial town. For some of the sequence the camera is situated inside the van in very close proximity to the faces of the chief protagonists of the micro-drama at the film's heart. But at other moments the van is held in extreme long shot, a small object amongst the massive, hollowed out factories. Because none of its characters have access to a totalizing discourse of analysis or opposition, the film cannot directly engage with the causes of what it shows. But by holding two contrasting spatialities in tension, it can invite us to make connections between the bigger story that has ended and the smaller story enacted in its ruined décor while underlining the claustrophobic intensity of the latter.

Something similar can be said about much of Guédiguian's work. The characters of all his films tend to move in spaces that have become too big for them but serve to explain their smaller foreground dramas. Thus, for example, *Marius et Jeannette* places a good deal of its action in the massive, decaying space of a cement works with long shots emphasizing the shrunken scale of the story. Panning shots from the works show us the Mediterranean and remind us of Marseille's role as an international port and major industrial city. The film's other chief locale, the courtyard occupied by Jeannette and her neighbours, has more adequate dimensions for the small group drama at the film's heart. The contrast between the two locations reminds us that the small drama has its roots in a much larger story. The pattern is the same in *A la vie, à la mort!* Its chief location, a nightclub, is of suitable size for the group drama at the film's centre, but the camerawork repeatedly lets us see the warehouses and ports which an organized working class once occupied. The consequence of this is that Guédiguian's films figure capitalist globalization as something that has passed through the social terrain rather than as ongoing global process. This failure to encapsulate the present, transnational dynamics of globalized capital might seem to underline the limitations of Guédiguian's work in particular and conventionally framed fictions in general. Yet, by attaching his small stories to the epic that went before them, Guédiguian holds on, *in extremis*, to the sense of totality that is essential for engagement with globalized processes. A similar analysis might be applied to other films considered in chapters 4 and 5. Films such as Jolivet's *Fred*, Vincent's *Sauve-moi* and Tavernier's *Ça commence aujourd'hui* also place their small-scale dramas in the hollowed out spaces of class struggle, thus bearing at least mute testimony to a totalizing causality that cannot be figured in their smaller foreground dramas.

Short-circuiting to the Global

Another way mobilized by the films considered to connect their narratives to a global frame that lies beyond their narrow spatiality is to effectively short-circuit from the fragment to the global by feeding off globalization itself. Tavernier's *Ça commence aujourd'hui* offers a prime example of this. When a locally based politician is delivering a speech endorsing the triumphant neo-liberal order, he is stopped by a social worker who complains that local social services have lost two posts, a nursery teacher and a psychologist, that they can ill spare. The politician replies with statistics, proudly boasting that their provision is 93 per cent of the national average. The social worker replies that these figures mean nothing on the ground. Two levels of discourse thus meet in a transparently engineered but eloquent collision. One is drawn from the currently dominant language of global competitiveness, the other rooted in the local and the immediate. While, the latter can only appeal to pressing need and suffering and not to any overarching principle or totalizing knowledge, it can reach the universal negatively by disrupting the confident claims of the former and simply saying, 'what you say works everywhere does not work here'.

Something similar happens in Kassovitz's *La Haine*. The film's three main protagonists are decidedly depoliticized and have no overarching language to connect to the global processes that contribute to their social marginalization but the film still finds a way to look beyond its own story space. The moment of short-circuiting occurs when Saïd, the *Beur* character, stops by something that his two companions, absorbed in argument, seem not to notice. It is a large advertising hoarding with a poster picturing the globe and a caption saying *le monde est à vous* or 'the world is yours'. Connecting to a different spatial frame, the poster gives what might seem a purely local drama a new resonance. The young men's painful and repeatedly constricted mobility already gives the lie to the utopian promise of a poster which offers access to the globe as commodified space. However, Saïd modifies the caption, crossing out the 'v' of 'vous' and replacing it with an 'n' so that it now reads *le monde est à nous* or 'the world is ours'. Although superficially tiny, the change is profoundly significant. It suggests a simultaneous refusal of the poster's consumerist interpellation and a minimalist but resonant reinscription of a political subjectivity that, having no universalizing language to oppose the current order, can only lay claim to the universal by appropriation of the code of the dominant. A similarly minimalist but telling connection to the global occurs in a scene we have already considered from *Selon Matthieu* where the hero discusses the impact of globalization with his wealthy mistress. As she explains its ruthless and apparently unopposable logics, the hero simply comments that it is disgusting, apparently a hopelessly personal, emotive response to systemic violences. But, because neo-liberalism presents itself as something that is universally valid, each local opposition or rejection punctures its hegemonic pretensions while at the same time turning its universal drive against itself. In their different ways *Selon Matthieu*, *La Haine* and *Ça commence aujourd'hui* all operate a short-circuit to the space of the global or the systemic from within their own relatively narrow spatial economies.

The Nation and its Failing Mediation

A range of the films we are discussing bear witness to the disintegration of the nation while some move beyond this stage to interpellate the state and to remind it of its failure to fulfil its traditional role of mediating between the local and the universal. Zonca's *La Vie rêvée des anges* is an excellent example to begin with. The film is set in the north of France, moving between prosperous Lille and decaying Roubaix and thus having an apparently tightly circumscribed spatial geography. As it starts, one of its two heroines, the rootless Isa, arrives at the house of an old friend to seek help. The friend has gone to Belgium to find work. Isa is then offered work by a Yugoslavian sweatshop owner. During their first conversation, he recounts how his daughter now works in the U.S.A. making military and police uniforms. This complex criss-crossing of boundaries suggests that the dividing line between national and non-national has substantially blurred. Isa, her absent friend, the Slav and his daughter are all part of a transnational, low-wage economy, a Third World that is no longer outside the prosperous West but which has become part of it. Isa is not only homeless literally but rootless symbolically, as the nation no longer provides her with a meaningful home. At the same time, the fact that the Slav's daughter is making uniforms underlines the transition from a protective to a repressive state.

Something similar might be said of *La Haine*. It is no accident that Kassovitz sends his protagonists on an abortive trip from their *banlieue* exile into the heart of their nation's capital. The threesome are not socially unintegrated. It is rather that they are no longer integrated in any meaningful way into a national space. Thus, it is noticeable from the start that far from being locked into their respective Jewish, African and North African 'ethnic' origins, they all share a post-national, essentially transatlantic culture and are thus, in Balibar's terms, tightly tied into the real universal. Vinz, the Jewish character, for example, imitates the famous 'Are you looking at me?' scene from Martin Scorsese's *Taxi Driver* (1976). More broadly, the youths' tagging, break-dancing and scratching are all absorbed from hip-hop, a cultural form that migrated from the U.S.A. to France in the 1980s and 1990s. However, what the abortive trip into Paris reveals is that they have no place in the capital, the nation's symbolic heart.

This is clearly signalled when, seeking to imitate a gesture by the hero of Eric Rochant's *Un Monde sans pitié* (1988), one of the trio tries to make it appear as if he has turned out the lights of the Eiffel tower by clicking his fingers at the time they are due to go out. He mistimes his gesture and the light stays on underlining his status as outsider. The group's marginality is also indicated eloquently by a scratched song in the film which mixes Edith Piaf's archetypically French 'Je ne regrette rien' with rap group N.W.A.'s 'Fuck tha Police'. The song would seem to be suggesting that it has become impossible for the young *banlieuesards* to integrate into a nation-state when their main relationship with it now passes through its repressive wing. Although the film shows a nation that no longer integrates, it can also be seen as an interpellation of the national. Kassovitz could have left his characters in the *banlieue* and registered an apparently narrow social drama but by sending them into the heart of the capital he very deliberately points to the failure of the state to create a cohesive national society. We are led to a not dissimilar conclusion by Siri's *Une Minute de silence*. Labour used to be one of the classic mechanisms through which French society integrated successive waves of immigrants. But what Siri's film shows is that deindustrialization has the capacity to undo the apparently complete integration of groups such as Poles and Italians who had once seemed so securely absorbed into French society. Tellingly, one of the hero's parents advises him to move on to Australia. France now only arouses the comment *che cazzo di paese!* or 'what a fucking country!'

The disintegration of the French nation is suggested in a different way by Poirier's *Marion*. As the film begins, people from the area where the action is set are mobilizing to prevent the closure of their local railway station, an event that would separate them from a network which has traditionally been one of the most powerful symbols of the connection of the national territory. Due to their poverty, the story's central family have a problematic connection to another national grid, the EDF (Electricité de France), an increasingly market-driven branch of public service. However, the local school seems to offer a last safe bastion of positive national integration. It is a place where republican values of civilization and civic solidarity are taught, apparently free from market pressures. However, as the rich Parisian couple in the film tell Marion's parents, it is only by sending their daughter to one of the leading Paris *lycées* that they can ensure that she gets the best possible education. Rather than ensuring integration, the school thus now seems to underline the effective detachment of local spaces from national networks of power. However, by his deliberate evocation of erstwhile agents of national connectivity, Poirier, like Kassovitz, is reminding the Republic of its duty to integrate its citizens. A parallel dynamic can be identified in Tavernier's *Ça commence aujourd'hui* with its deliberately orchestrated interplay of school, social services, politicians, police force and EDF. Rather than integrating the population into the

national as it might once have done, the school at the film's heart finds itself
sucked, as we saw, into the local, having to tend to immediate needs no
longer taken in hand by either political instances or social services. Things
are at their grimmest when the poor local family is disconnected by the EDF
and when disaffected children find themselves facing the police, the
repressive wing of the state, after vandalizing the school. Although
considerably more upbeat, the closing school fête tends to confirm the
detachment of the local from the national. Those involved are making a
personal commitment that serves to underline official inaction and the
effective detachment of the margins from the centre.

Reassembling the Fragments

Ça commence aujourd'hui is also notable for its use of a partially developed
choral structure. Built essentially around its hyperactive central figure, it
nonetheless achieves a relatively rounded picture of social implosion by
using the primary school at its heart to assemble a series of individual
stories. It thus shows that fragmentation can be at least partially resisted by
narrative structures that hold together several different strands and thus
retain some sense of totality. Guédiguian's *La Ville est tranquille* has a far
more fully developed choral structure. Its own ambition to hold on to a
sense of totality is indicated by the opening panning shots that capture the
whole of Marseille. By intercutting thereafter between the trajectories of a
range of powerful and disempowered individuals from different social
groups, the film retains a sense of a whole even as it notes fragmentation.
It thus reminds us that local miseries must be reconnected back to their
structural causes. But what it cannot of course do is to maintain that there
is, at the present time, an oppositional voice that operates at the same
spatial scale as neo-liberal globalization. This was the point underscored by
the derisory 'Internationale' sung in a range of languages by the lone voice
of the taxi driver (chapter 4). But the evocation of the 'Internationale' is
enough to remind us of the scope that an oppositional movement must
have. By developing a choral structure while underlining the absence of an
oppositional choir, Guédiguian's film finds its own way to resist debilitating
enclosure within the fragmentary without pretending that any particular
fragment has the ability to reach outside itself. Despite developing a
broader reach than other films considered it tends to underline how the
different fictions considered can only resist a politically debilitating self-
enclosure by working against their own raw material. As their characters
become forcibly detached from broader solidarities, as their struggles
become disconnected from struggles in other places, and as their voices are
silenced and their language lost, they must inevitably fight to reach outside
their narrow spatial frame thus forcibly raising the question of the

suitability of essentially realist fiction as a vehicle for critique. A similar question could equally be derived from Cantet's brilliant *L'Emploi du temps*, a film that, as we saw (chapter 5), is able to engage with both the powerful and the disempowered, the local and the international precisely because it partially breaks free from the constraints of realist narrative by placing a fantasist at its heart. Is fiction, especially its realist variant, simply the wrong vehicle for oppositional film?

The Global Reach of Documentary

For so long the poor cousin of fiction, documentary has recently experienced unprecedented box-office success within France. Some of it has been due to the tremendous popularity of nature documentaries, including such films as Claude Nuridsany and Marie Pérenou's *Microcosmos* (1995) and Luc Jacquet's *La Marche de l'Empereur* (2004). Some is owed to the box office power of U.S. films such as those of Michael Moore. But some is also undeniably due to the remarkable revival of indigenous critical documentaries since the mid-1990s. These can usefully be divided into two main categories that, for ease of labelling, one can call the anti-globalization film and the counter-globalization documentary. While the former sets itself the task of tracking the devastating consequences of factory closures and relocations, the latter is more interested in pinning down the operations of the powerful and in tracking emergent oppositions to them (Marie 2005). The two categories have clearly different spatio-temporal frames. Films recounting factory closures and resistances to them – Luc Decaster's *Rêve d'usine* (2002) and Ariane Doublet's *Les Sucriers de Colleville* (2002) being notable recent examples – tend overwhelmingly to focus on a single locale over an extended period and thus deploy a spatial economy not dissimilar to that of the realist fictions that we have been examining. Their strength and their weakness is to be committed to today's losers. Whereas contemporary capital is all too willing to sever its ties to any specific place or group of people, these films devote themselves to spatially grounded collectivities and refuse their silencing and their invisibility. They seem condemned to track capital only at the moment it withdraws from specific outposts and to record resistance only as it winds down and loses its collective voice. This might seem politically unproductive. However, one should not underestimate the cumulative effect of films that repeatedly bring the local damages caused by neo-liberalism to public view.

A distinctly different spatiality is deployed by those films that we have termed counter-globalization documentaries and that devote themselves to tracking both systemic logics and emerging transnational resistances. To begin with, they are more consciously investigative. That is, refusing to simply record events, they are typically driven by an inquiring narrative presence (usually that of the documentary-maker) and set out to track down some aspect of the functioning of the global economy or of international institutions. To achieve this, they have to imitate capital's own mobility by becoming 'road documentaries' that make transnational movement part of their own narrative or by cross-cutting between different places, thus underlying the simultaneity and connectedness of processes in different locations. Thus, for example, Marie-France Collard's *Ouvrières du monde* (2000) showed the operations of Levi's, the jeans manufacturer, not simply in Belgium and France, where the predictable cost-cutting factory closures were underway, but in Turkey, Indonesia and the Philippines, countries in which the multinational was able to find lower wages, low or non-existent taxation and weak worker protection and collective rights. While the film might seem to lead in some of the same pessimistic directions as others that recount factory closures, its broader frame allows it to bring the systemic to the fore and to underline the need for transnational action and resistances (Marie 2005). By establishing within its own framework the beginnings of a dialogue between European and Asian workers, the film avoids the pitfalls of national corporatism while pointing the way towards the kind of international solidarity that needs to develop. Jonathan Nossiter's *Mondovino* (2003) shows a similar mobility in its desire to track the impact of economic globalization on the wine trade, notably its tendency to produce a transnational homogenization of taste driven by *de facto* convergence between leading North American wine critics and dominant producers. The film is decidedly unhurried and allows the different figures it interviews time and space to express themselves. It is nonetheless notable for a transnational mobility that takes in the U.S.A., France, Italy and Argentina, recording local resistances, keeping systemic causal dynamics in clear view, while still finding time to figure the presence, at the edges of the narrative, of counter-globalization activists as they prepared for demonstrations in Florence. *Mondovino* feeds off very real but nonetheless spatially dispersed and not altogether homogeneous struggles but is able to develop a sense of an overarching conflict by deploying its central trope of collaboration and resistance and through a judicious cross-cutting between places and voices that brings divergences into clear visibility and concentrates antagonisms.

Vincent Glenn's *Davos, Porto Alegre et autres batailles* (2003) has less inherent need for transnational inquiry and mobility as its central confrontation had already been staged by the organizers of the World Social Forum (WSF) in the Brazilian town of Porto Alegre when they timed their event to coincide exactly with the annual gathering of the corporate and political luminaries of the World Economic Forum (WEF) in the Swiss resort of Davos. The film was nonetheless able to bring a variety of techniques to bear to sharpen the sense of a confrontation between forces.

At a more obvious level, it established clear but effective contrasts between the cold colours and wintry scenes in Davos and the vibrant summer colours of Porto Alegre. More subtly, it used images of closed doors and security guards to underline its inability to gain access to Davos. The resultant need to rely on television images of the WEF develops a sharp contrast between the top-down, one-way, mediated communication of one location and the more democratic, participatory and face-to-face debate of the other. Access to some of the leading voices of counter-globalization at Porto Alegre also allowed Glenn's film to bring forward an elaborated counter-expertise with a global reach. Although it relies on cross-cutting rather than on a now impossible face-to-face encounter, *Davos, Porto Alegre* starts to restore some of the elements of an overarching narrative of opposition. It identifies two clear camps each of which seeks to project its voice on a global stage. If one, the WSF, as yet has no clear programme and may not indeed want one, it can nonetheless confidently identify what it does not want and claim intellectual and political legitimacy for that position.

This brief and inevitably schematic turn to documentary might seem to suggest that it is far better equipped than realist fiction to come to grips both with systemic features of globalizing capital and with the emerging face of counter-globalization. If documentaries that commit themselves to registering the local effects of factory closures seem broadly similar in their reach to fictions, counter-globalization documentaries have a very different spatial scope to them. Fictions are not, of course, tied to one place. As we shall shortly see, many of the films discussed derive some of their political force from the mobility of their characters. But these mobilities are generally more local and, as we shall see, put to different political purposes. Concerned with small, relatively unchanging groups of characters, fiction finds it hard to pin down the systemic except in so far as it impacts on the group concerned and not in its more impersonal dimensions. Held back by the demands of verisimilitude and tied to characters deprived of an overarching oppositional language, it cannot easily develop a counter-expertise either by placing an inquiring narrator at its centre or by bringing in a range of expert witnesses. There are different ways in which one can figure this contrast between its spatial reach and that of documentary. One way would be to simply proclaim the superiority of the latter in this regard. Another would be to build on a demarcation established by Comolli (chapter 4) who suggested that, while documentary is suitable for recording active witnesses, only fiction can adequately engage with silence, defeat and demobilization (Comolli 2004: 526–44). Reconfiguring this analysis more positively, I suggested that fiction can work to bring hidden violences and mute struggles to the surface thus giving expression to resistances that can no longer call on an elaborated language. Introducing a spatial dimension, one might say that fiction shows a politically fruitful capacity to inhabit the spatial frames of small groups and individuals as long as it finds ways to refuse the debilitating self-enclosure of the purely local. One way it does this is to develop what one might call a micro-spatial dynamics based on local mobilities. It is to this that we will now turn.

Differential Mobilities

The films discussed here focus on small groups detached from broader national circuits of power yet open to the very real effects of global economic flows. The characters' powerlessness is underlined by their repetitive and purely local spatial trajectories that seem at best derisory and at worse meaningless in a world of global flows. Some trajectories are not only limited but are also painful or contested in a way that contrasts with the seemingly effortless mobility of cultural products or economic power. This is perhaps most obviously the case with the *films de banlieue* whose spatial dynamics revolve tightly around the narrow frame in which the urban underclass is obliged to move and the struggle of usually young male characters to inscribe their presence in public spaces. *Banlieue* films characteristically show characters walking through streets as if to underscore the slowness and local nature of their movements. Beginning with *Le Thé au harem d'Archimède* and continuing with *Etat des lieux* and *Wesh wesh*, they repeatedly figure characters pushing mopeds or motorbikes as if to underscore their struggle to retain mobility in a world of flows. *La Haine*'s story of the disastrous consequences of a missed train and an abortive attempt to steal a car could be considered a variant on the same theme.

However, it is not just the *banlieue* films that underscore the unequal mobilities of those at the bottom. Despite its generic identity as road movie and through its decidedly localized geography, Poirier's *Western* also highlights the dramatically restricted frame to which its heroes are condemned. The loss of mobility of the Spanish salesman is particularly striking. The start of the film sees him driving apparently effortlessly on main roads, but once his car has been stolen and he has joined the unemployed, his mobility becomes increasingly painful until, after the accident in which his leg is cut, he finds himself pushed along a country lane in a wheelbarrow. The servant in *La Cérémonie* has no car and her postmistress friend has an unreliable vehicle but the wealthy family for which she works has several vehicles and departs on foreign holidays. Similarly in *Marion*, the poor family at the film's heart seem condemned to circulate within the narrow confines of the village where they live while the wealthy Parisians move at will between the capital, their village retreat and the coastal resort where they go on holiday. In *La Ville est tranquille*, the heroine's movements are always constrained and local. We see her travel

back and forth on her little moped between the twin obligations of hard
physical labour packing fish and hard social labour caring for her drug-
addict daughter. Highlighting Marseille's self-promotion as global city, the
film underlines how the world has fragmented into two spatialities, one of
power, the other of powerlessness and frantic local efforts to keep afloat.
While the first continuously impacts on the second, the second seems
increasingly incapable of touching or even naming the first.

Similar patterns can also be found in Dumont's films. The action of *La
Vie de Jésus* is interspersed with images of the unemployed young men
riding singly or in a group on local by-roads. Their repetitive movements
underscore the futility and narrow framework of lives going nowhere.
L'Humanité's spatial dynamics are similar but more complex. Much of the
film revolves around the restricted trajectories and frequent immobility of
characters who seem condemned to move within a tightly local frame. We
see the hero sweat as he cycles up a local hill on his racing bike. The school
bus, upon which the murdered child at the heart of the film's action used to
travel, undertakes a repeated local journey. Yet the film's landscape is also
dissected with great violence by the high-speed Eurostar train as it takes
passengers from Paris to England. Significantly, the two potential witnesses
to the murder were on it but failed to see anything important due to the
speed at which they were travelling. The train is thus used to suggest the
inhuman spatio-temporal dimensions of the new world. But one could also
cite the film's announced factory closure and the mismatch it reveals
between a company's mobility and the characters' rootedness in a network
of local ties. Dumont's humans are frail, small, slow and clearly not at home
in a world that has become vast, violent and fast.[1] His film opposes that
which it figures through its slowness and painstaking attention to
characters' bodies and desires. Yet, being rooted as we saw in a profound
sense of the smallness of humanity, this opposition does not open
productively onto a politics.

Tracking the Powerful

If recent French cinema has seemed to devote itself above all to tracking the
painful and obstructed trajectories of those at the bottom of the pile, a few
films have begun to explore the spatiality of the powerful with Cantet's
L'Emploi du temps and Moutout's *Violence des échanges* being the most
prominent examples. Moutout's management consultant hero is a mobile
character, one of a group which moves from place to place and country to
country performing services for international capital. Employees of the
company that he has been sent to restructure live and work locally. Images
of him on the TGV stress his seemingly effortless mobility as he moves in
and out of the spaces upon which he visits so much harm. *L'Emploi du*

temps also stresses the mobility of the powerful. The hero, we may remember, is first seen by and on the road, while his wife, kept near the home by her children and by her job in a local primary school, is associated with fixity. The job that the hero pretends not to have lost took him from place to place, visiting decisions from elsewhere on locally lived lives. His invented job for the UN prolongs the same asymmetry of power and mobility at the global level, suggesting how an international elite take decisions felt around the globe. The same job and his subsequent employment smuggling contraband repeatedly take him across national borders while his Eastern European investment scam underlines the mobility of capital. Yet his journeys also bring him into contact with those – lorry drivers, migrant workers glimpsed in a sweatshop – whose mobility is tied to subordination and compulsion. His own lack of a job also focuses attention, as we noted, on the enforced exclusion of the marginal from sites – the hotel, the UN building – where the powerful circulate. The film thus provides a rounded examination of the connections between power and mobility under globalized capitalism. It also holds on to an association between movement and liberty to which we shall now turn.

Defending the Mobility of the Disempowered

In its opening minutes, *L'Emploi du temps* shows a sequence of apparent utopian freedom when the hero, a high-flyer within the capitalist economy, races a local train in his car. Yet, as we learn, his liberty was not fully realized until he lost his job (chapter 5). As long as he was constrained by the needs of capital, his mobility only seemed like self-determination. In the end family responsibilities and economic constraints clip his wings. In between, however, his trajectory reasserts a desire for mobility and self-reinvention that cannot be satisfied within the existing system. In a not dissimilar way, other films discussed defiantly hold on to the desire of the poor to move, both literally (by contesting their immobilization and exclusion) and figuratively (by refusing to accept the fixity of their social situation or identity). Perhaps the clearest example of the defiant mobility of the disempowered is seen in *Marion*. Although the film is more generally traversed by the contrast between the mobility of the bourgeois Parisians and the locally lived existences of the poor, the hero's libertarian brother defiantly takes to the road when he wishes, living poorly in order so to do. His niece, Marion's sister, asserts a similar refusal of the choice between the freedom to move of the rich and the constrained immobility of the poor by declaring her desire to neither live in Paris like the wealthy bourgeois, nor to be tied to the village like her parents. The final shots of Marion's family on holiday on a beach also underline the refusal of the poor's immobilization. A similar dynamic can be found in *Sauve-moi*. The taxi driver hero's circulation in Roubaix underlines the immobility of his situation. His driving is a purely local circulation that brings him back again to the same place, a place to which he feels bound by ties of friendship and family, even if it has nothing to offer him. However, another poor character, the Romanian woman, shows a defiant attachment to mobility, firstly by her initial journey to France, and secondly by her determination to move on when France offers her nothing.

The two Masson films previously discussed likewise revolve to a considerable extent around the poor's refusal of their immobilization. The first, *En avoir (ou pas)* is about a young woman who uses redundancy to break with what seems her destiny as a working-class woman. Rather than accepting another mindless job, she leaves the northern port where her family lives to resurface in Lyon. There she stays in a hotel that, temporarily at least, underlines her refusal of any permanent or fixed status. By the time the film ends, she has become attached to a working-class man and has found a job in a bar, thus being forced back into her subaltern social location. The same director's *A vendre* has something similar at its heart. Its heroine is a decidedly mobile character who, as we saw (chapter 5), turned herself into a commodity as a way of liberating himself from social ties. Her elusiveness is undermined by the fact that the man she was to marry, and whom she jilted at the altar, has to hire a private detective to track her down. While the detective's enquiries and a series of flashbacks, gradually pin down where she has been and what she has done, she still runs ahead of us. If she inevitably runs into the buffers, self-commodification leading to a loss of self not liberation, her flight carried a utopian dimension by showing how someone from the bottom end of society could defiantly refuse her allotted place and role and lay claim to the right to circulate and reinvent herself.

Suitably the most minimalist inscription of a recalcitrant mobility is to be found in Chabrol's *La Cérémonie*, the film where stripped of any positive expression, class was reduced to its essence, to struggle. Fittingly, the conflict to come is announced at an early stage when the rich woman goes to the station to meet her new maid. Instead of dismounting from the train on which she was due, thus appearing from the expected direction, the maid (who has caught an earlier train) comes from the other side of the station, catching her new mistress by surprise. This is, of course, entirely trivial on the surface. However, at a deeper level, it prepares for all that is to come, for it is only by not being where she is expected to be that the maid can resist. At a more general level, we might say that the films can only reopen the space of the political when they establish a gap between where the dominated are or would like to be and where others expect to find them. While frustrated movement, as we saw in the last chapter, plays a productive role in bringing hidden barriers and exclusions into melodramatic visibility, it also plays an important role in opening a gap between subjective desire and objective reality. This is a gap within which a politics can be built.

Conclusion

On a spatial level, as in other essential ways, contemporary political fictions seem condemned to work against their raw materials. As capital has become ever more elusive and developed the capacity to distance itself from its social and environmental consequences and outflank the shrinking demands of nation-states, it has become ever harder to pin down and confront. At the same time, opposition has seemed increasingly condemned to be local and found itself stripped of the kind of universal claims and totalizing vision that once allowed it to face capital or imperialism, if not on equal terms, at least in the same spatial frame and with the capacity to name and locate its enemy. The rise of counter-globalization suggests how some kind of symmetry may be restored, how the scope of opposition and oppositional knowledges might again compete with those of the dominant, allowing processes to be named and framed and globalizing counter-propositions again to emerge. Counter-globalization documentary has shown how this re-emergent symmetry can be put to use to restage a collision between actors and visions that no longer occupy the same space but can still be forced to collide when film-makers imitate the mobility of transnational capital, when montage allows different international spaces and actors to be brought together and when voices of international counter-expertise become cinematic witnesses. But, constrained undoubtedly by its traditional attachment to individuals, small groups and places, fiction has predominantly chosen to pin itself tightly down and to inhabit the spaces of fragmentary struggles. It is productive when it can invent new means to make these spaces speak of something beyond themselves and short-circuit neo-liberal globalization's utopian claims. But it is also productive in its deployment of what we might call a micro-spatial politics, one that uses the purely local movements of characters to bring obstacles into visibility, to underline the profoundly unequal nature of contemporary mobilities and to open a gap, no matter how small, between the dominated and the location to which they have been allocated.

Notes

1. Dumont's films echo others discussed earlier in this chapter by underscoring the effective loss of the national as a meaning-giving framework and symbolic home. In *La Vie de Jésus*, as we saw, the national has collapsed into a xenophobic neo-tribalism. Rather than rescuing the characters from their primitive passions, it has been sucked into them. *L'Humanité* might seem on the surface less preoccupied with

the national. It is, however, surely not accidental that, when it takes its leading protagonists on a day trip to the seaside, they visit a disused coastal fortification facing England that once signalled the rigid boundaries of national space. Given that the central murder story figures the Eurostar train and its routine high-speed border crossing, the film would seem to be underlining how the evacuation of the national leaves characters suspended between local lives and global networks with no way to connect the two productively.

CONCLUSION

The cinema discussed in this volume finds itself located between the elaborated politics that was and the politics yet to come. There are undoubtedly better and worse ways to occupy this difficult position. One way is to focus exclusively and unproductively on defeat and to generate angry, nostalgic or even folkloric representations of a now dismantled working class. Another equally unproductive possibility is to passively reflect contemporary social and political disarray, locking the dominated into their subordination and silence, holding them up as objects for humanitarian contemplation or for voyeuristic delectation and disgust. But contemporary French fiction film has also shown that there are more productive solutions. One is to perversely refuse to accept the finality of defeat and to put the shattered pieces of the old dramaturgy of class to work, disrupting the surface calm of political consensus, bringing struggle back to the surface, restoring grounds for critique and demonstrating the necessity of resistance even when the resources – the collective values and solidarities, the shared language – seem lacking. Another productive solution has been to move fully into the desolate location between two politics and to inhabit the fragmentary spaces of isolated individuals and residual groups deprived of traditions, evicted from social solidarities and condemned to raw suffering, voiceless struggle and incipient meaning-lessness. This latter solution is only productive to the extent that the films resist the processes that they show by connecting the violence of the margins to the centre and reasserting the ethico-political agency and recalcitrant subjectivity of those cast as dominated social objects.

Thematically and stylistically, the films can broadly speaking be cast as realist. More specifically, their generally unpolished aesthetics, loose episodic plots and recourse to amateur and non-star performers suggest clear affinities with Italian neo-realism. However, their more profound affinity to their precursor relates to a capacity to rebuild in the ruins, drawing not on a pre-existing politics, values or meanings but making us react to the absence of such things in a way that drives us back towards a politics. What they also have in common with their precursor is a sustained recourse to melodrama that is not an unfortunate adjunct to their realism but its vital complement, for it is only through the deployment of a range of melodramatic strategies that a real made silent by the loss of an oppositional language can once again be made to speak to us. The kind of critique of realism, developed for example in the pages of *Cahiers du Cinéma*, whereby a realist cinema is seen to merely reflect the surface of the real, give us back the already known or sustain and immobilize the status quo, would seem to miss the point of films whose shared drive is to rupture a superficial consensus by bringing domination, alienation, oppression and struggle back to visibility. The critique of formal conservatism, of a return to the vices and devices of the old civic fiction or *fiction de gauche*, also substantially misses the point of films whose turn to melodrama and to individual and family-centred stories shows a real capacity to bite upon contemporary reality by making embodied struggle eloquent and dramatizing social implosion, the failure of inter-generational transmission and the impossibility of real individual autonomy, notably for those at the bottom of the pile.

If it seemed possible, in the post-1968 period, to draw a sharp line between genuinely progressive films and those whose formal conservatism betrayed an apparently radical content, such clear differentiation now seems much more problematic. This does not mean that we should draw back from evaluation, but it does suggest that we need to develop criteria that are both more nuanced and more adequate to dramatically different times. Thus, while part of the films' political work might seem to consist in an unphotogenic focus on marginality, exclusion and the world of work, this of itself is not enough. If politics begins, in Rancière's terms, when there is disagreement about the distribution of social roles and places and the allocation of the right of public speech, then the films only become political in a real sense when they inscribe disagreement within their narratives, soundtracks and *mise-en-scène*. While a raw, naturalist *mise-en-scène* might seem sufficient to distance them from much of commercial cinema, they must move beyond this to place struggle at their core. This implies a focus on characters defined not by a substantive, immobilizing identity but by active refusal of their allocated place and their political silencing. It also implies a focus on central processes and the systemic, rather than on marginal states and the purely local. It necessitates moreover a probing of a real that must be worked upon to bring socio-economic violences, divisions and barriers back into visibility in a way that allows the voice of refusal and alternative values to be heard and make sense (or their silencing to be seen and understood). A real reconfigured by struggle and by the expression of oppositional voices and values is, as Rancière (1995) has underlined, one that is fissured so as to reframe the status quo and allow alternative possibilities to begin to re-emerge. It is according to their capacity to fissure the real, to figure agency, to inscribe struggle, to recreate possibility and to rebuild systemic critique that we should judge the films.

Of course not all the films are equally effective from a political point of view. Some bring social struggle and economic violences to the surface but show inadvertent complicity with dominant discourses by objectifying their popular characters. Some work to rebuild a sense of ethical agency through a forced encounter with the other but nonetheless limit their potential political impact by staging this collision without the presence of an oppressive third party against whom self and other could unite to restore, at a minimal level, the kind of antagonistic construction of the social necessary for an oppositional politics to take root. Other films use the family to dramatize the crisis of social connectivity and of working-class transmission but neglect to problematize roles and hierarchies within the family unit. However, perhaps the greatest potential weakness of the films is the difficulty they face in bringing oppressor and oppressed into confrontation and in figuring the underlying dynamics rather than the local effects of neo-liberal globalization. To avoid abetting capital's ability to distance itself from its social impact, they have to find inventive ways to reach outside the narrow spatial frame to which their characters are usually condemned. Unable to feed off a totalizing discourse of opposition, they cannot propose either a global critique or a global alternative. Nonetheless, their capacity to puncture neo-liberalism's utopian claims has its own undoubted effectiveness, as does their ability to figure the dramatically unequal mobilities of the powerful and the disempowered and to use the limited movement of the latter to bring socio-economic barriers to light and assert the defiant right of those at the bottom to change social and physical locations. Overall, the limitations shown by the films and the necessarily inventive strategies to which they are obliged to have recourse to compensate for them remind us of the emergent rather than developed state of an oppositional politics.

A political cinema needs to be contemporary of its times. We should thus not have the same expectations of one that emerges at a moment when radical socio-political transformation seems potentially imminent and one that comes in the wake of a political defeat and which must of necessity exist in the space between the politics that was and newly emergent political possibilities. Given this essential proviso, we can say that current French cinema is effectively contemporary of its period in that, not only does it put the shattered pieces of the old political dramaturgy to productive use, it also helps prepare the ground for a new politics. If we seek in it a radical break, a totalizing politics or an already existing oppositional project of the sort to be found in post-1968 cinema, we will inevitably be disappointed. But if we judge it in terms of its capacity to resist a defeat and to prepare the ground for renewed opposition (allowing it to make sense, to 'bite' upon the real), then we will see it much more positively. Faced with a major defeat and forced to digest the accumulated disasters of the twentieth century, a leftist politics can clearly no longer hold to any vision of inevitable historical progress. It has to come to terms with historical contingency, the sense that outcomes are never guaranteed, and with a discontinuous emancipatory narrative, with moments of progress interspersed with periods of stasis or regression. If we are not to suggest that a properly political cinema can only exist in a sharply discontinuous way, limiting its appearances to periods of transformatory social struggle, we must develop a sharper understanding of the counter-hegemonic work a cinema can do when radical change is not an immediate prospect. The way in which current French cinema has worked to undermine the neo-liberal consensus, to restore eloquence to mute struggle and to re-ground a sense of political possibility may carry lessons that are more generally applicable to other contemporary cinemas.

There is another important way in which current French cinema is contemporary of its time. Even when they deployed techniques designed to produce an actively questioning audience, earlier models of committed cinema had a developed vision of the sort of utopia that they looked towards. In contrast, contemporary films are characterized to a considerable degree by their capacity to configure the real in such a way as to drive us in an active search for a politics yet to be found. They are thus eminently suitable tools for an oppositional politics that is characterized not by the old hierarchical structures, nor by an elaborated project to be transmitted to the masses, but by a decided preference for participatory deliberation. To the extent that the films show popular characters that actively reinvent values and possibilities (rather than receiving them from above), they mirror the kind of active, democratic publics that characterize the social movement in France and beyond. They find their ideal public when, as now not infrequently happens on the French arts circuit and in the burgeoning number of festivals, they are used as a stimulus for public debate. But their more general capacity to bring urgent issues of shared concern to public attention can be seen as a defence both of cinema's status as public art and, more broadly, of the kind of dynamic public sphere in which a radical oppositional politics can emerge.

FILMOGRAPHY

Information is given as follows: film title; director's first name and surname; country or countries of production; year film officially registered with French release date in brackets when known. The information is taken, wherever possible, from the data provided on the website of the Bibliothèque du Film in Paris.

2084, Chris Marker, France, 1984
A bout de souffle, Jean-Luc Godard, 1959 (1960)
Air de famille, Un, Cédric Klapisch, France, 1995 (1996)
A l'attaque!, Robert Guédiguian, France, 1999 (2000)
A la vie, à la mort!, Robert Guédiguian, France, 1994 (1995)
A vendre, Laetitia Masson, France, 1997 (1998)
Bicycle Thieves, Vittorio De Sica, Italy, 1948
Ça commence aujourd'hui, Bertrand Tavernier, France, 1998 (1999)
Cérémonie, La, Claude Chabrol, France, 1995 (1995)
Coup pour coup, Marin Karmitz, France/Germany, 1971 (1972)
Davos, Porto Alegre et autres batailles, Vincent Glenn, France, 2001 (2003)
De l'amour, Jean-François Richet, France, 2000 (2001)
De l'autre côté du périph', Bertrand and Nils Tavernier, France, 1997 (1997)
Discrète, La, Christian Vincent, France, 1990 (1990)
Drôle de Félix, Olivier Ducastel and Jacques Martineau, France, 1999 (2000)
Electrons statiques, Jean-Marc Moutout, France, 1998
Elle est des nôtres, Siegrid Alnoy, France, 2002 (2003)
Emploi du temps, L', Laurent Cantet, France, 2001 (2001)
En avoir (ou pas), Laetitia Masson, France, 1995 (1995)
Enfant, L', Jean-Pierre and Luc Dardenne, Belgium/France, 2004 (2005)

Etat des lieux, Jean-François Richet, France, 1994 (1995)
Fils, Le, Jean-Pierre and Luc Dardenne, Belgium, 2001 (2002)
Fond de l'air est rouge, Le, Chris Marker, France, 1977 (1977)
Fred, Pierre Jolivet, France, 1996 (1997)
Full Monty, The, Peter Cattaneo, Great Britain, 1996 (1997)
Gazon Maudit, Josiane Balasko, France, 1994 (1995)
Glaneurs et la glaneuse, Les, Agnès Varda, France, 1999 (2000)
Haine, La, Mathieu Kassovitz, France, 1994 (1995)
Histoires de vies brisées – les 'double peine' de Lyon, Bertrand and Nils
   Tavernier, France, 2001 (2001)
Histoire(s) du cinéma, Jean-Luc Godard, France, 1989
Humanité, L', Bruno Dumont, France/Belgium, 1998 (1999)
Inguélézi, François Dupeyron, France, 2003 (2004)
Je pense à vous, Jean-Pierre and Luc Dardenne, Belgium/Luxemburg/
   France, 1992 (1992)
Jean de Florette, Claude Berri, France, 1985 (1986)
Level five, Chris Marker, France, 1996 (1997)
Lorsque le bateau de Léon M. descendit la Meuse pour la première fois,
   Jean-Pierre and Luc Dardenne, Belgium, 1979.
Ma 6-T va crack-er, Jean-François Richet, France, 1996 (1997)
Ma petite entreprise, Pierre Jolivet, France, 1998 (1999)
Ma vie en rose, Alain Berliner, France/Belgium/United Kingdom, 1996 (1997)
Marche de l'empereur, La, Luc Jacquet, France, 2004 (2005)
Marie-Line, Mehdi Charef, France, 1999 (2000)
Marion, Manuel Poirier, France, 1996 (1997)
Marius et Jeannette, Robert Guédiguian, France, 1996 (1997)
Microcosmos, Claude Nuridsany and Marie Pérennou, France, 1995 (1996)
Minute de silence, Une, Florent Siri, France/Germany/Belgium, 1998 (1998)
Moi, un noir, Jean Rouch, France, 1958 (1959)
Monde sans pitié, Un, Eric Rochant, France, 1998 (1999)
Mondovino, Jonathan Nossiter, U.S.A./Argentina/Italy/France, 2003 (2004)
Nadia et les hippopotames (longer, cinematic version of *Retiens la nuit*),
   Dominique Cabrera, France, 1998 (2000)
On n'est pas des marques de vélo, Jean-Pierre Thorn, France, 2002 (2003)
Ouvrières du monde, Marie-France Collard, Belgium/France, 2000
Part du ciel, Une, Bénédicte Liénard, France/Belgium/Luxemburg, 2001
   (2002)
Péril jeune, Le, Cédric Klapisch, France, 1993 (1995)
Petit Voleur, Le, Erick Zonca, France, 1998 (2000)
Pour que la guerre s'achève, les murs devaient s'écrouler (Le Journal), Jean-
   Pierre and Luc Dardenne, Belgium, 1980.
Profit et rien d'autre, Le, Raoul Peck, France/Belgium, 2000
Promesse, La, Jean-Pierre and Luc Dardenne, Belgium/France/Tunisia,
   Luxemburg, 1995 (1996)

Regarde Jonathan, Jean Louvet, son œuvre, Jean-Pierre and Luc Dardenne, Belgium, 1983.

Reprise du travail aux usines Wonder, La, Pierre Bonneau and Jacques Willemont, France, 1968

Reprise, Hervé Le Roux, France, 1995 (1997)

Ressources humaines, Laurent Cantet, France, 1999 (2000)

Retiens la nuit (made for television version of *Nadia et les hippopotames*), Dominique Cabrera, France, 1999 (2000)

Rêve d'usine, Luc Decaster, France, 2002 (2003)

Rien à faire, Marion Vernoux, France, 1999 (1999)

Rosetta, Jean-Pierre and Luc Dardenne, Belgium/France, 1998 (1999)

Sauve-moi, Christian Vincent, France, 1999 (2000)

Selon Matthieu, Xavier Beauvois, France, 2000 (2001)

Seule, Erick Zonca, France, 1995.

Shoah, Claude Lanzmann, France, 1985 (1985)

Sitcom, François Ozon, France, 1997 (1998)

Sucriers de Coleville, Les, Ariane Doublet, France, 2002 (2004)

Thé au harem d'Archimède, Le, Mehdi Charef, 1985 (1985)

Tout va bien, Jean-Luc Godard and Jean-Pierre Gorin, France/Italy, 1972 (1972)

Tout doit disparaître, Jean-Marc Moutout, France, 1996

Vie de Jésus, La, Bruno Dumont, France, 1996 (1997)

Vie rêvée des anges, La, Erick Zonca, France, 1997 (1998)

Ville est tranquille, La, Robert Guédiguian, France, 1999 (2001)

Violence des échanges en milieu tempéré, Jean-Marc Moutout, France/Belgium, 2002 (2004)

Voleuse de Saint-Lubin, La, Claire Devers, France, 1999

Wesh wesh, qu'est-ce qui se passe?, Rabah Ameur-Zaïmeche, France, 2001 (2002)

Western, Manuel Poirier, France, 1996 (1997)

BIBLIOGRAPHY

Agard, S. 2004. 'Chômeurs et précaires: l'enjeu de l'image', *CinémAction* 110: 214–17.
Agard, S. 2005. 'Les cinéastes et les "sans-papiers": contester ou filmer?' in G. Hayes and M. O'Shaughnessy (eds) 2005. *Cinéma et engagement*. Paris: L'Harmattan; pp.241–53.
Amarger, M. 2003. 'Entretien avec Rabah Ameur-Zaïmeche'. *Arte Vidéo* (included in DVD of film).
Austin, G. 2004. 'The Amateur Actors of Cannes 1999: A Shock to the (Star) System', *French Cultural Studies* 15: 251–63.
Badiou, A. 1985. *Peut-on penser la politique*. Paris: Seuil.
Badiou, A. 2005. *Le Siècle*. Paris: Seuil.
Balibar, E. 1997. *La Crainte des masses: politique et philosophie avant et après Marx*. Paris: Galilée.
Baumann, Z. 2003. *Liquid Love: On the Frailty of Human Bonds*. Cambridge: Polity.
Bazin, A. 1990 [1958–62]. *Qu'est-ce que le cinéma*. Paris: Editions du Cerf.
Beaud, S. and M. Pialoux 1999. *Retour sur la condition ouvrière; enquête aux usines Peugeot de Sochaux-Montbéliard*. Paris: Fayard.
Benoliel, B. and S. Toubiana 1999. 'Il faut être dans le cul des choses' (interview with L. Dardenne and J.-P. Dardenne), *Cahiers du Cinéma* 539: 47–53.
Beugnet, M. 2000. 'Le souci de l'autre: réalisme poétique et critique sociale dans le cinéma français contemporain', *Iris* 29: 53–66.
Blouin, P. 2003. 'Où est le cinéma politique?' *Cahiers du Cinéma* 578: 10–12.
Bluher, D. 2005. '*Wesh wesh, qu'est-ce qui se passe?* Le cinéma hip-hop, relève du cinéma beur et du cinéma de banlieue', in G. Hayes and M. O'Shaughnessy (eds). *Cinéma et engagement*. Paris: L'Harmattan; pp. 271–85.
Boltanski, L. and E. Chiapello 1999. *Le Nouvel Esprit du capitalisme*. Paris: Gallimard.
Bratton, J., J. Cook and C. Gledhill, (eds). 1994. *Melodrama: Stage, Picture, Screen*. London: British Film Institute.
Breton, E. et al. 2000. *Nous avons tant à voir ensemble: cinéma et mouvement social*. Montreuil: VO Editions.
Brooks, P. 1976. *The Melodramatic Imagination*. New Haven: Yale University Press.

Burdeau, E. 1998. '68/98, retours et détours', *Cahiers du Cinéma* numéro hors série 68: 43–46.

Burdeau, E. and F. Ramone 1998. 'Penser le surgissement de l'événement' (interview with A. Badiou). *Cahiers du Cinéma* numéro hors série 68: 10–19.

Butler, J., E. Laclau and S. Zizek 2000. *Contingency, Hegemony, Universality: Contemporary Dialogues on the Left*. London: Verso.

Cadé, M. 2000. 'A la poursuite du bonheur: les ouvriers dans le cinéma français des années 1990', *Cahiers de la Cinémathèque* 71: 59–72.

Cahen, J. 1997. 'Cinéma et politique: beauté de la mise en scène', *La Lettre du Cinéma* 2: 72–73.

Caillé, P. 2004. '*Ressources humaines*: lutte de cinéma et critique des classes', *CinémAction* 110: 201–7.

Castel, R. 1995. *Les Métamorphoses de la question sociale: une chronique du salariat*. Paris: Fayard.

Castel, R. and C. Haroche 2001. *Propriété privée, propriété sociale, propriété de soi: entretiens sur la construction de l'individu moderne*. Paris: Fayard.

Cohen, C. 1997. 'Le rêve du bonheur: *Marius et Jeannette* de Robert Guédiguian', *Cahiers du cinéma* 518: 54–57.

Comolli, J.-L. 2004. *Voir et pouvoir, l'innocence perdue: cinéma, télévision, fiction, documentaire*. Lagrasse: Verdier.

Crettiez, X. and I. Sommier, (eds). 2002. *La France rebelle: tous les foyers, mouvements et acteurs de la contestation*. Paris: Michalon.

D., I. 2001. 'Vingt ans après, Guédiguian court encore' (interview with R. Guédiguian), *Le Monde* 24 January.

Danan, M. 2000. 'French Cinema in the Age of Media Capitalism', *Media, Culture and Society* 22 (3): 355–64.

Dardenne, L. 2005. *Au Dos de nos images 1991–2005*. Paris: Seuil.

De Bourbon, T. 1999. 'A Roubaix, le noir donne des couleurs à la vie', *L'Humanité*, 20 November.

Deleuze, G. 1985. *Cinéma 2: L'image-temps*. Paris: Editions de Minuit.

Delorme, S. 2003. 'Engagés et enragés', *Cahiers du Cinéma* 578: 13–15.

Denis, S. 2005. 'Du plateau à Millau: Le souvenir du Larzac' in G. Hayes and M. O'Shaughnessy (ed.), *Cinéma et engagement*. Paris: L'Harmattan; pp. 99–123.

Derobert, E. and S. Goudet 1997. 'Entretien avec Robert Guédiguian', *Positif* 442: 42–48.

Dogme 1995. 'The Vow of Chastity'. http://www.dogme95.dk/menu/menuset.htm, consulted 11 September 2006.

Garnier, J.-P. 2001. 'Le social sans la politique', *L'Homme et la Société* 142: 65–89.

Gauteur, C. and G. Vincendeau 1993. *Jean Gabin: anatomie d'un mythe*. Paris: Nathan.

Gauthier, G. (ed.) 2004. *CinémAction* 110 (special issue: 'Le Cinéma militant reprend le travail').

Groupe Lou Sin d'intervention idéologique. 1972. 'Les luttes de classe en France. Deux films: *Coup pour coup, Tout va bien*', *Cahiers du Cinéma* 238/239: 5–25.

Guérin, N. 1998. 'Entretien avec Erick Zonca', *Jeune Cinéma* September–October: 20–21.

Hallward, P. 2006. 'Staging Equality: On Rancière's Theatocracy', *New Left Review* 37: 109–29.

Harris, S. 2003. 'Cinéma du look' in E. Ezra (ed.) *European Cinema*. Oxford: Oxford University Press; pp. 219–32.

Harvey, S. 1978. *May '68 and Film Culture*. London: British Film Institute.

Hayes, G. 2005. 'Multiplexes et résistance(s): à la recherche d'Utopia', in G. Hayes and M. O'Shaughnessy (eds), *Cinéma et engagement*. Paris: L'Harmattan; pp. 199–222.

Heller, T. 2004. 'ATTAC: une approche pédago-militante du film' (interview with J.-C. Victor), *CinémAction* 110: 221–26.

Heller, T. 2005. '*Charbons ardents* et *Tower Opera*, ou les formes contrariées de l'engagement du spectateur', in G. Hayes and M. O'Shaughnessy (eds), *Cinéma et engagement*. Paris: L'Harmattan; pp. 125–46.

Hewlett, N. 2004. 'New Voices, New Stage, New Democracies?', *Modern and Contemporary France* 12(1): 9–22.

Higbee, W. 2004. '"Elle est où, ta place?" The Social-realist Melodramas of Laurent Cantet: *Ressources humaines* (2000) and *L'Emploi du temps* (2001)', *French Cultural Studies* 15(3): 235–50

Homer, S. 2000. 'Le syndrome de l'hippopotame' (interview with P. Corcuff), *L'Humanité*, 22 March.

Houba, P. 2003. 'Dans le dos de l'ange de l'histoire' (interview with L. Dardenne), *Multitudes* 11: 145–57.

Ince, K. 2001. 'Queering the Family? Fantasy and the Performance of Gay Relations in French Cinema, 1995–2000', *Studies in French Cinema* 2(2): 90–7.

Jeancolas, J.-P. 1997. 'Une bobine d'avance: du cinéma et de la politique en février 1997', *Positif* 434: 56–8.

Jeancolas, J.-P. 1999. 'Requalifier la politique', *Positif* 455: 46–8.

Laclau, E. and C. Mouffe 2001. *Hegemony and Socialist Strategy: Towards a Radical Democratic Politics*. 2nd. edn. London: Verso.

Lazar, J. 2000. 'Cinéastes: de nouveaux "intellectuels"?' *Le Débat* 112: 48–53.

Le Roux, H. 1998. *Reprise: récit*. Paris: Calmann-Lévy.

Lyotard, J.-F. 1984. *The Postmodern Condition: A Report on Knowledge*, translated by G. Bennington and B. Massumi. Manchester: Manchester University Press.

Marie, L. 2000. '*Reprise*: la mémoire retrouvée de Mai 68', *French Studies Bulletin* 75: 17–21.

Marie, L. 2005. 'Le réel à l'attaque: French Documentary and Globalisation', *French Politics, Culture and Society* 23(3): 89–104.

Masclet, O. 2003. *La Gauche et les cités: enquête sur un rendez-vous manqué*. Paris: La Dispute.

O'Shaughnessy, M. 2000. *Jean Renoir*. Manchester: Manchester University Press.

O'Shaughnessy, M. 2001. 'Republic of Cinema or Fragmented Public Sphere: The Debate between Film-makers and Critics', in J. Marks and E. McCaffrey (eds). *French Cultural Debates*, Melbourne: Monash University Press; pp. 65–79.

O'Shaughnessy, M. 2005. 'Suffering in Silence: Bodily Politics in Post-1995 French Film', *French Cultural Studies* 15(3): 219–33.

Osganian, P. 2003. '*D'Amerika rapports de classe* à *Rosetta*. Sortie du naturalisme et subjectivation du réel', *Mouvements* 27/28: 51–7.

Powrie, P. 2001. '*Marius et Jeannette*: Nostalgia and Utopia', in L. Mazdon (ed.) *France on Film: Reflections on Popular French Cinema*. London: Wallfower; pp. 133–44.

Ramone, F. 1998. '... et le peuple aura été', *Cahiers du Cinéma* numéro hors série 68: 24–6.

Rancière, J. 1995. *La Mésentente: politique et philosophie*. Paris: Galilée.

Rancière, J. 2000. 'Il est arrivé quelque chose au réel', *Cahiers du Cinéma* 545: 62–4.

Royer, P. 1999. 'Bruno Dumont, cinéaste de l'humanité' (interview with B. Dumont), *La Croix* 27 October.

Tarr, C. 2005. *Reframing Difference: Beur and Banlieue Film-making in France.* Manchester: Manchester University Press.

Tarr, C. and B. Rollet 2002. *Cinema and the Second Sex: Women's Film-making in France in the 1980s and 1990s.* London: Continuum.

Toubiana, S. 1997a. 'Entretien avec Hervé Le Roux', *Cahiers du Cinéma* 511: 50–55.

Toubiana, S. 1997b. 'Retour du politique (suite)', *Cahiers du Cinéma* 511: 28.

Verhaeghe, M. 2001. 'Bénédicte Liénard et Séverine Caneele à propos d'Une Part du ciel'. http://www.cinergie.be/entrevue.php?action=display&id=139, consulted 21 September 2006.

Zimmer, C. 1974. *Cinéma et Politique.* Paris: Segher.

INDEX